FREEDOM FROM FASCISM:

A CHRISTIAN RESPONSE TO MASS FORMATION PSYCHOSIS

MICHAEL J. SUTTON

ISBN: 978-0-6455671-0-6

Published by Hidden Road Publishing

DEDICATION

To those to whom it has been said: 'sit down, shut up, and do as you are told,' to those with no voice, those who have been silenced, those who dare to stand up when all are seated, know this, you are not alone, you have never been alone, and you will never be alone. Those who stand for the truth, never stand alone, for the Truth stands with them.

CONTENTS

ACKNOWLEDGMENTS

To those ministers, priests, pastors, and bishops who stood at the church door and turned people away because they did not have a 'vaccine passport,' this book would not have been possible without you. Your actions during Covid Hysteria support my perspective on Christian Fascism. Thank you. To those who decide to read this book, please remember, freedom matters today because you matter to God.

1 IS MASS FORMATION PSYCHOSIS REAL?

Freedom Matters Today is committed to the study of freedom from a Christian perspective. This book is the first in our series examining six aspects of freedom: freedom from fascism and tyranny, freedom from fear and despair, freedom from guilt and shame, freedom from war and conflict, freedom from past and prejudice, and freedom from sin and death. But I am treading on dangerous ground. I have already mentioned the word *'freedom'* nine times. No doubt I am therefore already on somebody's list. It is a sad day when I must justify why I am talking about freedom. Even to suggest these days that *'freedom is under attack in our society,'* is to be accused of peddling misinformation and fake news.

I know what some of you are thinking. It is not the season for freedom. It has fallen out of fashion. It is out of date. It is time to put it away for a while. Public health is more important. Freedom is a luxury for days long gone. I don't believe that. I still believe in freedom. That is why I started *Freedom Matters Today* in September 2021 at the height of two abysmal years of martial law in Australia. We at *Freedom Matters Today* are in the freedom business. I make no apology for that. If you feel uncomfortable with my use of the term *'freedom,'* then that is your problem and not mine.

Why does freedom matter today? It is an important question. I believe it is one of the most important questions for us today. *Freedom* matters today because freedom comes from God and not from us. Freedom *matters* today because it has been distorted by misinformation and fake news. Freedom matters *today* because we need to be free.

The Bible talks a lot about freedom. Freedom is at the heart of God's message to us, especially from the New Testament, though the Hebrew Bible has a lot to say about freedom as well. A well-known saying of Jesus is found in the Gospel of John, chapter 8, and verse 36. Jesus said: *'So if the Son sets you free, you will be free indeed.'* The Bible proclaims that the work of Jesus was to bring freedom. In the last few years during Covid Hysteria in the West, the churches have been falling over themselves trying to tell us that Jesus doesn't talk about freedom. Instead, churches widely proclaim that Christians are to be subservient to the state. Nowhere does the New Testament teach that Christian freedom is subordinate to the government.

What was even more remarkable was that so many conservative evangelical Christians suddenly ceased to preach the good news of God's grace and became outlets for government public propaganda, bringing into the pulpit sectarian political philosophy. Many went further and closed their doors to people who had not been injected with Covid jabs, embracing so-called *'vaccine passports.'* To sweeten the deal, thousands of religious practitioners during the lockdowns in Australia received financial remuneration from the state. It was the largest transfer of direct funds to the church in Australian history. To quote the ancient proverb, *'he who pays the piper plays the tune.'* How this was done was scandalous. This capitulation was just the latest in a long history of awful decisions by church leaders. For many in the church, it is not *'what would Jesus do?'* but *'what do we need to do to secure our financial future?'*

What does the Bible really say about freedom? It is quite possible you are a victim of misinformation from priests, pastors, and ministers who want to keep the Bible closed. Instead, they tell you to sit down, shut up, and do as you are told. It is sad but true. Our goal at *Freedom Matters Today* is to do something radical, subversive, and counter-religious, and that is to open the Bible and let God speak today to us about who we are, who he is, and why he sent Jesus Christ. Our goal is to break the hypnotic power the ruling class may have over you, your life, your choices, and your freedom.

You have a mind of your own. Think for yourselves. Let God speak through his Word and make up your own mind.

There has never been a more crucial time for genuine, authentic, real freedom. At the beginning of the second decade of this century, the best our world can offer is a menu of poisonous delicacies crafted after years of preparation. Take your pick: fascism, fear, shame, guilt, prejudice, sin, evil, or war. Human freedom is often a synonym for living in chains. Liberal democracy, always tenuous and fragile, is now morphing into fascism.

Freedom matters today, more than ever, and no more than in dark places, perhaps where you are, right now. I do not know your situation. I do not know your pain, your heart, or your life. But I speak to all of you with what I can, with words, ideas, encouragement, and hope. I hope that this book becomes a resource of hope, encouragement, and refuge for those in our world who suffer in silence in all the dark places. You are not alone, and you are never alone if you know God and God knows you.

It is time to step out into the light.

It is time to wake up.

It is time to be free.

Today, freedom is needed because we are not allowed to speak freely about many things. There are many new heresies. It is a difficult job keeping up with what is true and what is misinformation. The result is of course that people are bullied into silence by material interests. A 'heresy' is an interesting word. It was used by the Roman Catholic Church and Protestant Churches to legitimize murder for centuries. Heresy is simply a view that diverges in some way from the commonly accepted position. In religious parlance, heresy is a view about God that challenges the political and economic power of the Church. Most heresies were innocuous, many were misunderstood, and for a thousand years, Europe was a slaughterhouse. This was all before Benito Mussolini rediscovered fascism in the 1920s in a small European state that had suffered a millennium of religious fanaticism, murder, war, and three complicated wars of independence, in a newly formed nation called Italy.

A modern heresy is holding to or expressing a different point of view on a current topic. If you hold to an alternative view on one or more subjects, you are a heretic. These days debate is over, as there is only one acceptable political view on an increasing number of issues. If I stand for freedom, and that freedom comes from God, then I am happy to be a heretic. I am also completely opposed to fascism and all its versions, past and present. This is also a heresy. This is also probably the time to nail my colors to the mast as the saying goes and utter the third heresy. Let me say something else we are not allowed to say: *Mass Formation Psychosis is real.*

That is my confession. I have written one of the unforgivable sins, the words that many in the ruling class don't want us to utter, or even mutter under our breath: mass formation psychosis. The old-fashioned word was propaganda. Synonyms include brainwashing, indoctrination, and psychological manipulation. Merely stating the existence of this form of propaganda is career-ending heresy, these days. What remains of Western academia, long the bastion of free speech has fallen silent unless one is parroting government narratives and propaganda. It is a world gone mad, but it has been mad for years. Let me supply context.

In December 2021, Joe Rogan, the king of podcasting, invited Dr. Robert Malone, one of the inventors of the mRNA technology (used for some of the COVID-19 injections), to share his views on science and public health. It is episode *#1757 Dr. Robert Malone, MD*, and runs for over three hours. It was an entertaining, interesting, and controversial conversation, the best podcasts always are. I enjoyed listening to it. I admit that freely. Malone is a world expert in his field, and he knows what he is talking about. He speaks well, slowly, and methodically, doesn't ramble, and he is careful and articulate. Malone has what you might call a 'quiet charisma.' We need more people like Dr. Malone in our world today. Joe Rogan is one of the best interviewers alive. If some 'journalists' were like Joe, their ratings would not be so low, and the 'news' might seem more like real news, instead of fake news. Joe doesn't ignore hard questions, and he also knows what he is talking about.

During that three-hour conversation, the term 'mass formation psychosis,' came up, which is the latest term some social scientists have used to describe what we know happens all the time, which is propaganda. The term 'mass formation,' was coined by an academic by the name of Mattias Desmet, though these ideas have been around for a while. I have heard of his book on the subject but have not read it.

What offended many people in power was the statement that the response to Covid was hypnotic indoctrination. Through the focus on the now debunked 'bat story' of a lethal virus, in some obscure place in rural China, Western governments were able to use this event to overturn, suppress, or strangle representative democracy. This is exactly what happened. There was a mass delusion. There was mass indoctrination. Parliaments shut down, decisions were made in secret by unelected officials, misinformation was rampant, government narratives changed constantly and inexplicably, and this insanity has led to a world in chaos. Intelligent, educated people turned off their moral compass and their brains and stopped thinking for themselves. They chastised and condemned anyone who asked questions, presented alternative opinions, and chose to stand against conventional wisdom. There was a hysteria called Covid Hysteria. It was diabolical and evil.

We are still living with the consequences of this Hysteria as well as the continued devotion of many of its disciples in academia, the medical establishment, politics, media, and the church. Two years on, these disciples are looking more like members of a cult than impartial, rational thinkers, especially since the narrative around vaccine efficacy is collapsing. The Covid injections don't work. Regular boosters are now needed but do not decisively prevent infection, transmission, or illness. People have been lied to since the end of 2019. Whatever your views of the vaccines, this world is now in a catastrophic mess, reflecting one of the greatest failings of the ruling class in many nations for generations.

Now, here is where I part company with many of those who agree that we have been experiencing Covid Hysteria. Many people who are horrified by the possibility of mass formation psychosis believe that a small group of powerful people has been able, through Covid, to interfere with our 'free society.' They believe our society is pure, it is the highest form of society, a democracy, with power residing in the people. For them, there are the naughty people who have sought nefariously to overturn our freedoms. There are the usual suspects: corporations and groups like the World Economic Forum, even Marxists and Critical Race Theory.

I take a different view. It is true, Covid Hysteria is a form of propaganda, but we do not have, nor have we ever had a 'free' society. We have always been the target of propaganda from people in power. Democracy is just another form of government run by flawed people who are neither angels nor demons. Covid Hysteria is just the latest of many coordinated propaganda exercises in the West. I would go further and say quite boldly, that propaganda is essential for the adequate functioning of a democratic society, it is at the heart of marketing and advertising, and is the soul of media.

People in power, the ruling classes, lie to us all the time, often for our good, or for theirs. To prop up our democracy, political deceit is essential. Covid was not the first time, nor will it be the last. It is just the latest episode. Scholars have written on propaganda for decades. The classic texts, in my view, are Jacques Ellul in 1965 *'Propaganda: The Formation of Men's Attitudes,'* and the 1988 book by Noam Chomsky and Edward S. Herman, *'Manufacturing Consent.'* Both are great reads. Both are insightful, though Chomsky is rather dated and simplistic. I prefer Ellul and as a Christian writer, I also find his views refreshing in that he had no difficulty traversing the boundaries of politics, life, and faith. There are many other books about propaganda. Many were influenced by the nightmare of Nazi Germany, European fascism, and the horrors of the Holocaust.

What I believe is that propaganda is to democracy what blood is to the human body, what sap is to a tree, and what heat is to the sun. Democracies use ideas to hold society together while authoritarian or fascist societies use force. It is as simple as that. You, the reader, must decide for yourself which is the best model. In my view, democracies have simply run out of good ideas. Existing ideas are not strong enough to act as a glue to keep society together. We are now hurtling towards full-blown fascism, and this is more likely as we slip into WW3 with Russia and China.

After the rather technical and intellectually stimulating interview on the Joe Rogan show, the media and governments in the West had collective, in-tandem dare I say *'lockstep'* apoplexy, announcing that the interview was peddling lies, misinformation, and falsehoods. Fine, that is their opinion, everyone is entitled to their opinion. But two extremely dangerous things came out of that response. First, calls came to expel Rogan entirely and shut him down for daring to question the official story promoted by people in power.

Second, many people in power in the media announced that there was no such thing as propaganda. There was a flurry of articles, all saying the same thing, that there is no such thing as propaganda. It was astounding. It was of course, complete, and utter nonsense. Their collective statement was collective deceit, their collective confession was collective complicity. Propaganda happens all the time. It is everywhere. Rogan's 'crime' in our once free and open society was offering a different perspective on the Western response to Covid, on a podcast *'The Joe Rogan Show'* that is renowned for offering different perspectives. Remarkable.

After that interview, anyone caught even mentioning the term 'mass formation psychosis,' was canceled, ostracized, or demonized. No doubt, people will try to silence my voice, especially from within the Christian Church. I can see them now, jumping up on their polished marble altar, in their Italian suits, and designer clothes, layered in their clerical garb, sweating profusely, clutching a piece of paper yelling at *Freedom Matters Today* and screaming, foaming at the mouth: *'I will put you on my list, I have a little list!'* I have images of Gilbert and Sullivan coming to me now. I don't know why.

These days, many people in power assume we (ordinary people) are stupid and need to be 'protected' or 'kept safe' from information that might 'harm' us. This is a lie. This is about power and control. This desire to prevent alternative opinions is fascism, plain and simple. The internet is full of unsafe information, and they allow it all, except information that undermines their power and control. In the past, there were always competing views on every topic.

One writer who greatly influenced my understanding of the West (aside from people such as Ellul and Marx) was the late institutional economist, J.K. Galbraith (1908-2006). I owe Galbraith and his way of thinking a huge intellectual debt. One of his many ideas was the concept of *'conventional wisdom.'* As I understood his teachings, conventional wisdom is not the truth but simply our way of making the sense of the current situation, which is effectively a set of facts associated with one another. A *'conventional wisdom'* in politics and economics makes sense of facts and statistical relationships rather than asserting any truthful absolutes. There are others, on the margins of this conventional wisdom who have a different point of view. Eventually, the conventional wisdom collapses when it cannot be sustained by new facts or statistics. There is therefore a shift to a new conventional wisdom. Sometimes this shift takes place after much argument, conflict, and anxiety. Sometimes, the change takes place overnight and no one even notices.

If Galbraith is right, and I think he is, there needs to be the *existence* of alternative points of view to allow the conventional wisdom to change. They are essential. They have been present in most societies, even in authoritarian regimes. Prisons are often the boarding house for new generations of leaders. Political prisoners are often future political leaders, just look at Nelson Mandela.

For some reason, our faltering democracies cannot accommodate these differences of opinion. In our newly fascist West, however, anyone with an alternative point of view is condemned as a conspiracy theorist and their views banned or censored as fake news and misinformation. I believe, as many Marxists and Libertarians do, that our Western democracies have morphed into fascist societies. Unless there is a renaissance of politics, it is all downhill from here. What will happen to our fascist society? There are four options for a nation that is opposed to alternative points of view: decline, death, war, fire, or a combination of the four. It is pointless to talk about political freedoms now, they are out of season, but I will continue to talk about the goodness of God's grace and the freedom that comes from knowing God.

What was even more surprising then about the media's reaction to Joe and Robert was that the people in power who condemned them were themselves well versed in the reality of media and politics, notably the politician problem. What is the 'politician problem'? This is the accepted wisdom that political figures regularly lie and engage in misinformation, I mean, they are flexible with the truth, or they tell us what we need to know when we need to know it.

Politicians own the patent on misinformation. Politics is the art of curating truth, crafting stories, and culling news. Politicians wrote the book on the subject. If you call a political person a liar, you are simply using a synonym, not making any allegation or moral turpitude. An honest politician is like looking for the Tasmanian Tiger, I am sure it might still be there, hidden in one of the mountains of Tasmania, but chances are you will have to look for it for a long time. If you want to know all there is to know about politicians, I recommend the classic British comedy, *Yes Minister*, and *Yes Prime Minister*, starring the late Paul Eddington and Nigel

Hawthorne. You can learn more about politics in those delightful comedies than in any degree on public policy and government.

Who decides what is true and what is false? That is the question isn't it. If mistakes are made by people in power, who holds them accountable? According to them, nobody, because they are like God, they don't make mistakes.

What is the Christian view on all of this? *Freedom Matters Today* presents a Christian response to issues relating to freedom. We are non-sectarian and apolitical. That is a pillar of our methodology. As a result, I am not interested in defending the church, or church history, or traditions, but have an interest in presenting a biblical response to freedom, a Christian response.

Many radicals who talk about propaganda tell us that we need to protest, overthrow the government, vote in a new government, engage in acts of violence, or impose our counterpropaganda on others, whether they like it or not. All these options have taken place over the years, and everyone thought at the time they were doing the right thing, with the best intentions. They all said the same thing, that it would be different this time, that we will not the mistakes of the past, but yes, they did, and yes, they always do, in a never-ending cycle. Violence, protests, or politics are not the answer to any problem of significance in life. Gandhi was right. Non-violence is the way. Jesus believed the same. All Christians are called to a life of peace, as one of the fruits of peace with God.

I think it is time for a new approach and a unique perspective. How does fascism relate to freedom, faith, and life? *Freedom Matters Today* is non-sectarian in any way shape or form, other than the fact that we approach freedom from a Christian perspective, and I make no apologies for that. We are not on the left or the right (that is true) we do not represent a denomination or a religious group. I expect to make enemies on both sides and no doubt a few friends.

Many Christians also love labels, mainly because they need to know whom to hate. I don't like labels; they tend to lose their stickiness and fall off at some point, or they smudge or fade. I am simply a Christian, a follower of Jesus. At *Freedom Matters Today*, we have a saying 'don't go to church, follow Jesus instead.' This has upset so many people in the church and no doubt they see me as a heretic. Incredible. We are not forbidding people to enter a church building, no that would be what governments do, instead, we point people to Jesus Christ and ask them to ponder what it means to follow Jesus, not just for the one hour of church on Sunday, but for the rest of the week, when no one is looking except God.

Why court controversy in the first place? Why not simply keep your head down, take the soup, and keep quiet? I know many people in churches who have been simply doing that. They took the government handouts in the lockdowns, biding their time, waiting for the smoke to clear and they could get back to business as usual, which is a life of tax avoidance, a closed Bible, and the clenched fist of prejudice.

My answer is simple, I follow Jesus. Jesus wrote the book on courting controversy. Google it. Too many in the church are staying quiet on Covid Hysteria, hoping it will all go away, and they can emerge from their bunkers and get back to business as usual, no pun intended. These Christian leaders have lost their voice. They lost their authority long ago. Few like them or trust them, and why would they? History never goes backward, no matter what people think. There will be no going back to the past, especially in a world run by the church. That nightmare is over, thank God, but we must resist every effort by fascists in the Church to return to the past.

What have the churches been up to during Covid? It is a tragic story. It is about betrayal, money, and power. Few dare talk about it and those that do need to confront evil in society, and it is not what you think. There is a specter that is on the move in Europe and North America, though it exists in Australia as well. Mass formation psychosis did not originate with Covid or with capitalism. There is another narrative most of you know little about, and yet it has been in plain sight for decades, and no, I am not talking about the Great Reset. I am talking about a great evil and one of the greatest threats to freedom in our world today.

2 ARE WE THE VICTIMS OF MASS FORMATION PSYCHOSIS?

The lifeblood of democracy is propaganda

In chapter 1, I mentioned that propaganda is essential for the adequate functioning of a democratic society and that we are lied to all the time by people in power either for our good or for theirs. In a democratic society, lies from people in power weave fabric or a tapestry of beliefs, values, and ideas, across social, political, economic, and religious life. When a crisis comes, like Covid, the vulnerability of democracy is exposed, and a light is shone into that darkness. That tapestry or web of deceit is exposed to the light for all to see, and a national fine print emerges.

If a society is ultimately a good one, it leaves certain doors closed and when the crisis is over, life returns to normal. Whether or not those key doors stay open or closed depends on the integrity of the people in power. Human nature suggests the temptation to open those doors is too strong for most, and once open, those doors are rigged to stay open. They cannot be closed again. They were closed for a reason because evil lurked on the other side. There was something there trying to get in.

People in power are still people, subject to all the weaknesses of human nature, no matter how educated or wealthy they are. Covid Hysteria opened the door for some people in power to use the crisis as an opportunity to influence others adversely for their own political or personal gain. This is typical behavior for people in power in a democracy. It happens all the time. In the context of Covid Hysteria, we see this in the lockdowns, the police brutality, the suspension of human rights, the vaccine mandates, and the creation of a new class of people, the so-called 'unvaccinated.'

I also suggested earlier that Jesus Christ is essential in understanding freedom from a Christian point of view. A personal faith in God is the only way to see the world clearly and when you do, it does not matter what hypnotic nonsense people promote, it does not affect you. You can see through the propaganda, or at least discern it, or ensure it does not affect you adversely. The way to break the hypnotic imprint of people in power is to open the Bible and consider the words, life, and deeds of Jesus Christ, to ponder what he has to say about who we are, who he is, and who he is in relation to God. The answer to mass formation psychosis or propaganda is not political, or sectarian, but it has all to do with Jesus Christ.

Have we been lied to, indoctrinated, brainwashed, and hypnotized by people in power? Are we the targets of propaganda, persuasion, and manipulation? The only answer is yes, without any shadow of a doubt. Covid Hysteria involves hypnotic power over others. All forms of hysteria and propaganda do. Democracies rely upon propaganda. To deny the reality of propaganda is delusional. Covid Hysteria is a mental illness, and many have suffered from it in the last three years. Many will never get over it. Millions of people will carry the emotional, economic, social, and political scars of Covid Hysteria for the rest of their lives, some remaining true believers, while many will live in regret, and shame.

Covid Hysteria was and is curated fear, cultivated fear, from people in power, involving wild exaggeration of the threats of Covid, the manipulation of data, the censoring of alternative views using authoritarian mechanisms that only exist in wartime, and the sowing of division, hate, and suspicion.

Allow me to give a relatively simple example. Omicron is a Covid strain that has shown that the original vaccines were ineffective in stopping transmission and infection. If you are inoculated against a virus, then you should not get the virus. That is science. Many who are inoculated, even with booster shots are still getting the virus. As of August 2022, Covid is now rampaging across the community. This presents a logical problem. How do many people overcome this contradiction? They don't, but they have been provided with a script. They say: *'I got covid, but it would have been worse if I had not been vaccinated.'*

This phrase *'would have been worse,'* is an example of brainwashing. If you are close to someone, you and that person will often become like each other in mannerisms, expressions, points of view, and so on. It is highly unlikely for strangers to express anything using the same vocabulary, the same words, and the same phrases. The common response to Omicron Covid cases for vaccinated individuals is exactly that, proof of propaganda, as people are reciting received texts from others. This is classic, but simple propaganda.

Contrast this with Trump's slogan *'Make America Great Again,'* or his latest one *'Make America Great Again, again.'* It is a sectarian slogan. It appeals to Trump supporters and is a trigger for Trump detractors. Most political slogans are like that. They are ineffective. They are for true believers, slogans always are. They are meant to offend and locate political affiliations. It is a form of propaganda but crude. You like it and wear his slogan on your clothes, or you roll your eyes and avert your gaze.

The vaccine ideology in Covid Hysteria is a different form entirely because it crosses party affiliation. The language, intensity, and frequency of statements around the vaccine cross party lines. Anything that brings Left and Right together is effective propaganda because people do not realize that what they are saying is the received wisdom. To use Galbraith's term, it is a conventional wisdom. These words and phrases are not their own, they are not organic, and they are sourced from others. They are phrases used to convey certain emotional responses and reactions to the event, a traumatic response to something that should not have happened at all, namely post-vaccination covid infection.

Why use those words at all? Why not say things differently? Why not explain one's experience differently or not at all? This is old-school propaganda from people in power. Nothing new to see here. Whether it is for our good, or theirs, that is a different question, but to deny that it is happening is plain wrong.

Much of the Covid vaccine discussion is old news and I have no intention of rehashing it all. That is not my focus here. I have a different intention. You can blame *Freedom Matters Today* on the apostasy of the Christian Church. I was happily writing novels and books during martial law in Australia, but the mass failure of the Church brought me out of early retirement. I would not have written this book if the Christian Church had stayed faithful to the Gospel of Jesus Christ or at least stood up for the vulnerable, the weak, and the dying during Covid.

Overall, they didn't. They supported the state entirely, completely, and effectively. There were a few exceptions I grant, but for the most part, the church sat down, shut up, and did what they were told. This behavior was a disgrace and not only was it a disgrace, but a mass apostasy, a repudiation of their faith in Christ. To sign their names to this apostasy, some even dared to create Covid Theology. It is a scandal, and the Church hopes that you have forgotten all about it.

What does apostasy look like?

During the lockdown, many politicians argued that Christians had to support Covid lockdown policies:

'You Christians must act in love and since that is what you believe, you have no choice but to accept and obey our policies. After all, Jesus told you to love your neighbor and if you do not get vaccinated, then you are not loving them.'

This was the sort of rhetoric that was used by the ruling class. Politicians crossed the line. Imagine them quoting the Quran to berate followers of Islam. It is deeply offensive for politicians to use Holy Books to promote their policies. No one in power has a right to use their official position in a secular nation to tell people of faith how their faith is defined and how to follow it. The churches, overall, said nothing except words of affirmation.

The church amid Covid Hysteria was proclaiming peace where there was no peace, friendship with the world, where there was only enmity, and the goodness of humanity when a person's heart is wicked. If you see the world as God sees it, then you are not surprised at the state of the world, because you see things clearly. The last thing the church wants is for you to see at all. What was going on behind the scenes? As you know, the Western church is in deep trouble, and they need friends to prop up their dying institution. Behind the scenes, some people in power in the church are hard at work trying to forge a new alliance, an unholy alliance between ancient power and new power, between what's left of the old state churches and the state, both with the same goal, to deny us our freedom.

It is not only people in power in the state that long for the good old days. You were not watching, you were too busy looking at Trump or Putin, or Xi, or the World Economic Forum, but there are others in our society, people in power, who long for the good old days, and they include many in the Christian church. They want their positions of power back, the days when the church held the sword, and Covid Hysteria is one of the stepping-stones to that end. Now they want 'religious freedom' and more power and more money and the right to persecute children who do not live up to their definition of a 'child.' Religious freedom for the church is a license to abuse, it is the right to persecute, and it is a recipe for violence against the vulnerable, all in the name of a God they pretend to believe in.

The silence of the Christian Church on Covid Hysteria and in many places the continual patronage of vaccine ideology is a disgrace. Enough is enough. Let me speak to the Christian church plainly. My message is to you who claim to be leaders and important people. Whether you are or not, I do not know, only God knows:

The creation and demonization of the so-called unvaccinated is a sin against God. God has not and will not forget what has been done in his name. The silence of the church is an astounding evil. It is apostasy, a betrayal of Christ.

Innocent people (the so-called 'unvaccinated') were, and are persecuted every day, and the church says nothing. It is not surprising. The church always says nothing when it needs to say something. The complicity of the church, their silence, and their support for yet another persecution, is, it seems to me, the latest sign that God will destroy what is left of the institutional church in the West.

Covid Theology revealed the true heart of the Western Church. It is clear to me, that the church in the West is running out of time. I wish it was not true, but it is. The die is cast. Blaspheming the name of God is now the native language of the church. Covid Hysteria is just the latest in a litany of failures. Almost every single time the church had the chance to stand up for truth, it didn't. It never does. It is a disgrace. The failings and corruption of the church is the greatest obstacle to the proclamation of the Gospel. The early Christians were known for their love, the church today is not known for that. It is known for other things, things that have become synonymous with the church: corruption, nepotism, abuse, and irrelevance.

The Western Church was given the glory of God, the promises of faith, the covenant of peace, and the Spirit, but the churches here have done nothing but build kingdoms on earth. Nero fiddled while Rome burned. The church counts money, while people suffer. The Western church has always been on the side of power, and they are silent, unless their wealth is threatened, or they see the opportunity to extend their power. Jesus said that his kingdom is not of this world, so why does the church think that it is?

Nothing shows the revival of church fascism more than the creation of the so-called *'anti-vax'* or *'unvaccinated.'* The creation of a new group of people to hate is the hallmark of fascism. A group of innocent people targeted by society. The creation of this class of people (and all others) is wickedness. To the church leadership, or those who claim to be leaders, I say this about them: their lack of compassion and love and their silence are testimony to their fall from faith and their blindness to the reckoning that is coming. They are oblivious to the future of the church. Perhaps they should open the Bible they pretend to hold up as their book of faith to find out what will happen. They will be in for a few surprises. Now that Covid Hysteria has been shut down, these churches are crawling out of the spiritual sewer with cap in hand, pretending that the last three years never happened, and hoping that you will keep quiet about it, along with everything else.

Let me speak plainly to the church, to both leaders and those who sit in the pews and hate the unvaccinated who might spread disease, and to whom you closed your doors:

You brought partisan politics into the pulpit, again. You took sides, again. You were used and lied to, again. Next time, you will do the same thing to another group of people. It looks like that group will be gay kids or gendered minorities, or Russians. That is your legacy to God, being simply a mouthpiece for the state. Nothing in politics is scientific. Every political decision, even if it is claimed to be scientific, is based on a political calculation to promote the personal and political interests of those in power, nothing more. Public health departments are political entities, the Covid policies were partisan politics.

None of it has any place in God's church, you hypocrites. Those of you who used the pulpit to preach vaccinations are a disgrace, those of you who preached vaccine passports, get out of the pulpit, and get out of the church. God is against you. You put limits on the proclamation of the Gospel, and you violated your oaths and betrayed your calling. You betrayed your Savior, and you betrayed your flock. Now, when Covid is rampaging through the nations, you keep your churches open, and sit back, counting your money hoping that the next pandemic will come with more money to keep churches open, empty churches with dusty pews, stale air, and forgotten memories.

He who pays the piper plays the tune

I follow Paul when I am critical of those who claim to follow Jesus. Whom am I to speak to the behavior of those who do not call Christ Lord? (1 Corinthians 5: 9-11). Churches claimed to speak for God but said nothing to protect the vulnerable. They might dare to claim that they were looking to protect the vulnerable from Covid, but their churches are open while Covid still rages through the nations. They closed their doors to people and turned them away, often in return for economic and political privileges. If that is not moral corruption, what is? For example, how many priests, pastors, and ministers in Australia, spoke out against the lockdowns, martial law, and mandates while in receipt of their Job Keeper handouts? I would love to know. How many refused to take the government handout and decided to live by faith, not by welfare dependency?

Some priests, pastors, and ministers were simply cowards because they stood up in church and told their congregation to get vaccinated and take an injection they did not support privately. The Bible calls that hypocrisy. What Christian leaders say in public and what they believe must be the same. They are not politicians. They should not behave like them. Those who say publicly that the unvaccinated should be excluded but privately have reservations are hypocrites and not walking in the truth. They should have quit their job and kept their faith so they would not sin against their conscience.

The author of covid passports for churches was not God but the Devil, they knew that, but they did it anyway. Those same people celebrated the opening of churches not when the crisis was over but when Covid began to rampage through the nations. Where was this true concern of the church to *'keep us safe,'* when it is more dangerous than ever to contract Covid?

Now that monkeypox is a global health emergency, will these hypocrites close their churches or will they keep the *'contagion chalice,'* I mean the common cup spreading diseases every Sunday? Many churches must be licking their lips with joy as it seems that monkeypox is spreading through some gay communities. Maybe they will ban them from attending church as well, maybe churches will insist on new passports, showing gay people the door. Given their track record, the churches will do nothing unless more money is dangled in front of them. How much will be enough this time?

In Australia, thousands of teachers, nurses and doctors, and other workers were forced during 2021/2022 to leave their profession because they refused to take the Covid injections. That is why there are shortages in the workforce for teachers and hospitals, along with the thousands suffering stress, anxiety, and overwork. How many priests, pastors, and ministers refused to be injected? How many priests, pastors, and ministers lost their livelihood due to Covid Hysteria? My guess is very few. They will make a stand against transgender or gay children but not when their hip pockets are under threat.

But some Christians simply hate the unvaccinated. I know they do. They say so publicly. I have heard their speeches of abuse in Parliament, and I have read their articles. Christians who genuinely hate the unvaccinated are apostates because they are not walking in love. It is as simple as that. Sorry, that means you are not a Christian at all. Christians who also use the pulpit to preach against the unvaccinated are no longer people of faith, plain and simple.

For those Christians who claim to be leaders, know this:

There is no place for hatred in the church and no place in the leadership. Like many, I know about your hatred. You have a whole list of people you hate; it is an exceptionally lengthy list. The unvaccinated are just another number on that extensive list of people you despise. You wonder why your churches are empty, you hypocrites. Use the brain God gave you to work it out.

Covid Hysteria was the latest weaponization of misinformation. *At Freedom Matters Today*, we oppose misinformation about freedom. We aim to equip you with the right questions and information to enable you to make up your own mind. You might reach a different conclusion. That is fine. God allows us to ask any question we like, and to express any doubt we have, so who are we to behave differently? What people hear when they read the Bible might also be different depending on where they are in life, and what they need at that time. We just want you to think for yourself because that enables you to live a fuller and happier life. After all, the choices you make will be yours and not those decided for you.

Misinformation is a product of people in power, from above, not below. Only people in power, that is, the ruling class, can engage in misinformation, those who control the conduits and filters of information, the search engines, the media barons, and the political landscape, not the ordinary person and their website or social media account. Your friend down the road who does not like you cannot engage in misinformation. You might have said something, or done something, and now they are telling everyone about it. They are engaging in gossip or slander. People gossip, people slander, and people in power misinform. People in power engage in misinformation.

The propaganda behind the Covid Hysteria was pathetic, poorly conceived, and problematic. The people behind it were careless, they got too excited, too enthusiastic. They had never tasted absolute power before and many of them did not know how to handle it. The Hysteria led to the revelation of things kept secret, undisclosed, hidden, cloaked, now in plain sight. We know what they want. We know who they are. We know to whom they are loyal. Most of it is now out in the open. Watching the Covid crisis unfold in real time was fascinating. There were so many mediocre politicians and bureaucrats clearly out of their depths, you could see it in their eyes. Theirs were the eyes of fear, desperation, and uncertainty. Most were elected hoping to do very little but were thrust into the limelight, and many saw it as a chance to advance their agendas.

From my perspective, the goal behind Covid Hysteria was a simple one: to take down freedom and elevate tyranny. Put in plain language, the architects of Covid Hysteria hate true freedom, in all its forms, their goal was to overturn freedom and bring in tyranny, in the only way they know how by copying religion. Some people call it the Covid Religion. It certainly resembles one. There is a belief in a new form of public science or political science, what can only be described as religious fervor, devotion, rituals, high priests, liturgies, choruses, and creeds. I have even heard people saying, 'I will go on a holiday next week, Covid willing.' This is blasphemy. Covid is a disease, it is not a personality, and it is not a deity, stop calling it one. Covid Religion is pantheism for bored agnostics, living in opulence, bread and circuses, and an escapist culture.

Covid Hysteria is, however, only a symptom, not the cause. Only a corrupt western ruling class could create Covid Hysteria. Diseases come and go. Covid Hysteria reminds me of the witch trials of Massachusetts, the Reds Under the Bed scare of the 1950s, or the Russophobia of today. Many sane people these days have also gone crazy, they are engaged in crazy talk, they are screaming and yelling in public, friendships have ended, families have broken down, enmities have been sown, hatred cultivated, and divisions exploited.

There is rampant fear everywhere, fear of a virus, fear of others, fear of those not wearing masks, and fear of the unvaccinated. Covid Hysteria has given us another opportunity to divide ourselves once more as if we needed more reasons. The hatred for the unvaccinated, the venom, the spitefulness, and the anger is unlike anything we in the West have seen for decades.

Covid Hysteria brought fascism out of the shadows

I have said that national crises often open doors that should never be opened and when they are opened, they cannot be shut. The pandemic brought out fascists lurking in the shadows of power. These are people who saw an opportunity to use fear, lockdowns, mandates, and ideology to promote their political agendas. We all know who most are, and I will not name them. Their names are not worth repeating here. They are, overall, small-minded, mediocre people, and they are petty fascists or democratic despots, but pretenders all the same. In other words, there is no Franco or Salazar among them, not yet, not even in North America or Europe. There is no Mussolini or Hitler in the wings, at least not yet. These are all pretenders.

I started *Freedom Matters Today* in September 2021 in the middle of the second lockdown in Sydney. It was, like all lockdowns, a waste of time, and it failed, like all lockdowns to stop the spread of Covid. Millions have Covid currently and most of these are at varying degrees of vaccination. The lockdowns were like the vaccines, unable to stop the spread of the disease. Now, we are told by the same people in power that the vaccines will not stop the spread of covid and that we will all get the disease anyway, which means the vaccine mandates and exclusions were at the very least, a waste of time. The ideology and the lies however continue to be told by some people in power, worried that they might go to prison or be prosecuted in the future for criminal negligence. Maybe they will, eventually, time will tell. Who knows the future?

The lockdowns, mandates, and passports were a severe assault on human rights in the West and an appalling shift in values towards the abrogation of human dignity. During the lockdown, freedom was defined as something that needed to be taken away for our collective benefit. I was told that my freedom was not essential. I was told that my freedom depended on the decisions and wisdom of people in power. I was told that my freedom had nothing to do with my faith in God and his Son Jesus Christ.

Like many people, I was mocked and insulted, demonized, and patronized. I was told by many church leaders that any talk of freedom was unchristian. Any talk of freedom was the adoption of foreign, American values, proof that I had been indoctrinated with American right-wing thinking. Church leaders repeatedly said that only fascists believe in freedom. These were astounding statements to make, but not surprising. Don't expect intellectual sophistication from the church.

These church leaders said with one voice that my views were misinformation and out of touch with Australian Christian values. Apparently, freedom is not a Christian value in Australia. Like others, I was told to denounce freedom and submit to people in power because they had been ordained by God, and by obeying them, I was doing what God wanted me to do. I was told that the

Bible teaches our absolute submission to the state, and we must obey the state because any opposition is opposing God who appointed our leaders. Every time the government demands obedience, the churches said we must obey.

The war against freedom, however, was not scientific, it was political and came straight from America's public health officials. Australia's response was American-inspired, a product of partisan political thinking and yes, Australian churches were not adopting impartial truth but political truth, following American advice that suited their agenda of using unscientific means to stop a virus, such as lockdowns and mask mandates. Lockdowns did not make people safer, they did not kill the disease, and they did not bring people together.

There was nothing original in Australia's Covid response. Australia simply copied America. It always does. American values that uphold freedom were seen by the church as 'fascist.' American values that uphold the welfare state, lockdowns, and mandates were viewed by the church as 'science.' Church leaders told me that the heart of my faith was not to be found in freedom but in obedience to people in power whom God had decided would make decisions on my behalf. My role was to sit down, shut up, and do as I was told.

That thinking was not only wrong, but it was also sinful. It was demonic. Nowhere in the Bible are Christians instructed to obey public health directives from the government or any directive from the state. Nowhere are Christians to compromise their faith because people in power tell them to. The churches that embraced lockdowns, mandates, and passports were what we call apostate churches, churches that have fallen. They are not Christian churches anymore, except in name only. Their loyalty is to the state and not to God.

But many of us knew that anyway, and many Australians are simply voting with their feet and leaving the churches. This demographic dynamic will drive churches further into the arms of the state and toward a revival of public morality. Covid Hysteria and Covid Theology are two more ingredients for the rise of Christian Nationalism in America and the West.

Covid Theology

Covid Theology is the garbage that many Christian leaders invented to justify their submission to the state during Covid Hysteria. It is complete nonsense. It belongs in the dustbin of history. Covid Theology says that all government is ordained by God and must be obeyed without question. Even resistance, speaking out, or offering an alternative opinion to *'the science of the state,'* is a sin. This Theology was used to shut down churches when the virus was waltzing along through the community during the lockdowns, mask mandates, and vaccine passports in 2020-1. Then suddenly Covid Theology went on vacation in 2022 when the churches reopened at the same time the virus turned the waltz into a rampage. Now in mid-2022, the poisoned chalice of the common cup is passed around in many churches like Russian Roulette in a cocktail of potential infections due to the capriciousness of the state and their lackeys in putting money ahead of lives. The churches are laughing all the way to the bank as they return to *'business as usual,'* a religious life shaped by a panoply of tax exemptions. At the height of the church vaccine passport nonsense, someone could go to church with the flu, hepatitis, syphilis, herpes, and early onset of Ebola, if they had their Covid Vaccination Certificate. They could partake of the Contagion Chalice and share the love with all and sundry.

Covid Theology makes no sense at all. In Australia, after the money dried up, churches put Covid Theology away because 'the science' of zero-Covid was rejected by a government facing recession and rising inflation, as well as the inevitability of defeat at the polling booth. The 'science' was thrown out in 2022 for economics, and political expediency and the churches reopened. The reopening of the churches in 2022 is proof that their closures had nothing to do with science. They were simply loyalty tests. The Australian government must be pleased with itself. Most churches will do whatever they are told now. They will only speak when asked to speak, and if they keep to the script their money and their assets will be left alone. Whatever narrative the state adopts now, the loyalist churches will sing to their tune. We see this in the approved political narratives where churches are *'speaking out'* on social issues but staying silent on anything that challenges political power. In Australia, many of these vile religious hypocrites will condemn from the pulpit the alleged human rights abuses of the Russian army and yet say nothing about Julian Assange who exposed alleged human rights abuses committed by Coalition troops in the Middle East (including Australia). The West lives in a perpetual state of sinless perfectionism. How fortunate.

On every level, the logic of Covid Theology was ridiculous. Two logical extensions must follow their reasoning. First, the Protestant Reformation was a sin against God because it involved overthrowing the legitimate political authority God had ordained. That authority was Rome and the Holy Roman Empire, established by God. Covid Theology tells us that all Protestants are still sinning against God since they rebelled against the authority God had established. Remember Luther who said: *'Here I stand I can do no other!'* His appeal to Rome was over his conscience that he could not follow the God-ordained government anymore and their puppet pope and so he sought freedom. According to the church today, Luther was wrong. He should have obeyed God-ordained authority. He claimed that he could do nothing else. Well, he was wrong, he could have simply obeyed God and submitted to the state.

Second, according to Covid Theology, the American War of Independence was a seditious rebellion and was therefore a sin against God since the colonies rebelled against God's ordained authority, namely Britain. The Civil War, the breaking of the ties with Washington over the question of state's rights, according to Covid Theology, was also a terrible sin. The South, according to Covid Theology should have simply obeyed Washington and done what they were told. According to Covid Theology, the entire Civil Rights movement was a sin because it involved active opposition to legislation that discriminated, excluded, and ostracized African Americans. The Civil Rights movement promoted civil disobedience but according to Covid Theology, God was opposed to it, he was against it, and logically, God supported slavery and still does. What the Australian church is saying, following their idiotic logic is something quite offensive but I will say it anyway so they might be rightly condemned for suggesting it. If their logic holds, then America as a nation was conceived in sin. If you are an American, next time you meet an Australian Christian, ask them why they think that your America was a nation born in sin.

The leaders of the Australian church knew their reasoning was complete incoherent rambling nonsense, but they needed to say something to justify their silence. The churches had to say something, to cover up what was going on, and they needed a cover story. That was their first mistake. If only the church was honest, people might respect them more. The church is, however, like the little boy who has his hand stuck in the cookie jar and the mother has entered the room, and on the table is the jar on its side with the boy's hand in there grasping one too many cookies, and he is trying to pull his hand out, but his fingers are stuck. Now, the cat is out of the bag here, or rather the cookies are still in the jar, and whatever the consequences, the only sensible response for the kid is to admit what the mother can see with her eyes.

The problem with the Christian Church in Australia is that honesty has never been their strong point. They have a history of complicity, cooperation, and collusion in most of the horrors of Australian history from genocide to the abuse of children. It is a sordid story, mirrored in other Western nations conceived in the British Empire. Giving churches any form of political power is like giving a drug addict access to free cocaine. The result is a catastrophe, every time.

After the Covid Hysteria cover story went out, and the money started rolling in from the government, the churches brought partisan politics into the church, into the pulpit, and the liturgy, and then they fell. Game Over. I never thought that any church would ever close its doors to anyone, at least not officially. I never thought that the church would ever accept vaccine passports, but many did, and some still do, even after the end of martial law. Those churches are dead. They are lost. We can never trust them again. Stay away from them. They are not safe churches. Just get up and leave and stop giving them money. Any church that receives government money is not a Christian church. Their loyalty must always be questionable. He who pays the piper plays the tune.

The only way to fight 'misinformation' is to return to the Bible, and the revelation of God, Jesus Christ. Propaganda is about the mind, and for the Christian, the mind is the seat of the Spirit and therefore a precious place that needs to be protected. But who cares what Jesus says? It is a fair question. I have another: if Jesus rose from the dead, who cares what the government says?

I believe in the physical, literal resurrection of Jesus Christ from the dead and that fact of history changes everything. The freedom of *Freedom Matters Today* is spiritual, freedom of the heart, the mind, the soul, the center of the being, what makes us, us. We are in that freedom business, and the only real freedom that matters is the freedom God brings. We are committed to the proclamation of freedom as is found in the good news of Jesus Christ.

Jesus came not to bring a new religion or trap people in a dead weekly ritual. He came to bring genuine faith and a life of freedom. For Jesus, freedom is why he started talking and made that incredibly life-changing decision to be baptized by John in the river Jordan. He came to see us free. Faith and freedom are so deeply intertwined in the life and work of Jesus. The goal of Jesus was to bring freedom, true freedom. You know when you are in the presence of someone who is a fake Christian: they mock freedom, they downplay freedom, they qualify freedom, and eventually, they try to rewrite the words of Jesus.

For me, I am going out on a limb. I started *Freedom Matters Today* during martial law. The state in the West may talk about 'freedom' but they don't want it. Churches may talk about 'freedom,' but this is code for a license to abuse and discriminate. Arguing for true spiritual freedom is a dangerous thing to do. I am not sure whether people in power are smart to know the difference between a Christian view of freedom and the political version. True freedom comes from God. Maybe some do. Time will tell.

Talking about freedom in the West is now a dangerous thing to do as you probably know. It is no longer possible to utter an opinion on a wide range of topics without being called a proponent of fake news and the author of misinformation. In Australia, we were under martial law for almost two years only to come out of it, just in time for a national election. We endured the *'War on Terror'* for over a decade, then Trump for four years, and then Covid Hysteria for two years, and now the war in Ukraine for less than a year. In every case, people in power have argued that there was only one legitimate, possible view, and every other view was fake news or misinformation.

We are now expected to express confidence, admiration, and unquestioned loyalty to people in power. Anything less than that is increasingly seen as treason. These days everyone is expected to show our leaders the utmost respect, with every word being a word of praise and adulation. Criticism of our leaders is no longer allowed. We are told that any criticism comes from a place of misinformation. Our leaders are too pure to make mistakes. The purity and holiness of our leaders must remain the object of our devotion. These are lofty standards.

As I write, the world has been rocked by the war in Ukraine. But we are already at war. It has nothing to do with Moscow or Beijing. It has nothing to do with the democratic despots. They are dust. They are scattered by the wind on a summer's day. Just watch them fall like dominos. Democratic despots always do. This is an ancient war. We are not fighting for our nation. There is nothing wrong with a nation, but nothing is right with it either. It is an arbitrary creation.

There are no 'Christian' nations

God doesn't save nations, he saves people. There is no such thing as a Christian nation. There never was and never will be. We are fighting for our minds, our hearts, and our souls. We are fighting for the freedom to think, reason, ponder, question, doubt, criticize, oppose, and love. They are simple things, but they are what makes us human and that is why people in power are trying to deny them to us. They want to dehumanize and destroy us. The tragedy is that many in the church left us and no longer walk with us. They no longer walk in the truth, nor do they walk in love.

The Christian church had a voice in society, and people in power knew that voice needed to be silenced to promote their partisan political agenda. The church fell for it again during Covid Hysteria. Christians love it when important people talk to them. They love it when the rich turn up to their meetings. That is the problem. Priests don't care when ordinary people turn up. It is the rich who turn heads. When people of wealth and power walk past the church, the church gets excited, and they forget about God. This is what happened in Covid Hysteria.

But like the persecution of the unvaccinated, the church went further. The church was recruited by the state to do its partisan bidding. In some denominations, the silence was deafening. Conformity was enforced. Rebels were demonized by churches eager to do what they were told. Like rabid dogs they fell over each other salivating at the lips trying to outdo each other in the hit pieces they wrote against those who refused to toe the line of partisan politics. Your clever work will not be forgotten, my friends. God will not forget what you did and what you continue to do against his people. These hit pieces targeted fellow Christians who refused to bow to the state. Clever work. A high point in your journalistic career.

However, the capitulation of many priests and ministers, and pastors during this partisan political time is not surprising. As I said earlier, I do not believe Covid Hysteria is a pimple on the smooth skin of democracy. Many priests, bishops, and ministers had no problem lying to their congregation about Covid because many of them lie for a living. Many church leaders do not believe in the central ideas of the Christian faith such as the actual bodily resurrection of Jesus Christ. Most priests I have met over the years privately believe Christianity is complete nonsense. They are just waiting for retirement and the pension. When you sit them down and ask them for their personal views, they will tell you that they don't believe a word of it. They might be honest with you, but not in public.

I have had many of these conversations over the years with priests in Australia. They all have a different spin. There are at least four versions. They say, *'if Jesus rose for you, then he rose spiritually,'* or that *'the resurrection is theologically true but not literally true,'* or they talk about the contradictions in the Gospels or the mystery of faith. They are entitled to their opinion as we all are, but if they do not believe, why are they priests or bishops? I don't understand why they bother. Every Sunday they stand up and say that they believe in the resurrection. They recite the Creed and say every week they believe in something they do not. They are hypocrites. Lying about Covid was not a big deal, as lying is just something they do every Sunday.

Some denominations struggle to find belief at all and that is not a surprise. Unbelief is strongest in the church, especially churches drowning in tradition and ritual. They are more museums now than a living testimony of faith, eager to please everyone, but ending up pleasing no one. All the churches are in serious trouble. The axe has been at the trunk for some time, the blade is sharp. People see through the façade, and they are sick of the hypocrisy. They vote with their feet and leave. That is a good decision. Leaving a church is a vote for personal spiritual safety. The church only limps on by the patience of God. It is only God that holds back the decisive chop.

The great weakness of the church is its love of money. It is at the heart of their kingdom on earth. Just go to church and see their love of money in action. The church is not Christianity. Test what Christians claim not according to their traditions, but according to their Holy Book, the Bible, and I guarantee you will be shocked. Many of these Christians assume you will never open the Bible. Jesus had nowhere to sleep each night and died with only the shirt on his back, and yet he changed the world. In the church, you will not even get change. They will make sure your money stays safe in their pockets. Don't go to church, follow Jesus instead.

3 WHAT IS THE ANTIDOTE TO MASS FORMATION PSYCHOSIS?

What will Christians do for money?

From the beginning of 2020 until the beginning of 2022, the West was in the firm grip of Covid Hysteria. There was no justification for the end of the Covid crisis as deaths, hospitalizations, and post-vaccination transmission continued. In Australia, deaths from Covid rose dramatically as did post-vaccination transmission. Throughout this politically defined crisis, the church in the West, overall, sided with the state. This was despite the changing narratives, the cover-ups, policy failures, the social and psychological wasteland, and the apostasy that this capitulation required. Church leaders invented Covid Theology, the latest perverse twisting of the New Testament to justify financial transfer from the state to the church. The church regularly comes up with other Theologies to justify state policies, such as support for the War on Terror (the Twenty-Years War as I call it), and the Vietnam War to name a few. The Western Church is usually a great defender of war, which helps to explain the plummeting social support for Christianity since the 1920s amongst war-weary generations. Jesus was a man of peace and yet the church is militant, not for God and the gospel, but as a salesperson for bombmakers and warmongers.

Covid Theology was probably the first time this corrupt

institution strayed into public health. They said little during the AIDS epidemic, except to condemn gay people, though there were many Christians who stood with and supported those who suffered. Covid Theology was driven by monetary concerns, the only imperative of churches in the second decade of this century. The Church's Covid response was more to do with money than with public health. Overall, the churches with more to lose were the most supportive of draconian government policies.

From a Christian perspective, the silence of the Church in Covid was and remains a sin. It was an apostasy, a betrayal of Christ who touched the lepers, healed the sick, and visited the dying. There was similar prejudice during the first century towards illness, but no vaccine passports and no synagogues were closed to the ill. For all their faults, it seems the Pharisees allowed the infirmed and paralyzed to attend some gatherings. Even they would be astonished at the evil of churches turning people away if they did not hold a government-approved set of papers to prove their capacity to enter the building.

The mechanics of how churches capitulated, fell, and were bought off, is beyond the scope of this book, but it is a sordid story worth telling. No doubt those responsible have been deleting their cell phone records and emails and crawling back into the swamps from which they emerged, but God knows their hearts and all their dirty little secrets.

I have not been privy to such privileged information, but I have a few suspicions. I suspect that it is a ruling class dynamic as the church overall in the West functions in this way, as a defensive mechanism to protect privilege and power, certainly not to promote the Gospel or the good news of God's grace. Certain experts crept in from the government and private sector. There were 'backroom meetings,' where church leaders were taught the 'secrets' about Covid. These 'secrets' have all been discredited now, as you know, but church leaders love to be groomed by the state and state functionaries. It gives them a sense of self-importance.

Their allegiance to the king of kings is nothing compared to the honor of being spoken to by a powerful government bureaucrat asking them to betray their faith, especially for the money. These meetings with the 'experts' were crude instruments to enforce conformity. As was the case with the Omicron rhetoric, there is evidence of propaganda in these churches as everyone repeated the same arguments for complicity as if reading from a received script. Someone needs to write a detailed history of this awful apostasy for posterity.

What is God's response to the Christian church in the West during Covid Hysteria? It is simple. God will tear the Western church down, brick by brick, cathedral by cathedral, troll horde by troll horde, bank balance by bank balance, property by property. Where your treasure is, that is where your heart is, and the church loves money above all else. Their fingers grip their wealth tightly, the whites of their knuckles strain as they hold onto the money bags, and their eyes furtively glance back and forth, eyeing suspiciously anyone who might dare to threaten their wealth. The apostle John told us to keep ourselves from idols (1 John 5: 21). The church says that don't have any idols while counting their money.

Many churches were silent during the pandemic because of their love of money. They have built a kingdom on earth and hope Jesus will not return because if he does, there goes the wealth. The church in the West covets money and power. The veneer is Christian, the façade, but the heart is greed. Christianity is just the wallpaper, covering the gold and the silver.

The future of the Western institutional church is clear:
God will strip the church of all its wealth until all they have left is him.

If you have God, you have everything, but it is difficult to look at God when your hands are full of cash, you are treading over the poor and the weak, in search of more money. These church leaders are happy to betray their Savior for a dime and yet unable to part from one percent of their vast financial fortune. Marx said something like that a long time ago. He was right.

True freedom doesn't come from democracy

You will have to look hard to find churches in love with money and cherishing freedom. The love of money enslaves. Churches that love money have a lot of rules, which is not surprising. Covid Hysteria was designed to overturn freedom and usher in tyranny. This suited many Christians whose lives are anything but free. Many

Christians hate freedom, even true freedom. The idea that God brings freedom fills them with disgust. They want the rules and the regulations, and the stipulations and the restrictions.

The war against freedom is ancient, fought no more strongly than in the church. People have been fighting this war for a long time and will do so until the return of Jesus Christ and the end of all things. Jesus arrived on the scene with one intention, to bring freedom to the soul, the heart, and the mind. It is no wonder the church hates freedom because of what Jesus came to do, they continually oppose it, and it is no wonder the Christian disciples of Covid Hysteria rallied against freedom. Jesus said in the Gospel of John: *'If the Son shall set you free, you shall be free indeed' (John 8: 36)*. The apostle Paul said in a letter to the church in Corinth: *'...where the Spirit of the Lord is, there is freedom' (2 Corinthians 3: 17)*. To the Galatians, he wrote: *'It is for freedom that Christ has set us free' (Galatians 5:1)*.

None of these verses have anything to say about democracy. The early Christian assemblies flourished in the first century under the Roman Empire ruled by dictators, such as Caligula, Tiberias, and Nero. This was 1800 years before Western democracy, before elections, and long before America. Freedom is ancient. It is not new. It predates modern democracy. It has no language barrier, it is not patented by anyone, and no one nation or party can claim ownership of it.

We are the freest when we know God and God knows us. Freedom that comes from God is freedom from sin and death, guilt, and shame, and fear and despair. To know God is what it means to be a Christian, it is not about obedience or regulations or morality, but it is knowing God, who he is, and what he has done for us. The starting point and endpoint remain the Bible, which is where God speaks to us today in words we can understand. God speaks to our hearts, our minds, and our souls. True freedom does not come from democracy. True freedom is a gift from God. When we know God, we can know ourselves, and the world around us.

Covid Hysteria shone a light on the tapestry of deceit in our society and highlighted what is true and what is false. It once again showed the lie of democracy, that democracy and freedom are synonyms. They are not. Many people believe that freedom is about the state and our relationship with the government. It is not.

Freedom is about us and our relationship with God.

The only freedom worth having is one that is real, and for everyone, regardless of who they are. Freedom cannot only be for a small group of people, it must be for all, or at least offered to all, otherwise, it is not freedom. True freedom needs to be such that it cannot be taken away, censured or censored, restricted or removed, suspended or withdrawn. True freedom exists regardless of circumstance, social standing, wealth, or position in society.

Covid Hysteria promoted Counterfeit Freedom

One of the first tasks in stripping back misinformation is to go after *counterfeit* freedom. When many people talk about freedom, they are not talking about true freedom, though they are using the same word. Counterfeit freedom is what people in power offer those whom they hold in contempt, those without power. People in power neither live by the standards they demand from others nor do they grant true freedom. They lord their position over others (Luke 22: 25). They use their power to abuse others, climb over others, exercise power over them, and control them. People in power in democracies have no idea how you live, have no intention of living like you, and will never emulate the standards they continually demand of you. They demand everything but give little in return.

We also see counterfeit freedom at work since late 2019 as governments scrambled to cover-up the origins of the original Covid virus. When you are playing God, you need to know everything, but no one does, and no one can. Poor innocent bats in some market somewhere got the blame. They didn't have any good defense lawyers since they have no human rights. The same with monkeys in monkeypox. They have no access to lawyers to defend their reputation against such unwarranted character assaults. The coverup over the Covid lab leak made no sense, nor did the fantastical nonsense of trying to pretend it jumped from nature after hanging around with humans for thousands of years. Research into viruses is a global effort. Nations want better technology and the edge, driven by profit and power, they push forward, cut corners, and mistakes invariably happen. The bizarre ambiguities, questions over American involvement in Wuhan, and the vehement denial by the same institutions that ran the Twenty-Years War, the so-called 'War on Terror,' are a trinity of fake news about Covid origins. They lied for twenty years about American involvement in the Middle East so why would these institutions suddenly tell us the truth? If the world admitted the truth back in 2020, the response to Covid, the creation of Covid Hysteria, might have been different. Once again, it is all very human, it is about fear, guilt, and responsibility.

But Covid came at an interesting time. It is why America is trying to destroy Russia through the proxy war in Ukraine and why the Americans want a war with China. Something is different this time, something has changed since bird flu or swine flu, or even AIDS. The high point of American global rule is over. America is falling. The world is in flux. Had there been no anxiety over the future of America, the pandemic would have been approached differently, but America is in trouble. Everyone knows that the global tectonic plates are shifting.

This coincided with another trend which is what people in power never tell you and that is that many of them don't believe in democracy. Just look at the American ruling class. Democracy, the idea that everyone has an equal say in the running of a nation, gets in the way of their agenda. They simply tolerate it. The ruling class are fascists or elitists and believe that political power belongs in the hands of a small group of experts who should rule the nations and compel everyone to obey. They believe that ordinary people are stupid and irrelevant. This has been the prevailing view of the American ruling class throughout the twentieth century to the present.

A fragment of this broader disenchanted ruling class decided to push the envelope. They think highly of themselves. A small group of people in power came up with a way to advance an agenda to destroy what is left of liberal democracy in the West, to push it further toward the abyss. They wanted to see how far they could advance their scheme using the existing structures, laws, and systems. These people believe in a better future if they make the decisions. Covid is just the continuation of their century-long struggle to produce better quality people and fewer people if possible. Just watch them tear America apart today. It is fascinating to watch. Twenty years ago, the ruling class ignored the nation responsible for 9/11 and demonized all Muslims instead. Now, the

Biden administration has called all Trump voters fascists and enemies of democracy. A nation that cannot exist without 'enemies within' is doomed to fail.

Despite all their pretensions, they are not leaders, they are not young leaders, nor will they be real leaders. A true leader is a person of the people, who lives alongside them, and goes into battle with them. A true leader is a servant, a friend to all, and is always prepared to die for their people. A true leader is a person whom even their enemy respects. Such a person anyone will follow. I am not talking about fake leaders or false leadership such as wearing army fatigues and unshaven before the camera before posing for fashion magazines. The troops loved Napoleon, the redcoats loved Wellington, and the Civil War generals on both sides were adored by their men. Why? They fought on the same battlefield together, and some died.

The problem with these fascists is that they could not come up with a perfect model for indoctrination. Too many people saw through it, and too many problems emerged with the tools they employed to promote it. The Covid Hysteria lasted about a year and is now falling apart at the seams. It was poor hypnosis, based on dodgy science and faulty technology. The vaccines are unable to stop infection, transmission, hospitalization, or death. None of the vaccines have been able to stop Covid and tragically Western governments have gone to the other extreme and seem content if everyone contracts the disease. Bizarrely, by mid-2022, Covid Hysteria was closed, just after the Winter Olympics, just in time for the Ukraine War. The people who created it were the ones who shut it down. The cost has been horrific. The fascists who invented it now want us to forget about it and 'go back to normal.' We are not even allowed to talk about it, even though more people today are dying of Covid than during any of the lockdowns and most of the victims are fully vaccinated.

But what about the followers they have left behind, the new converts to fascism? They were exploited and led astray. Many of these converts were lost souls anyway. They exist in a dazed state and are easily manipulated. This includes many in the chattering classes and the middle class. A cacophony of voices competes for their minds. People live with a constant factory of fear and manufactured anxiety. These fear factories target our entire system, our minds, hearts, and memories, they sow anxiety to unsettle, undermine, and overthrow our ways of thinking. Fear of the unknown, fear of others, fear of Covid, and fear of the future have become the new normal. This is not freedom, it is tyranny.

A word to those new converts to state authority

I have a few words to say to the new true believers, the ones who believe that loyalty to the state is the highest virtue, those who trusted the government without question for the last three years, those who are convinced the government never, ever lied to you:

Maybe you are one of these true believers. Two years ago, you didn't trust people in power. Now you do. You cannot be swayed from your conviction that people in power are always right, and they will never, ever lie to you. You are devout in your belief. You listen to people in power because you trust them completely and absolutely, there is no chink in your armor, no Achille's Heel. Daily you listened faithfully to the new Mass, and the daily covid briefings, you line up for whatever booster shot is on offer and will not hear anyone who presents an alternative point of view. You have become a weapon, a tool of people in power. You were brainwashed in less than a year. Your beloved leaders represent absolute truth, and they can be trusted implicitly and completely. You know they will always tell you the truth because they want to protect you. You don't need to question, doubt, or disagree, because you are not an expert and only the government knows the truth.

'You don't want to be wrong. You don't dare to admit you were wrong and you keep believing the lie. Some of you will eventually wake up, but many of you will believe that you were never lied to for the rest of your lives. You rant and rave at the unvaccinated, you avoid them, you break friendship and fellowship, and you cast them out of your homes and your churches.

One day, you will be in the nursing home or hospital dying alone because your children and grandchildren are ashamed of you and what you did. You will hold stubbornly to your belief that life was perfect before the unvaccinated came along. It was all their fault because they questioned our beloved leaders. The unvaccinated were to blame, they made us sick, and they were selfish. Our leaders were the cure.

History will not be kind to you. You will die alone, unloved, and forgotten objects of shame, and targets for ridicule. Kids, children, they don't like the kind of person you will become, angry, regretful, bitter. Remember that when you continue your rant about the unvaccinated in the years to come and condemn every question as a conspiracy theory. You make fun of Christians, but you have your own religion now. You will obey and trust the government and bow on bended knees to the state. Why would they lie to you? But if they do lie, then what then? Will you give up your faith? Probably not. Even their faults will become virtues.'

History will record Covid Hysteria as one of the great crimes of the last hundred years, the latest sordid eugenics nightmare in response to Covid whose origins are just as elusive as its cure. A change is coming. Evil is always exposed eventually and then the prosecutions begin. Triple-injected or quadrupled-injected individuals should not be contracting the virus at all. Each day we step further away from Covid Hysteria, and it is quickly vanishing from view. We will be told *'this is old news, and we have more important things to talk about,'* or we will be told to *'stop dredging up the past,'* or *'governments were only trying their best with the information they had at the time,'* or *'please forgive us, we didn't know what we were doing,'* or *'we were just following orders.'* We will be told *'accidents happen or that we are only human.'* We are being told *'it is only the flu,'* and *'there is no need to isolate,'* and *'we knew the vaccines don't work, but don't get obsessed by it.'*

People in power lied for two years about this pandemic. They are still lying. People continue to believe even when the narrative changes and new truths are declared, and old truths are declared no longer true. What we have seen is a half-dozen sudden backflips in the Covid Hysteria, in unison, or tandem around the world. These sudden shifts in the covid paradigm of truth have occurred regularly and are rarely questioned. The shifts are indicative of a failed narrative, and a false narrative. The sudden departures and shifts in the narrative should have the warning sign that people in power were lying but people in power got away with it. They usually do. Instead of leading to a new conventional wisdom as is normal in liberal democracies, Covid Hysteria has simply evolved to protect the political and economic authors and beneficiaries of the crisis.

The Starting point is to think for yourself

The starting point is to think for yourself before you get dragged into the next bout of mass formation psychosis. This is the war in Ukraine. The timing is amazing. America knew the invasion time down to the hour. Russia politely waited until after the end of the Winter Olympics. Many people in power in the West have not been this excited since 9/11. Many are ecstatic, as they hide the body bags, and the blood banks and sign the defense contracts. Ukraine is also a testing ground for new weapons and technology to prepare us for the next war. Google it. This is WW3. The slogan *'Stand with Ukraine,'* is a declaration of war with the world's largest holders of nuclear weapons. This means Australia, Canada, the EU, America and Britain are officially at war with Russia.

Your kids, the ones you want to keep safe, so you got them vaccinated, they might get called up and in the next war, they can do their bit for freedom. Like the insanity of the Great War, your kids will be blinded, maimed, and blown to pieces, while your rich and wealthy leaders and their children will remain safe and at home, drinking chardonnay and waxing lyrical about human rights. There are already Western troops on the ground in Ukraine. This includes personnel from America, Britain, and Australia, some fighting, some *'training'* just like Vietnam. It is a proxy war. Many people will now happily send their kids to die. They did last time. Remember the War on Terror, the Twenty-Years War, or as we also know it, the Great American Defeat. That war was an exercise in propaganda. Name one individual we fought against in the two decades of that war, aside from Osama Bin Laden. Bet you can't. By the time most people cotton on to any of these propaganda schemes, it is too late for the victims. That is how propaganda works. It is a painkiller, to dull the senses while the death merchants move in for a profit.

The problem for the American ruling class is that the American people will not stomach a drawn-out conflict. Wars should be like the movies they watch easy to understand, and simplistic, with an ending where the goodies win, and the baddies die. Unfortunately, life is not like American movies. Mass formation psychosis is a form of propaganda but people in the West are not like the beaten broken people under Stalin or Mao. They think for themselves. Many people in Western nations, however, also suffer from collective attention deficit disorder. They cannot keep their attention on anything for long enough. Just look at the West and the Ukraine War. People are sick of hearing about it already, only a few months later. They want another distraction. Time is essential for indoctrination, but Westerners are easily bored and always looking for something new. Thankfully, the September 2022 counteroffensive in Ukraine was branded by the media as a decisive defeat for Russia heralding the end of the war. This gives Americans a sigh of relief so they can forget about a conflict that has been raging in that part of the world for almost a decade. The facts on the ground, the truth, and the awful tragedy are irrelevant. The media has decided 'nothing to see here friends, move on.'

This is what I call the 'misinformation' of misinformation. In other words, propaganda exists, but we still have a choice, and we can choose to ignore it. The misinformation about misinformation gives more power to propaganda than it deserves, and we are being lied to about its power over us. We are giving it far too much power in our thinking and in our estimation of its power over us. Controlling someone's mind is a difficult thing to do because life is difficult to control. Take a virus. Viruses are tricky things, they, like us, just want a place in the sun. Like all living things, they want to live, they escape and bypass vaccines, mutate and change. So do we, and so can we, change. People choose to be indoctrinated; they choose to be hypnotized by the state. They willingly forfeit their freedoms. People enjoy being lied to, or they prefer not to look too closely into things to avoid personal responsibility. During the Holocaust, the classic excuses in Germany were: *'I didn't know what was going on,'* or *'I thought the smoke and smell of something burning was just the factory down the road.'*

Our world is a dangerous place. In our world a few eagles are moving around from one prey to the next, the eagles have a pecking order, and behind them are the little birds along for the ride, the influencers, the commentators, journalists, the strategic analysts, the 'experts' bought and paid for, they scavenge, and they sort, and make their living from the titbits of the dead, moving from one corpse to the next. The internet is full of these little birds. They lie for a living. We are force-fed a steady diet of their poison every day. The benefits are large salaries, good jobs in think tanks and departments, respect from their peers, and a fast track to hell.

Covid Hysteria is just the latest propaganda exercise and don't worry when Mr. Covid has moved on, you will be able to believe in another manufactured lie to take its place, with a specific cause, a specific problem, and of course specific people to blame for it. You will do as you are told. Many of you always do. This mass formation is child's play. It is pigeon food. You were duped about the War on Terror. You were duped about Covid. You are being lied to about Ukraine, so after that mess, what is the next big thing to turn your mind, your heart, and your soul?

What does God promise us?

Some people in power in the church are now handing out the new script for Act 2. Act 1 was to support vaccines. Act 2 is to oppose Russia. Churches that opposed vaccination are lining up to prove their patriotism and love of war. It is amazing to see so many Christians who were opposed to Covid Hysteria were quick to denounce Putin and quick to support military intervention (war) in Eastern Europe. They want us to take sides and begin to hate. That is not a surprise. I cannot think of many Christian leaders who are calling for a negotiated peace in Ukraine or even peace. Most support war with Russia.

We need to protect our hearts, minds, and souls from misinformation. The only way forward in our world to combat deceit, delusion, propaganda, and indoctrination is to do the most subversive, radical thing possible: open the Bible and read it. The Bible? What are you talking about? Surely you mean to protest, violence, revolution? Surely you mean voting out people in power and putting in the right people? No, don't bother. You will fail, and you might end up dying for nothing, nothing at all. There is nothing more pointless than protests, and violent protests are useless.

One thing I have learned is that *God only promises what he promises*. He does not promise anything he does not promise and yet we spend all our time away from the promises of God. Be careful what you do, or you might find yourself fighting against God and his purposes. The answer is not to be found in political action, revolution, or violence. Because the target of propaganda is the mind, the only way to effectively combat these assaults is to defend the mind by opening the one book people in power hope that you never open, the Bible. Just listen to the church now. They have taken sides once again in another conflict, in a pattern that goes right back to the Crusades. In standing for Ukraine, as they stood for America after 9/11, the churches are standing against God. God does not take sides in a war.

As Christians, we believe that God speaks to us through the Bible, and therefore, we read it to understand what God is saying to us today. God's word is as relevant to our world as it was thousands of years ago. People have not changed. God has not changed. People are the same everywhere, predictable, and in need of saving from themselves. The Bible encourages us to renew our minds, to think about good things, and positive things, it encourages us to think about who God is, what he has done, and what he continues to do in this world.

I encourage you to do something far more dangerous than protesting, it is the most dangerous thing in the world you can do, and it is the one thing that people in power fear more than an army, and that is people who pray. Pour out your heart to God, plead with him for your nation, for your family, and your people, pray to God and claim his promises. Prayer is the most powerful weapon you have. Many in the church say prayer only changes the person praying, (their attitudes), because God cannot change a thing, but that is not true. God hears our prayers, and he is the God who answers them. He is the God who acts.

What is the greatest threat to faith in the world today?

Do not mishear what I am saying. I am not saying go back to church or go to church. The church is not the answer. The church is part of the problem and that is because church leaders are people in power as well. They have their own agenda which is usually money, and they crave to influence the souls of weak people for selfish gain. Overall, there are exceptions, but many churches are now unsafe places. The greatest threat to faith in the West is not the government, but the church, and the most dangerous institution in the world is the institutional church especially a church under state control or influence.

Many priests, pastors, and ministers are 'soul catchers.' They prevent the soul from reaching God and trap them. God wants us to know who we are and who he is. That is simply what a Christian is, someone who knows God and grows in their knowledge of God. To know God and Jesus Christ whom he sent is the Christian message. The church doesn't want that. The more you know of God, the weaker their power over you is. The more you read the Bible, the more you pray, the more you think for yourself, and the weaker their power over you is. God wants to know us so our souls can be free.

The church wants to prevent us from knowing God so our souls can be caught by them, controlled, and abused. Freedom for you is the last thing they desire. Many people go to church because they don't know who God is and they hope the priest does, but usually, he has no idea either and so he hides behind rituals no one understands, but they look good, and he can talk about the mystery of faith because he doesn't have any.

Many people in power in the churches covet political power. People in power who seek to recruit the church for their own political ends are naïve, they are better off recruiting vipers. The Church of England, the Presbyterian Church, Rome, and orthodoxy, among others, have enjoyed political power for centuries, real power, that overshadows anything political leaders have entertained in recent years. The Christian Church killed more people over time than Hitler, Stalin, and Mao combined. They caused most of the wars, and most of the famines and kept the poor in servitude and misery for hundreds of years complete with short-life expectancy, illness, and disease. There is nothing that excites the church more than the prospect of political power, the possibility of restoration, and the return of the sword. They want their places of power back.

Churches in the West were easily silenced in Covid because they want the power. They are easily silenced if they can gain more power and money. These things bring security and longevity. Their price is more power, more access to power, and more influence. They want a role, a seat at the table, an ear in the cabinet, the confidence of the PM, or a visit to the White House. They crave political power, not to promote the kingdom of God, but to ensure their continued power and wealth.

Many churches are no longer churches, they are corporations, powerful corporations, largely outside the tax system, and they wield a lot of power in the West. Christianity is just the face. The heart of the machine is money, lots of it, and it needs to be protected. I am sure the World Economic Forum has an agenda. Everyone does. Do not, however, underestimate the power of the church, and its ambition. It would not take much for the church to return to its places of power in the world. The deader the church is in the world, the more political power it assumes.

These days we are told that mass formation psychosis doesn't exist, or propaganda. That is a joke. The church has been at it for far longer than the CIA, MI6, or KGB combined. The church knows all about mass formation psychosis because they are the template, they are the expert craftsmen, they are the real deal, and they have been weaving their black magic for centuries. They are the compass, the foundation stone, and the architects of mass formation. They care little about the people under their control, they lure them in but do not enable them to think for themselves, or to reason, pray, or ponder. The local church was and is the microcosm of mass formation, where people are never set free, only controlled. The soul catchers have their methods, techniques, incantations, and spells, and freedom is a curse never to be uttered.

To those who created the Covid Hysteria propaganda exercise, I say well done, you did well, it has about a year to go, it is already falling apart, with the questions of myocarditis and cancer, deaths of the vaccinated, and so on. Two years, wow. Amazing. But listen to this: The state-based Christian church managed to run a mass formation exercise that lasted centuries, to foster hatred between Christians, Protestants, and Catholics. Even today, prejudices remain, with all the old hostilities and hatreds. The soul catchers run rings around anything governments can create. Sure, Mao ran his brainwashing for a generation, so what, Pol Pot for less time than that, even Stalin needed a slaughterhouse because, so few believed his brainwashing. Hitler's regime didn't last 15 years, let alone 1,000.

The fascists and communists of the twentieth century were aftershocks of the global earthquake that was caused by the

Christian church in the West. It would have been terrible to live in a world run by the Roman Catholic Church, or the Church of England. There was no compassion, no tolerance, no forgiveness, no love, only tyranny, and death.

Those of you who love a conspiracy theory have been misled. You have been watching the wrong thing for years. Covid Hysteria is but a ripple on the pond. The World Economic Forum did not drop the rock, they are an echo of the past. Their books are entertainment, craving accolades from the dead. They look back with envy on the true masters who in their glory shaped the world for centuries.

This was the Christian Church, the first fascists. They are the ones who wrote the book on misinformation, it is their language. It is their alphabet. They wrote the script. We still live in their shadow, and in many ways, suffer from their curse. We all danced to their tune at one point. We are just actors in their play and every play is a tragedy. Look at what they did in Northern Ireland. Look at the history of the Church of England. Look at the Religious Wars. That is mass formation. That is propaganda. If you can create a lie that transcends nations and generations for over a century, then that is impressive. The church has a dark history, a violent history, and one that has nothing to do with Christianity, and certainly nothing to do with Christ Jesus.

Faith and religion are not the same

When you read the Bible, especially the New Testament, you are struck with the great revelation, that the faith described is completely different from what the church promotes and lives out. Many people have said that they love Jesus but hate the church. The history of the church grieves God because it is always in his name. The history of the Western church is one long graveyard in a place called regret. Religion points to the church, while faith points to Jesus. They are not the same. I do not defend the church, nor its history of malice and hate. It is impossible. All the established churches have blood on their hands.

Most Christians rush to defend the history of the church or they try to whitewash it. Not me. Christianity for me was never about the church, it was always about Jesus Christ and a personal relationship with God. All church buildings should be sold, and the money given to the poor. Churches can gather anywhere and everywhere. Jesus would do that and so would I. There are no church buildings in heaven, so why should we have them here?

For me, I am interested in the person and work of Jesus, not the history of church fascists and their devotees. It all comes down to Jesus and what you think of him. Those who love Jesus but hate the church are right. Jesus and the church are different. They are in different worlds. Despite the nightmare of the church, I believe that we need to go back to an open Bible and ask ourselves three questions. First, what did Jesus say? Second, what did he mean? Third, what is he saying to us today?

I believe that the only essential thing in the world is to see ourselves clearly once we see Jesus clearly. The rest will take care of itself. I believe that by reading, pondering, talking, and discussing the Bible, you are engaging in the most powerful exercise you can do. The Bible is the most hated, subversive, radical text of our age, universally hated by people in power who want us to close the Bible and have us listen to them. Most people in power like the church, they just hate the Bible, and whoever opens it. Most ordinary people hate the church and like Jesus. That is the paradox of faith in our time. If you want to change the world, open the Bible, and read it. If you want to change the world, pray, pray some more, and then some more. Find another person who wants to read the Bible with you, and pray, and there you have the 'church' as it was meant to be.

The Christian church, especially when it bonded to states, creating state churches, was the Master of Mass Formation Psychosis, not the victims. The world it created, oversaw, and ruled, was one of violence, malice, and oppression and lasted for centuries. The various branches of this hideous leviathan, Orthodox, Catholic, Protestant, all drank from the same cup, a wine distilled from the blood of Christians who dared to follow Jesus. Therefore, the greatest threat to faith in this world is not the government, corporations, or the World Economic Forum, but the Church, the Christian Church, especially those people in power in the church who long for a return to their places of power in society when they had the sword.

The Church remains the source of true mass formation psychosis. Church leaders are masters of manipulation, indoctrination, and hypnosis, and we live in the ruins of the world they created a thousand years of tyranny, death, and suffering. The fascists, communists, and democrats of the twentieth century and twenty-first centuries are just copycats. When the fascists and communists spoke of freedom, a large part of it was freedom from the power and violence of the Christian Church.

There is a profound difference between religion and faith. They are not the same. People in power love to equate Christianity with religion. Christianity is about faith, not religion. Religion is about rituals, rules, and institutions. Faith is a relationship with God the Father and Jesus Christ whom he sent. Religion leads to the church, while faith leads to Jesus Christ. One is external, the other is internal, one is about membership, and the other is about identity.

Fascists within government are experiencing a renaissance in the West, and there is also corporate fascism. They all have their agenda, their plans, and ambitions, but the greatest threat to the Christian, to the life of faith, is the Church. The greatest evil in the church is their agents of hypnosis, the soul catchers, those men, and women who use their power in the church to prevent you from finding God, and true freedom. These soul catchers take advantage of weak-minded people, lure them in, keep them trapped in guilt, and shame, and make sure the money keeps coming. For many, religion is a deal that thinks they are making with God but in fact, it is a contract they made with men, and they didn't read the fine print.

It is very hard to be a faithful follower of Jesus in a corrupt Church. But there are some brave souls even in the darkest places. People of faith in those churches, few as they are, are the true warriors of our age. A true Christian standing up for Jesus Christ in any of these corrupt religious institutions is a sight to behold. They are there for true freedom found in Jesus Christ, but they fight a war on a dozen fronts, against monied power, against class distinctions and evils, against church tradition and ritual, against a culture of abuse and toxicity, against heritage and the past, against clerical power and abuse, against malicious gossip and slander, and against racism and prejudice.

These few men and women are the saints of the faith, fighting in the darkness with the light of Christ in dark places, places of oppression, misery, and despair. There are no darker places than in some churches today. Many leaders in the church care nothing for

Christ and nothing for God. It is about power, their power over others, their money, and their reputation.

The goal of mass formation psychosis is the evil intent to influence others for pernicious gain. The target of propaganda is the mind, the seat of the Spirit, a sacred place. Propaganda is foreign, intrusive, and invasive. The goal is a distraction, to shift our attention to new topics, ideas, and principles. Nobody has access to the mind, except God, not even the Devil has access. But propaganda is about distraction, shifting attention, and creating habits of the mind. We are told to remember some things and forget others.

An example of this is the way we think about the world today. The past is to be forgotten as quickly as possible. Before 9/11, in the West, we lived in a world of relativism, a *'live and let live'* world. There was space for different points of view to flourish, compete, and coexist. Those days are gone. Since 9/11, the West, which I assume to include America, its satellites and allies, Britain, and Europe, has rejected relativism in favor of absolutism. Absolutism teaches that there is only one answer to every problem. Most modern problems are technical or administrative, reflecting the growing complexity of society. Modern problems have no clear answer, we must swim and navigate in a world of ambiguity. Most problems in our world today could be managed effectively or solved.

We all, however, are living in a world of post-traumatic stress disorder created by America. After 9/11, America was traumatized by the fact that they had enemies in the world and not everyone in the world loved and adored them. Absolutism killed Relativism and reintroduced 'good and evil' into politics. First, it was Osama bin Laden, then the Taliban, then ISIS, then Trump, then the unvaccinated, and now Russia. America changes its mind so often now we have a hard time catching up. We are told that Trump is the Antichrist and once people accept that, he is already gone. Now, Putin is the Antichrist. Who will it be tomorrow?

The shift in mass formation psychosis is seen clearly in the ditching of Covid Hysteria in favor of War in Ukraine. Putin is now the new Trump, the embodiment of pure evil. We are all told to hate Putin. This is the new loyalty test, like the vaccines: *Prove your patriotism to the nation. Sit down shut up and do as you are told. Forget about Afghanistan, Iraq, Syria, and Libya. Stop talking about the Taliban, collateral damage, and civilian deaths. Forget Julian Assange. That's 'yesterday's truth,' the new truth is that war is bad, and nations that go to war are 'evil,' like Russia.* The hypocritical West condemns Putin for doing what the West was doing for twenty years. They talk of war crimes in Ukraine. What about war crimes in the Middle East? The war in Ukraine is a blood feud, this is a family dispute, nasty, brutal, it is all about revenge, the worst conflicts always are.

The Ukraine civil war is a distraction from the recent disturbing revelations about the adverse effects of the vaccines, and the lies told by many people in power during Covid Hysteria. Nations shut down over 1 case of covid and now thousands of people have the disease, everyone is vaccinated, and the lockdowns are over. That does not make sense.

The only truth in the world is a person

You must take a side, Michael, why are you not condemning the new Antichrist? Why should I? Don't I care? Of course, I care about the 15 or so conflicts in progress in the world today. Ethiopia is being torn apart by the Tigray civil war, which began in November 2020. Thousands of civilians have been killed or massacred, there are over 2 million displaced people, thousands of soldiers killed in combat, and there is a humanitarian catastrophe. Yemen has been in a civil war since 2014. There are civil wars in Myanmar, Libya, Mali, and Syria, and ethnic conflict in Sudan.

Those of you who know the mind of God and know that Putin is evil, which side is God on in all these conflicts? Is their suffering any less important than Ukraine's? Are children in Africa less important than Ukrainian children, does the color of your skin and the wealth of your nation still determine the attention and priority of the West? How sad that it does. Do we see #Ethiopia, or #Africapeace? Maybe. Do corporations stop credit cards in these nations, or go after the filthy rich oligarchs? No, they don't. Who is selling weapons to all sides in all these wars? Soon after the Russian conflict with Ukraine began, the American Congress approved 40 billion dollars to go to the Ukraine war machine. Where is the money to help the starving children in Africa? Who knows?

Innocent children are forgotten if they were born in the wrong part of the world. If Ukraine was not in Europe, you would not have known about the war, and many people would not care one bit. People in power in the West today believe the life of a White European is worth more than the life of an African, an Asian, or anyone else. They have for centuries. But God doesn't. God sees all human life as the same and he sees everyone the same. Everyone is on the same level and of the same importance, and that is perhaps why people in power hate God, he sees them in the same way he sees the most irrelevant of those under their power.

Propaganda is always about deceit. It is why it is used. Hypnotism in Covid focused the world's attention on the now debunked 'bat origin' theory. The world was transfixed upon this natural mystery of a runaway virus, elusive, intangible. Since it came from a lab, this is just another sordid human-created catastrophe. The convenience of the bat origin meant that the world could blame it all on a freak of nature. Since it came from a lab, then we need to ask what they were doing in the lab in the first place. There are too many people whose careers and reputations are bound up in the continuation of the fake bat theory, and too many people whose careers and reputations are bound up in Covid Hysteria, its promulgation, continuance, and promotion.

Once we know this, the search for the truth is more predictable. Like the kid with his hand in the cookie jar, the myth of Covid is that this is about a virus. Wrong. This is about pride, arrogance, presumption, and opportunism. The Covid disaster has human fingerprints over all of it. Bats deserve an apology. They are always hanging around so apologize to them next time you see one.

As propaganda targets the mind, and is external, and is clothed in deceit, it is possible to resist. Most choose not to. It is easier to go with the group, to do as you are told, to follow the crowd. Now and again, you meet someone different, who doesn't follow the crowd, who thinks for themselves, who is settled in their mind, walks free, says things you cannot believe, challenges the status quo, is humble, and genuinely cares about you. They don't have an agenda, and they live ordinary lives.

That is the kind of person Jesus was. His time was a time much like our own, propaganda was rife, there was political intrigue, conflict, war, chaos, people took sides, people knew how to hate, and divide, and they knew who was to blame, and who was guilty and who was innocent. Jesus was different. That is one reason they killed him.

When Jesus arrived, he broke the hypnotic spell that rested on the minds of a few people who were going about their lives, doing ordinary things, living ordinary lives. Jesus spoke clearly and lovingly to people in words that destroyed the hypnotic power that oppressed their minds, and he can do that today to us.

Jesus speaks to us in words that can destroy the counterfeit freedom so cherished by the world today. There is one verse that comes to mind. Jesus said many things and they are recorded in the four Gospels and scattered through some letters but one saying spoke to me and when I read it, I realized this kills propaganda. is a saying that is an antidote to any form of mass formation psychosis that the world or the church throws at us.

This short saying of Jesus is found in one of the books written by a man called John who followed Jesus for three years, probably written in the middle to the end of the first century. It is a fair assumption that the words were probably spoken by Jesus to his disciples at that time, and there is no reason to expect otherwise. They are not words that would be easily forgotten. It is also likely that Jesus repeated himself on many occasions and there is no reason to expect that he would not, as this is the way of all good teachers. John was a close friend of Jesus. He was the one who was given the care of Mary, the mother of Jesus in front of the crucifixion as her son lay dying. He liked to refer to himself as the disciple whom Jesus loved as a brother. This verse is only short, and it is: *'I am the way, and the truth and the life. No one comes to the Father, except through me.' (John 14: 6).*

Jesus said this to eleven of his disciples while he was enjoying the evening meal, the night of his betrayal by his close friend Judas. The disciples of Jesus had asked him where he was going. Jesus replied by saying that he was returning to his Father, to God. His disciples did not want him to leave. They were his students and friends. It was a shock to them that Jesus was leaving them. He answered that all who desired to follow God could only go through him. He was the way to the Father, he was the truth about the Father, and he would bring life to all that the Father gave him.

It was a strange response. That one verse is the entirety of the

Christian message. It is a little summary of the good news about Jesus. Jesus did not say that he was a way or one of many truths, or that he came to preach a new truth or teach a new way, but that he was the way, the truth, and the life. What Jesus said was deeply radical, controversial, and subversive, especially these days.

What Jesus says here in these few words is the heart of the Christian message. Notice what he does not say. He does not say that church is the way, the church is the truth, or the church is the life. Jesus does not say that a code of behavior is the way, the truth, or the life. Jesus does not say that a set of rules, regulations, or doctrines are the way, the truth, and the life. The focus is himself. He is the way to the Father, he is the truth about the Father, and he is the source of life. The Way, the Truth, the Life.

These are words for our time, words about freedom. This verse is a direct attack on those who want to control our minds, our hearts, and our wills. This verse is the antidote to the spell of Covid Hysteria. The power to change your life is contained in that one sentence of Jesus Christ. Your life depends on your response to what Jesus is saying. The only thing that matters in life is what you think of Jesus. The rest is background noise.

But our minds have already been infected, affected, and attacked, and this verse makes little impact on us because our immediate reaction is that it is not relevant to our lives. That part of our brain and mind that used to think about important things, things that matter, has long been occupied by something else entirely, an invasive, intrusive thing, and that is called politics. Let me explain how the world was in the past, before 9/11. Politics was on the margins of life. We used to have this system called representative democracy. In this system we appointed people to act on our behalf. These people would do a job, for us, on our behalf and then a few years later we would assess their performance and judge whether we should allow them to continue.

Everyone knew that real power in democracy resided with the bureaucracy, people who never leave, who are unelected, unaccountable, and impossible to challenge. Government officials are the ones who run the state, not political parties, or politicians. The public officials have their own agendas, their own factions, their own fiefdoms, and to a large extent, much of the political debate and conflict is simply a turf war between various factions within this larger political structure. Parties and civil society are recruited to play a role in this largely hidden political process.

Bureaucrats run the wars, and they ran the Covid Hysteria, and we saw this in the unscientific, arbitrary nonsense of the rules around the Covid Hysteria, done to the minutest detail of our lives, pages, and pages of rules governing every step, every breath, every conversation. Only an unelected bureaucrat could write those crazy documents. Bureaucrats and their corporate masters are the real sources of power in any democratic system, but we have known that for years. Bureaucracy and corporate power are the engines of democracy.

But something happened. I don't know exactly when the change occurred, but we have been infected with a disease, a disease of politics. We cannot let politics go. We are obsessed with politics. Perhaps it is because we are paranoid narcissists. These days, elections are irrelevant because we can neither let elected people do their job nor remain silent about every decision they make.

We scrutinize their every move, their every decision, their every thought, and their every relationship, holding them up to standards not even the best of us could attain. We want to hear from our politicians every day and we want to talk about them every day. They want us to talk about them every day, and we listen, and we listen, and we listen, and we are the experts on everything.

What this means in practical terms is that we no longer believe in representative democracy. This means that most people, deep down despise democracy and everything it stands for. The election is just another episode in our political madness. Few trust elections these days and so it is what happens between elections that matter. This obsession with politics is a result of a deeper problem in America that has been around for at least a century. America is the center of the Western system and so this problem has spread everywhere, wherever American ideas and culture are significant. This is what we know as the Culture War.

The Culture War is faith's terminal illness

The Culture War is the source of most division in America. It is the political language of society, and the way society defines itself, how it views itself, and the export of that view to the rest of the world. The Culture War has made the West a global insane asylum. The Culture War is not about real cultures, be they ethnic or geographical, historical, or spiritual. The Culture War is about national culture or the values of the elites, the rules of behavior, and the expected norms for people in power and how they view themselves. People in power often live boring, uneventful lives, and many are simply marketed products and brands. If you strip off the outer layers, they are like the rest of us, normal.

The Culture War is about how nations define themselves, and the cultural views, laws, and regulations of society. In the absence of a monarch, or the lack of faith in democracy, the Culture War has stepped in to become the gel, the glue that holds the nation together. It is at best, a crude caricature of any society, even the simplest. If we step back, we see the holes and the cracks. If we stare at it for too long, the entire edifice will crumble. It is an illusion, a mirage, a fiction. The Culture War is therefore the wallpaper to cover over the growing mold on the wall, it is the bandage to cover over the gangrene leg, it is the face powder to put over the face that is drained of blood.

Sadly, many Christians are deeply involved in fighting the Culture War. They cannot tell the difference between their faith and their political struggles anymore. They fight it every day: abortion, same-sex marriage, sex, gender issues, climate change, feminism, and the list goes on. Most large churches and established churches are also involved. Many Churches effectively use mass formation psychosis in the culture in the same way governments and media do.

The goal is to make you angry, make you point fingers at who is to blame and scrounge around for the simple solution that will make the problem go away. Usually, the problem is said to be a group of people and the churches cultivate hatred and loathing of them to the point where families are divided, relationships are fractured, and hatreds grow. None of this is Christian. Churches weaponize their people. Pastors whip their people up into a frenzy. For Protestants, the enemy used to be Roman Catholics, but now it's Russia or gay people, or Muslims.

The main point of mass formation psychosis in the church is to distract you from Jesus Christ. The Church loves the Culture War because church leaders view it as stepping stones for the church's return to the sword and their places of power in the West. The church is always aiming at using politics to force people to behave in a certain way or hold to certain social values. This was the old way Churches used to force conformity, through threats of violence, actual violence, and social exclusion. It was never about freedom.

Millions of people today live frail and broken lives thanks to the church and the scars they received at church. Many Christians simply don't get it. Most people will never go to church and most who have left will never return. They do not go to church because they know the people who do and know what they are really like when the church is over, and all the smiles and false piety have retreated as quickly as they do from their weekly meeting with God.

Let me get to the point. Jesus doesn't care about the Culture War. He is not interested in it, he is not taking sides, and he did not come to fight it. The Culture War is fake. We should follow him in this and have absolutely nothing to do with the Culture War. Instead, we should listen to what he is saying and what is he asking us to do, about who he is and why he came.

The only thing we need to know is what Jesus said in that verse during his meal with his friends that night. Jesus makes an exclusive claim about who he is, and who we are, in relation to him. Jesus makes it very clear that we are to either accept or reject his claim. He sets the terms and the boundaries. He says this in the middle of a meal, as Jesus said many of his famous sayings 'on the go' as we would say – they were not prepared speeches to a select audience, but conversations among friends or in smaller groups.

We have experienced during the Covid Hysteria what people in power mean when they speak. They usually follow up their words with threats or promises for what rewards might follow obedience. It is what people in power do. *'Do this, or else,'* they often say, or *'do this and you will get your freedoms back,'* or *'here, you have been good children, we will end the lockdowns but if you are naughty, then daddy and mommy are going to shut down society again.'* Jesus is not like that. He gives us a choice. Unlike people in power, Jesus does not lie to our faces. He is upfront. He tells us how it is, what the cost is, and what needs to be done. He does not hide anything, nor does he give us smooth talk, false hope, or hide the fine print.

Jesus is not trying to distract us from what is important, but he is simply asking us to ponder his statement and respond accordingly.

The Christian faith is not about what others do, but about your relationship with him. It is what you think of him, and what he thinks of you. Jesus did not come to save nations, but people, individuals whom he treats as individuals and with respect. The Culture War is not about us, fighting some cultural war together, faith is about you and me, and it comes down to personal decisions about who Jesus is. No one else can make that decision for you.

What is God's only concern?

Many people in America say: *'God bless America.'* I do not know why they say it, or what they mean when they say it. It is often code for membership in a particular worldview or party, but it is not Christian, even though many Christians believe that it is. God doesn't take sides in our petty squabbles, or national conflicts.

He is no more on America's side than Russia's or China's. America is simply another nation to him. God however cares a great deal about what we think of Jesus. It is his chief concern. It is why Jesus came, to do the work of his Father in heaven. The relationship between Jesus and the Father is at the heart of what it means to know God and follow Jesus. What we think of Jesus Christ is the main concern of God.

His disciples asked Jesus the question which prompted Jesus' statement because he built up a culture of questioning around himself. They were always comfortable asking questions. They felt that no matter how stupid the question was, it was never stupid for Jesus. Jesus never condemned any of his disciples or his enemies for any question they asked of him.

The Gospels record some intense confrontations, but at least from the point of view of conflict resolution, Jesus is incredibly honest, clearly spoken, respectful, and present. He answered them all plainly and with respect. Sometimes he indeed grew weary with his disciples, as all teachers do, as they were sometimes not listening at the time. But Jesus turns no question away.

How much of a contrast is this to people in power today? They don't like questions or queries of any sort. These days, most people in power condemn anyone for asking questions of any sort. Our democracy used to be a place where any question was permitted.

Those days are gone. The days for questions are over. It is the time for loyalty tests, unquestioning obedience, and silence. Is that because the writing is on the wall, that they know our democracy will not last forever?

Democracy has a time limit. It will eventually die. Democracy as it exists today, full of contradictions and problems will end and God is not on the side of democracy. Those in the church or involved in the Culture War who tell you that Jesus is on the side of democracy are liars. Often questions in the church are met with answers like *'you need to have more faith,' 'you should just forgive, or love others,'* or *'that's the mystery of faith.'* Jesus is a breath of fresh air in a stale church building clothed in old memories and caked in the sweat of past anger.

We need to know Jesus better and in knowing him better we can know ourselves and others. All that matters in life is what you think of Jesus. Jesus doesn't care about our politics. He does not take sides. He never has, and he never will. The idea that Jesus after the resurrection is now a man you can enlist for your political agenda is so laughable that it is tragic. He is not here to save our democracy, and he is not here to return your nation to its Christian roots. He is not here to bless your Culture War or your latest crusade against the latest minority. If you try to prop up democracy or fascism, in the name of Jesus, then you might find yourself fighting against God.

4 IS DEMOCRACY WORTH SAVING?

Covid Hysteria was no accident

Democracy was the eldest child of the family of nations that were the progeny of a world run by the Christian Church, a thousand years of living hell, superstition, murder, genocide, and suffering. It is not surprising that the twentieth century was a violent one, as many nations crawled out of the abyss only to falter, fall, and fight, groping in the dark. All the criticisms of early American and English democracy are historically accurate. These infantile forms of liberal democracy were simply new forms of exclusion and disenfranchisement. Yes, the *founding fathers* were often slave owners and misogynists. By our standards, their world was nightmarish, but a pale reflection of the horrors of a world run by the Church, which kept most of humanity in abject poverty, ignorance, and illiteracy.

The emergence of liberal democracy was largely accidental and forever incomplete. No Western nation embraced ancient democracy, adapting to material interests a more limited form called 'representative' democracy. The English and American elites reluctantly adopted this form of governance in the nineteenth century, though it would take another century for there to be genuine enfranchisement. There are people living today who suffered exclusion before African Americans were *'accepted'* as human beings and allowed to vote. Representative democracy is the system where people are elected every few years to run the state, a system where bureaucrats ostensibly act on their behalf to implement policies decided by the electoral victors.

Few people seriously believe in this system these days, as it is more ideological than practical. The proposition that these representatives decide, form, and direct policy is a quaint and romantic fiction. In America for example, Donald Trump, it seems, believed himself to be the one who made decisions, after all, he was elected. Vested corporate and political interests buy and sell the Presidency and have done for a long time. The corruption of political office is not a scandal, it is an expectation. The great deceit in the West is complicity in the fiction that elected officials genuinely represent their electorate rather than material, corporate, or special interests.

Since late 2019, there has been clear organization and coordination between governments and media over the creation, promotion, and sustaining of Covid Hysteria. There was more global cooperation on Covid than there was in response to 9/11. After the twin towers fell, parts of the American state that deal with defense, technology, and foreign affairs, effectively took the reins of power, and along with their operatives, proxies, disciples, and propaganda, drove an illegal, unproductive, and catastrophic war in the Middle East, toppling four sovereign nations. The Twenty-Years War, otherwise known as the 'War on Terror' was designed, ostensibly to 'keep us safe,' from the villains, fundamentalist Muslims like the Taliban. After 20 years, the Taliban are still there in Afghanistan, and America was defeated.

Whatever the reason for the lab leak or variation of this theme, which caused the spread of this man-made virus, the villain this time was an innocent bat in an obscure Chinese market down the road from China's virus laboratory, kept open and running by Western money. Once again, we needed to be kept safe from this virus. Now two years later, everyone is vaccinated, but people are contracting Covid at an exponential rate. Many continue to be hospitalized and die. In the same way, the elements in the American state that dealt with technology, public health, and medicine took over the state, with their proxies, operatives, disciples, and propaganda running a remarkably successful indoctrination exercise that created Covid

Hysteria. Now, with Covid Hysteria in tatters, those who benefited financially from Covid are looking for the next virus to promote, but there is a shift once again, in the state, a backflip, pivot, whatever you would like to call it.

The weapons manufacturers who make all the bombs in the world were deeply saddened that America was pulling out of Afghanistan. During the Obama years, future conflicts were being laid in embryonic form around the world involving the nations that threatened American global dominance such as Russia and China. This agitation was done to ensure a continual supply of contracts to the bomb makers who keep America safe by starting wars around the world.

America toppled the democratically elected government of Ukraine in 2014 and cultivated and supported neo-Nazi elements in the Ukrainian military such as the Azov Battalion and Right Sector. The Western media kept quiet over the civil war in the Eastern war Donbas region, a war that has been going on for 8 years. The War in Ukraine between Russia and Ukraine is the best news America has had since 9/11 which brought the so-called neo-con fascists to power on the coattails of George W. Bush. The neo-cons who have not died or retired are still in Congress and the think tank circuit in Washington DC. Most were sidelined by the Trump Train or trainwreck, depending on your point of view, but now, crucifying Trump and MAGA, they are back onstage again, salivating, and hollering for WW3, and they expect to be handsomely paid for their efforts. This time the villain is Putin, who must be denounced, from whom we need to be protected. Once again, the operatives, the disciples, and the proxies, long silent due to Covid have been reactivated and the pendulum in the state has swung back to the war economy, away from the health economy.

In all three cases, the state weaponized the population against minorities, in the War on Terror, the enemy was Muslims in America and the West, in Covid Hysteria, the enemy was unvaccinated people and in the War in Ukraine, the enemy is anyone who supports or does not denounce Putin.

The Covid Shuffle, the pinpointing of a market, not any market, a wet market in Wuhan was the indoctrination point, the same as Colin Powell holding up a small tube of something and then showing pictures of so-called WMD (Weapons of Mass

Destruction) in Iraq to justify two decades of war, that resulted in America's defeat in Afghanistan last year. Representative democracy in America or old-fashioned democracy died after 9/11 and it has been dead for years. The 2000, 2016, and 2020 elections all have problems associated with them. That is three national elections in a generation. The fake bat story of Covid Hysteria confirmed it. We are in the last days of liberal democracy now unrecognizable from what it was a few years ago. We are witnessing the last gasps of the old regime, suffocated by neglect, forgetfulness, and narcissism.

The West, with its moral crusades, and holiness movements, will consume itself, tear itself apart and destroy itself as it moves from one national sin to the next. Now Putin is the West's new Anti-Christ, and the unvaccinated have been granted a reprieve. Soon, even Putin will gain a reprieve and the American elites will tell us whom we should hate next. These days, there is only one truth. As a result, people in power are always right, not only about Covid but everything. Dissent is crushed or dismissed as misinformation, by the same people who have run all three propaganda exercises – the media, corporations, and the state. The Christian Church is delighted to be involved. They want to be recruited. After all, they know all about the wonder of political power.

By the time everyone hates the new evil, the people in power have shifted to the new enemy and we begin all over again. Consequently, representative democracy is on life support until they decide to turn it off permanently. When that happens, most people won't even notice. The average westerner could not care less about democracy. They just hate Trump and will do what they are told. Revived fascism in the ruins of liberal democracy will reshape the world and is already leading the west to a nuclear war with Russia and China. After all, people love fascism. They did last time.

Covid Theology was an Apostasy

Churches should have shown more sense, but most church leaders were keen disciples of the War on Terror (because they fear Islam) and it fed into the natural and inherited xenophobia felt in the West, the fear of migrants, and the hatred of a multiethnic society.

Even the so-called 'liberal' churches that boast a record on migrant protection only discovered multiculturalism after it was forced upon them by circumstances. Liberal, national churches are notoriously racist in the West, open to all people, as long as they have clean teeth, speak well, and graduated from the right colleges. Few churches stood up for the rights of minorities before 1945, so religious support for 'migration' is a consequence of the economic imperatives in the post-war era that drove such trends in the first place. It is a comfortable place to argue for something when large swathes of the ruling class are on your side. Apologists point to the abolition of the slave trade by Wilberforce, but this was not freedom at the expense of tyranny, the government simply bought off the slave traders, a large financial transfer that continued to occur for decades.

These religious hatreds are deeply embedded in nationalist churches, especially the older churches. This enmity exists in Britain, America, Australia, and so on, but it flourishes in other nations in Eastern Europe such as Hungary and Poland, nations with a strong history of political fascism. 9/11 and the endless war doctrine, laid the basis for future propaganda such as Covid. As a result, Covid Hysteria produced in the churches, one of its intended objectives, gross apostasy.

Apostasy simply means the giving up of one's faith, the rejection of one's faith, or the departure from one's faith. There are many types of apostasy and many reasons why people have and often give up their beliefs. Apostasy is because of external pressure, or internal conviction, or a combination of the two.

It is impossible to be a genuine follower of Jesus Christ and willingly and knowingly places limits on the proclamation of the Gospel. Christians tell others about Jesus. Christian Fascists tell other people what to do and in Covid, they did just that. They shut their Bibles and turned people away. What many thousands of ministers and priests did was to preach the Gospel only to those whom the government approved worthy of entering the building on Sunday. The government does not decide who gets to listen to the Gospel and no one could honestly open the Bible and speak with any sense of human decency with even the most liberal interpretation of scripture a view that excluded some people because of government regulation. They decided that the government could tell them who was worthy to enter their building and all those who were present were there because the government approved of their presence. These distinctions were unscientific, political, arbitrary, and ridiculous.

The closure of the churches was religious persecution for two years, but most Christians embraced this policy with the view that 'the government is keeping us safe.' The fact that it was the government claiming to keep you safe should have been the warning sign, but you were lied to, and this lie was promoted in the churches by operatives, disciples, and proxies from the state and the corporations that run the government.

Two years of intense Christian persecution and Christians not only fell for it but welcomed it. The Church also invented Covid Theology which was, as usual, the twisting and corruption of a few selected verses to suit a political objective. This was classic church, and they do it all the time, finding some verse, taking it out of context, twisting it contorting it, giving it meaning it doesn't have, and then beating everyone over the head with it to force obedience. The consequence of this crazy Covid Theology is that America was conceived in sin and so were the Church of England and all Protestants because they overturned legitimate political authority, not through disobedience, but direct war.

The only Christian response would have been to resist, oppose and refuse to obey government directives, but the Church didn't want its ministers to pay fines or go to prison. In the Bible that is called the fear of people. Now we have the truth from the mouth of the former Prime Minister (in Australia) who said on March 12, 2022, that Covid is like the flu and should be treated as such. Now we know that when Morrison was demanding that all Australians obey the martial law directives of the Biosecurity Act, he was personally and secretly accumulating political power by becoming co-minister of every strategic portfolio in the cabinet.

This was an effective coup, more deadly to democracy in Australia than the chaotic goon show and fake insurrection on January 6 in the American capitol. Hypocritical church in Australia leaders still condemn citizen Trump and his movement but say nothing about the real coup that took place in Australia. If Australians knew the truth about this power grab before the election, both major parties would have been decimated at the polls. This was genuine election interference, and the media is silent.

A message to the church: Will you hypocrites close your church doors every winter for the flu? After all, you need to keep people safe. How about other diseases that can be transmitted using the common cup in the Mass? Will you close the doors on those people as well? Will you be consistent and shut out people who are triple vaccinated and yet have Covid or anyone with a sniffle or a cough? No. You will do as you are told, right, and the ones who run your theology are people in power in the state. We get that now. We know where your loyalties lie, and we will not forget.

Every single priest or minister who closed their doors to the unvaccinated betrayed Christ, but most still think they did the right thing. The history of the church has shown that most apostates believe they are faithful to God, even the ones who supported Fascism in Europe. Apostasy is simply giving up faith, turning away from God, deserting, repudiating, rejecting, or abandoning one's faith. People do it all the time because of internal or external pressure or a combination of the two. Mass apostasy is rare, but Covid Hysteria certainly produced it. Seeing the number of Christians who supported the War on Terror and still lament the departure from the Middle East but are now denouncing Putin as evil is further proof of this deeper apostasy and the source of their authority being the state and not God.

The Anatomy of Apostasy in Australia

I was surprised that so many evangelical churches supported vaccine passports, but when you factor in human frailty, it is obvious what was going on, a mixture of fear, greed, and ambition. Many in various churches didn't want to stand up and stand with Jesus, they feared what others would say, they feared the bishop, and they feared the loss of income. For others, it was greed, they 'took the soup' as it were, they took the government pension and decided to promote the vaccines in the pulpit. This is what we can a quid pro quo. For those people in church power, their ambition was to return to their places of power and their control over people's hearts, minds, and souls. To get that power back, they would sell their soul to Satan. Many do. The biggest black market of souls is in the church, where denominations outbid each other in the auction of eternity.

The Christian Church in the West, albeit with some areas of defiant rebellion, toed the official Covid Hysteria line, especially the churches associated with all those old buildings steeples, chapels, and schools. You are probably aware of this tiny group of rebels, and their stories need to be remembered, documented, and celebrated. Google the Ezekiel Declaration as one such example, widely condemned by the wealthy fake evangelicals, and Christian fascists who run the major denominations in Australia. The rest didn't want to stand with Christ, be persecuted, and face losing their vast financial empires. Theirs is a propertied religion, a religion of real estate and steeples, of money and investments. They said nothing when martial law came and its consequences and pretended it did not exist, for money and power, in the hope that this might be their ticket to return to the good life. They made fun of protestors and kept quiet over the police brutality, and the severe social and economic effects of the lockdowns. The mainstream churches were spiritually and politically emasculated.

Most churches will never stick their neck out and stand for something unless someone else supports it first. I will tell you what will happen when Christians are persecuted next time, their bishops and priests will have another set of clever arguments to justify apostasy. Church history is full of apostasy – the betrayal of faith, it happens all the time, and it is one of the reasons people simply do not trust the Church because they don't stand for anything, when times of testing come, they are just like everyone else.

In addition, people in power have churches over the barrel, and churches for their part have been tiptoeing around these days, following the revelations of systemic child sexual abuse in the churches. If churches made a stand for Jesus, then they might have lost their properties or their estates or been faced with further fines, which they could not pay. Then they might have to go to prison or face the loss of their properties and estates. The financial costs of compensation for victims of child abuse are astronomical because of the number of poor children affected.

Facing certain extinction, these ancient, corrupt institutions would sell out to anyone offering to bail them out of their financial difficulties. They need the money, otherwise, their empires will close, and they will end up with nothing. They might have to live like Jesus, the one they often talk about but hope they never resemble in practice. For the rich protestant ministers, their children will not get that free education at good schools then, nor will they live in that nice house provided by the parish. Financially, many denominations refused to stand up for Jesus to prop up their empty churches and cover the massive costs stemming from several generations of systemic child sexual abuse. All churches that have a history of child sexual abuse are facing extinction but their desire to survive is remarkable. If only their desire to survive was as strong as their desire to protect vulnerable children from abuse.

Democracy is not worth saving, you are

Fascism is experiencing a renaissance in the West. Trump didn't invent it or bring it into vogue. These political movements are superficial. The Trump movement was a brawl between fascists from various factions, not a war between fascism and democracy. American politics is now just a turf war between different departments of state and the material interests behind them. Marxists and Libertarians, in other words, the far-left and far-right agree on this, which I find quite interesting. Fascism is deeply rooted in the polity. Fascism is not a pimple on the skin, but it is in the bones, it is the hot blood that pumps through the veins of American democracy.

Representative democracy is too far gone now to be salvaged. It is over twenty years since 9/11 and the triumph of American neo-fascism. The system is irrevocably broken, and Covid Hysteria helped to push that agenda forward. This generation wrecked their democracy with the lockdowns, the martial law, the lies, and the suspension of human rights on the back of the War on Terror. The hypocrisies in the American ruling class are staggering. The feigned horror and condemnation of former President Trump and the 'coup-lite' goon show on Capitol Hill on January 6, 2020, is contrasted with the deafening silence as both Republicans and Democrats regularly decide which nation and society to send back to the Stone Age.

However, if you take a deeper look into it, democracy always had a dark side to it, and it is becoming more difficult to defend with such an appalling legacy. Those who still believe in democracy and think we can go back to the past, have their list of villains such as the transhumanists at the World Economic Forum and Bill Gates or the American military-industrial complex. Back in the day, it was the oil barons and before that the merchants. Bill is just the latest big fish. He speaks because he is rich and is a philanthropist. There is nothing wrong with being a philanthropist. Even Jesus was the recipient of funds from wealthy women who supported his work (Luke 8: 3).

The American economy is a war economy now so you must make a living somehow. Hundreds of thousands in America, if not millions rely upon war either directly or indirectly. If America adopted peace, the economy would completely collapse. America's entire democratic system is based on continual wars abroad. America is sustained by overseas villains, in nations we know nothing about, otherwise, we would turn in on ourselves. Many warmongers in the West hope this war in Ukraine will drag out for years for maximum profit.

There is no way, I could save democracy. Look at how many democratically elected governments America has toppled in the last eighty years such as Ukraine in 2014 or Chile in 1973. Democracy is long gone, and it is not worth saving. What so many of those Republicans who have 'come to the rescue' during Covid Hysteria hope you forget is that they were the ones who supported the invasion of Iraq and Afghanistan and the phony 'War on Terror.' Today in America or tomorrow, whoever is in charge, the madness will continue. To restore democracy, you would need a violent revolution. But, why bother, it would be too much work and it would eventually collapse anyway, as nothing lasts forever. That is the problem with Empires. They all turn to dust.

As a Christian, I do, however, have an obligation to proclaim and live the Gospel, the good news of Jesus Christ for all people everywhere. I am compelled to show that with God there is true freedom, and freedom from all the things that bind us in fear, despair, guilt, shame, past, prejudice, sin, and death. *Freedom Matters Today* exists for all people but especially those who have been blessed not to have encountered the Church firsthand. This is most of humanity. Thank God.

I hope, therefore, through this book to encourage you to think for yourself and ponder what I have to say about freedom and faith. I encourage you to open the Bible and read for yourself the life of Jesus, who he is, and what he has done. I hope that you find true freedom and faith. If you have not encountered the church, then you are truly blessed, you have been saved from the soul catchers who trap people in their snare of guilt and shame, and cage everyone in the false hope of religion, rituals, and rules. Don't go to church, follow Jesus instead. True freedom is knowing God and being known by God. If God has set you free, then you are truly free.

There are many however in the church who question what is going on and notice the disconnect between what the priest or pastor says and the Bible that is carefully managed and interpreted. Most in Church are lost already. There is not much hope for them. Their hearts are too hard, they are stuck in their traditions, and the last person they expect to meet at church is God. They gave up their belief long ago. Many people go to church for social reasons, most churches are social clubs, a place to meet people, and connect with people who think the same way you do.

Churches are famous for cliques, the in-crowd, those in the inner circle around the priest, his devoted followers, factions, and those on the outer, who keep coming but everyone ignores. Every church is the same wherever you go. People are social animals, and many talk the talk so they will not be shown the door or the cold shoulder. If you are looking for faithful Christians, do not go to church to find them. It is dead easy to be a Christian at church.

I will not give up on the church however and there is also a chance to save some trapped in the church, the rules, the rituals, and the expectations. Democracy is not worth saving, but you are. I hope that this book might motivate some to leave fascist churches and return to Jesus Christ and the true freedom that he brings, leading them to open the Bible at home with their family or with their friends over coffee and start their own Christian gatherings and groups that reflect their lives and their experiences, not the lives and experiences of people long dead.

Most churches care more for the dead and their lives than for those who turn up each Sunday morning. Try changing something in your church and watch the resistance and the bizarre arguments as to why things must stay the same: *'this is the way we have always done it,'* or *'my father built this,'* or *'our family has been here for three generations,'* or *'this is our seat, we sit here, find your own place.'*

Christianity is about a personal relationship with God

A personal relationship with the living God is what real Christianity is all about. It is a personal relationship with God the Father and Jesus Christ whom he sent – that is the good news. All Christians are Christians. There is no true Church and those who claim that are liars. The orthodox, the Church of England, the Catholics, the Presbyterians, and the Baptists have at some point claimed that they were the true Church and only they were right. Christianity predates the state church, predates the rise of orthodox Christianity, and predates the rise of denominations and creeds and rules and regulations, and traditions.

A Christian is a Christian, and there is fellowship wherever you go and whenever you meet another Christian. I make no apology for making you question your denomination or church tradition, which is a good thing because your faith should rest in God, not in the church. They are not the same, and once you realize that, then you are on the path to true freedom.

When I am talking about *'the church,'* I am using contemporary usage. Therefore, this is the way ordinary people think of church, those who *'go to church,'* and many who do not *'go to church.'* This means a building or a place you physically go to on Sunday. At that geographical location, you participate in a *'church service,'* or liturgy. This church is usually a local branch of a denomination. This means, therefore, an institutional structure that shapes that physical encounter. Christianity, however, predates the church. Christian Fascism has divided the church between those who believe in Jesus and those who live in the past. Early Christians were called *'Followers of the Way,'* or Christians (first at Antioch). In the New Testament, they were often simply called the *'people of God.'*

The church as a geographical, physical, and ritualistic encounter, did not come first. Jesus did, and from that emerged Christianity. It was only later that Christianity became part of the state, leading to denominations. This was the rise of what we call the *'church'* in

English, and for many, the West and Christianity are inseparable. In addition, this change led to a long struggle between those faithful to Christ and nationalists within the church. This is what I call *'Christian Fascism.'* Not content with the Gospel, these 'Christians' sought to merge church and state, so that they became one. The control of the state and enforced conformity is the goal of Christian Fascism and is at the heart of the struggle between Christian Fascists and Christians.

While governments may have perfected propaganda, they are not the only institution employing the techniques and methods. Freedom Matters Today is more interested in freeing people from fascism in the Church. The theory of Desmet's Mass Formation (based on what I have discovered from his podcasts) is that there is a hypnotic point where people are indoctrinated or ensnared. Applying it to the Church, then there are two, depending on which tradition you support: for traditional services, the Mass, or Eucharist, for contemporary services, the sermon. These rituals act as a point of hypnotic indoctrination. These rituals are not Christianity, nor is membership in any brand of Christendom. One is simply a Christian or not a Christian.

Christians, before the denominations arose, met everywhere, and often in various contexts, sometimes by the river, sometimes outside, often in homes, and often in much smaller groups, some even met in the temple in Jerusalem until they were kicked out. The Church is not Christianity, and the Christian faith is simply a personal relationship with God the Father, and Jesus Christ whom he sent, in the power of the Holy Spirit. As Billy Sunday said, entering a church building does not turn you into a Christian in the same way that entering a garage doesn't turn you into a car.

Jesus Christ is the antidote to any form of propaganda because he is the Way, the Truth, and the Life. Christians who believe in God the Father, and Jesus Christ whom he sent, the foundation, the heart and the essence of their faith is a personal relationship with God, they know God, they want to know him better, and they want others to know God. Their faith is not wrapped up in some event that occurs for one hour on Sunday, but a daily, hourly, walk with God, as they seek to follow Jesus in their ordinary path through life. The church is one hour a week and for many people who claim to be Christians, this event is the heart and the soul of their religion.

The Magic Show

Churches might start as a simple gathering of Christians but then over time they become solidified and stuck, entrenched, and once ritualized and these churches act as a form of distraction away from the person and work of Jesus Christ. Some do this intentionally, many do this unknowingly, and some have no idea they are doing it. Many ministers or priests over the years have noticed this fundamental tension in the organization and have tried to return the church back to Christ, back to simple faith, back to the Bible, but what they find is resistance, factions within that church who support the rituals, the traditions, the rules. They often or usually prevail. This problem is compounded when national cultures have been shaped by Christian witness and participation, and this is known as nominal or superficial Christianity. I call this Christian Fascism.

The nominal Christians run the churches, they have no faith at all, but they wield incredible power and will destroy anyone who gets in the way of their church, their building, their traditions, and their rituals. The greatest enemy in the Western Church is the nominal Christian and the churches that allow them to flourish. Christian culture is a curse on faith, it is a wicked thing because religious people are not people of faith. The worst thing for the Christian faith is a Christian culture. Nominals have no faith and yet they make up the bulk of church membership in every single denomination. They come for the ritual, for the tradition, for the denomination, for their ancestor's memory, they come for the theatre, and they come for the Magic Show.

What is the Magic Show? It is the weekly church ritual that defines a person's religion. The main form of church propaganda or Mass Formation is a point in their services that is the focal point, where all eyes are focused. In the churches it is obvious. Every church has a central ritualistic event. In the traditional services, it is the Mass or the Eucharist, and in the contemporary services, it is the sermon. Most who attend church see this ritual as their means for cleansing, forgiveness, restoration, and rejuvenation for the week ahead, but it is not Christian. God does not appear in the ritual, nor is he present other than the fact that he is present whenever two or three gather in the name of Jesus. The ritual does not add anything extra in a spiritual sense aside from the social benefit of being together and the added psychological effects.

The Spirit is always pointing to Jesus Christ and reminding us of what Jesus said in the Bible (John 14: 26), but these charlatans don't care about the Bible or Jesus Christ. They take advantage of the vulnerable, the guilty, the weak, and the poor, and tell them that this ritual is their way to be close to God and be sustained by God and their presence is required because without the ritual performed by them, they are lost.

The most obvious ritual in the church that is hypnotic indoctrination is the Mass or Eucharist or Lord's Supper. The whole service is consumed (no pun intended) by the Mass, and everything is subordinate to it. The high point of the Mass, aside from the prayers, chanting, incantations, and hand-waving is the elevation of the two elements used in the Mass, the bread, and the wine. The chalice or cup is elevated, and the saucer of bread is elevated, and this is the point of indoctrination.

The ritual replaces God as the object of worship and people worship things made from human hands and created things rather than the creator. Watch the eyes of the people gaze upwards following the two elements of the Mass, their hopeful eyes, their expectant eyes, their eyes of worship and adoration of two physical things that are not God, do not transform into God, do not change into God. The elements stay bread, and they stay wine, and there is no mystery.

It is theatre, it is a Magic Show, and it is spiritual abuse. It is the heart of Christian fascism and has directly caused the deaths of millions of innocent people. What does God do? Well, as Paul says in Romans, he gives them over to their self-delusion, they worship created things rather than the creator and so God gives them what they want.

The function of the Mass is Spiritual Abuse

The function of the Mass is hypnotic indoctrination, designed to consolidate the power of the priesthood and the church, to keep the money flowing in, and to keep you in guilt and shame wallowing in your sin, living in fear of an angry God. You gaze at the priest who performs the rituals and chants the prayers, ancient prayers that invoke the Holy Spirit, bring him out of heaven and down to earth, prayers that rebuke heaven over the man-made altar. Altars are not mentioned in the New Testament at all, nor is the word priest mentioned except in the context that all Christians are priests (1 Peter 2: 9). Indeed, both John and Peter attest to this in their writings. There are no robes in the New Testament, no incense, – the church made them up by cutting and pasting various verses in the New and Old Testament to create a liturgy that is pagan and reflects the values of the pagan world at the time they invented it, around 300 or so years after the resurrection.

This cut-and-paste job was inherited by the Orthodox and Rome and so generations of priests would perform the Mass they believed came from the past. The worst cut-and-paste job was by the Church of England who in the 1662 Prayer Book generously plagiarized from the Roman Rites to create Anglican liturgy and did this again with the Oxford Movement in the nineteenth century where they simply made up a ton of rituals, they claimed were pre-Protestant liturgy. However, not even Rome with all its splendor could compete with the fictional make-believe of high church ritualism. High Church Anglican rites celebrate British Imperialism, the Rite of the Mass being the heart of a religious museum dedicated to white supremacy. The classic work of fiction was the textbook for the Oxford Movement, to revive 'English Catholicism' in England, Percy Dearmer's *The Parson's Handbook* (1899). What he didn't invent, he plagiarized from Rome. There are more historical facts in J.K. Rowling's Harry Potter literary universe than in the high church Anglican rites.

The church glorifies the priest because the priest has the hotline to God, that special connection, that purity, and he has the power to bring God out of heaven and into the elements so Jesus Christ can be sacrificed every day and every time you eat the bread and the wine, the elements magically transform into the body and the blood so that you are eating the crucified Jesus.

This is blasphemy for many reasons. Many priests do not believe in the actual bodily resurrection of Jesus from the dead, but they still do the Mass. If Jesus is lying in a tomb somewhere he is not going to pop out for the Mass, is he? Likewise, if you believe Jesus is alive, then it naturally follows that he is alive, that as the Bible says, he sits at the right hand of God and will come to judge the living and the dead, and that he is spiritually present in all believers and he is present when two or three gather together in his name to pray or read the bible, and that all believers are united to him by faith.

Therefore, he is not being cut up into a million little bits to be munched on or chomped on, or nibbled every Sunday. Each week, tuck into Jesus for a little nibble and chew on God for a bit. Jesus is not God's Magic Pudding, where we all have a slice once a week, or once a day. Which part of Jesus are we eating? Is it a good cut, a leg, an arm, or a toe?

John's Gospel excludes any mention of the Mass and never mentions it in any of his letters. John's focus is not fake ritual but practical Christian living. Not even Paul talks about the Mass, and the oft-quoted verses to prop up the Mass come from a fellowship meal that one assembly enjoyed together, an actual meal, where the rich were exploiting the poor. The church has turned a meal that was the heart of Middle Eastern hospitality into a ritual shaped by distance, silence, and separation, to shed the Gospel of its Jewish origins. Fortunately, after the Holocaust, many Christians rediscovered the Jewish roots of Christianity and tried to rebalance the faith that the Church's explicit Anti-Semitism tried to purge.

Those who insist that the Mass is mandatory because the early church did it are hypocrites because the early Christians also shared everything in common, like a form of the communist commune. Can you imagine the Greek or Russian orthodox churches sharing their wealth with the poor on an equal basis? Some of those places are dripping in gold and silver and wealth, and according to the early Christians, it needs to be held in common for all. Ask your orthodox priest if you can drive his Maserati, the catholic priest if you can enjoy a bottle from his wine cellar, and the Anglican priest if you can wear his designer clothes.

Jesus died once and he died for sin, and all who have faith in him have eternal life. It is as simple as that. Jesus is whole after the resurrection, and when you place your faith and trust in him, you are whole too, you do not have a dismembered Savior but a whole Lord. Read Hebrews if you have time, to see how Jewish Christians understood Jesus as their Lord and Savior.

We know that the Roman Mass is a sham now because of Covid

Hysteria. The Vatican revealed to the world that the Mass was optional to faith during Covid. The Pope said that since the lockdowns closed the churches, you did not need to go to church. Therefore, the church made a special dispensation so that you did not need to have the Mass. Hang, on, wait a moment, I thought Christ instituted the Holy Sacrament, not the church or the Pope. However, now we find out that it wasn't Jesus at all, but the Pope. Then the Pope said that if you do not take the vaccine, then you will be denied access to the Mass. In fact, you will not be allowed into the building. The Pope once again puts himself in the place of God and rules in his stead, making it up as he goes along. No one with any degree of self-respect could ever respect Rome again. Now, since the vaccines do not prevent the transmission of Covid, he can never be trusted again. The vaccines were supposed to keep us safe. I thought the Pope was infallible. How can you get Covid if you have been thrice injected? How can he be infallible? Maybe God didn't tell him that. What else is God not telling him?

Jesus does not promote a ritual, but a real life

When Jesus says that he is the Way, the Truth, and the Life, he is not talking about the Mass, nor is he talking about the sermons. Those rituals all take place in the church building, and they all are a kind of magical ritual. I call the church the Magic Show, where the theatre happens, it is fake, it is superficial, and a form of distraction away from the person and work of Jesus Christ. The Gospels make it very clear that Jesus is talking about faith as something real, something every day, and something that transforms all of life, not just the one hour on Sunday. Faith becomes real in life, not in church, faith is confirmed through life experiences, encounters with people, and through putting into practice what Christ taught.

We see this in the life of Jesus himself, certainly not the fiction the churches have invented, such as Jesus in a continual state of torment, hanging on the cross in the stations of the cross, or in a perpetual form of babyhood where Jesus doesn't cry lying as a white-faced ceramic doll in the manger.

Jesus wept when his friend Lazarus died (John 11: 35). He was broken emotionally when he was confronted with the horror of death, especially the death of his friend. He was physically affected by suffering, just read the account of his trial. Jesus fell asleep because he was tired and weary from all his walking and talking and praying.

Jesus was angry when he went into the Temple Courts and saw them making money out of their faith in God, much like so many in the church today, he had a right to be angry, church corruption is evil and it is awful to see people in power in the church use their power to exploit others and so he makes a whip himself, Jesus-made whip and proceeds to smash the money tables and kick everyone out of the Temple Courts. This is not little Jesus meek and mild (John 2: 15).

Jesus also was not afraid to speak the truth to power, instead of cowering to them, he spoke to them plainly and openly, and he did not mince words. He had full-blown arguments with the Pharisees in public, one against many, and he spoke with authority about God and life. Jesus wandered through the fields and plains of Israel and used everyday examples to demonstrate the kingdom of God and his relationship with the Father and our relationship with him. The world was his audience, and he was not contained in a building. His life was real.

Contrast this with the priests who hide away in their churches and vestries, who are not allowed to express emotion, or get angry with anyone or anything. What do they know of life? Surely you have more insights living your ordinary life so come Sunday, why do the priests ignore you? In the synagogue, Jesus asked to read the Hebrew Bible and then make a comment. He was not a priest or a pastor and yet the Pharisees had the practice to let anyone comment on the Biblical text. What freedom that was. Can you imagine that today?

Why should the priest be the one to give the homily? The traditional answer is that the priest suffers on behalf of the congregation, he is held up as the one who acts vicariously on behalf of his flock, so his flock can remain untouched, unmoved, and unregenerate, while the priest dies each week for his people. None of this is found in the Bible, the church just made it up to elevate the power of the clerics and priests. However, if you want to see freedom in church, open the sermon time for everyone to comment and reflect. After all, don't all Christians have the Holy Spirit or is it just the person out the front?

In the Gospels, Jesus makes it very clear that his followers, while they are to respect political authority, are not to align themselves with anything or anyone aside from God. The Pharisees and Sadducees would have agreed with Jesus on that, especially the Zealots. Jesus clearly says in the Gospels that all authority is from his Father in heaven and that is not saying or doing anything that does not come from his Father. The other Jewish leaders of various groups at the time disputed with him on his relationship with the Father, but they would have all agreed with him that God, not Caesar was the ultimate authority for God's people.

During the temptations with Satan in the wilderness, the Devil told him that he had the power to give him all the kingdoms of the world if only he would worship him. Jesus did not dispute the Devil's statement, and this is confirmed by all the other writers in the New Testament – Paul, Peter, John, the writer of the Hebrews, James, and the Gospel writers. State Churches are an abomination.

Jesus is not here to force people to believe, educate them, or drill them into belief, but that is what the state does, it forces people to believe, it compels people, it orders them, it directs them. Jesus is the opposite, he says: Behold I stand at the door and knock and if anyone opens the door, then I will enter, and we will enjoy a meal together (Revelation 3: 20), or 'Come unto me all you who are heavy laden, and I will give you rest' (Matthew 11: 28-30).

Christian Fascists want a kingdom on earth

As we saw last week, many Christians confuse their faith with politics and long for Christian culture and nation, thus giving birth to Christian fascism. At some point, they will need the sword to force belief. They always do. Christians who try to prop up states in the name of Jesus are going against God and working against him.

Nowhere in the Bible does Jesus look to create an earthly kingdom. All efforts to create Christian empires end in disaster because they were never ordained by God, none of the kings, none of the monarchies, none of the state religions. This includes the Church of England which recently buried the head of their religious order, Queen Elizabeth II. It was the sword, not God who put the

English kings and queens on the throne. Religion was to clothe a deceitful heart and turn attention away from the real agenda, power, and control over others. The soul catchers had a field day. They feasted on souls for a thousand years. During the brief interregnum of democracy, these ancient churches have grown hungry in desolate places, outside their places of power, and have been stirring again, and they want to return to their places of residence. What they will be, will be seven times worse than before. When the church and the state were friends, the world was a butcher's yard.

Politics is about deceit and Christians involved in the Culture War embrace that deceit. The opposite of truth is deceit, and the father of deceit is the Devil. The Devil is alive and well today. He might have visited your church, he might know your priest or minister or bishop, who knows, he gets around. His language is the most popular today, it is one of the fastest-growing languages in the world. He has been very busy in recent years, trying to murder as many of the unborn as he could because he failed to kill both Christ and Moses, and he is the architect of much of what we call political power.

The vaccine passports were and are Satanic and they were used to close the door to the proclamation of the Gospel, plain and simple. Churches got a taste of real political power, the power they crave, but the result was that they had to do as they were told because they do not have any real power anymore. Instead of being light and speaking truth to power, and standing up for the weak, they shut their mouths and turned away. Many people in power lied to us about the origins of covid, the treatments for covid, the adverse effects of the vaccines, the efficacy of the vaccines, the daily covid rates, the lockdowns, the masks, and social distancing, and the lies continue. Throughout this, most of the church was silent.

The truth is not to be found in politics or in the ritual of the Mass, but in the life and words of Jesus Christ. Jesus said that he was the way, the truth, and the life in the context of an evening meal with his disciples. It was not a grand speech. It was not before large crowds. It was and is personal. What Jesus is saying to his disciples on the night of his betrayal is that they do not need anything beyond the one they know, the one they were talking with, in that room, enjoying the evening meal.

Jesus claimed to be the truth. What he is saying is that he is the full revelation of God to the world, the complete, sufficient, and total revelation of the nature and character of the Father. If you see him, then you have seen the Father. The claim of Jesus here is radical, subversive, and dangerous, especially in a world where human power and ambition seek to mold our hearts and our minds. People in power try to get into your head, so they can control you, direct you, influence you, and lead you. Human power is about rules, and doctrines, whom to love, and whom to hate, what to do, and what not to do. Jesus is saying the complete opposite.

Truth is a person, not a set of facts about the world. Truth is about who God is and who we are in relation to God. The disciples spent time with Jesus, eating with him, living with him, talking with him, and following him. This is spending time with the truth and if there is any model in the New Testament, those who believe that Jesus is the Son of God are to follow him.

As the truth, this power of God radiates into our lives and our world. The person of Christ is the most powerful person in the world. Jesus is God, he claimed to be God and claimed to be God's Messiah, and these fundamental Christian beliefs are like the sun's rays that go out, radiating and warming the earth. Christians in tune with Christ can see falsehood more clearly. This is not surprising because people of power reign not because they are right, or truthful, but because they have, enjoy, and exploit the power they have secured for themselves.

I believe that Christians can see lies more clearly because the truth is not a set of doctrines, but a person, and once you know God and you can know God then your life is not based on human morality and rules, but on the person whom you know.

People in power rarely know the truth. Democracy for example cannot exist without deceit. It is based on deceit. Elections are based on marketing a candidate, exaggerating their virtues, minimizing their flaws, and hiding their failings. Most in democratic power believe in very little beyond themselves and their own importance. They crave power and want it to continue for as long as it is possible, and hope that no one outside their inner circle finds out what they are like.

In authoritarian societies, power is secured through violence. They do not need the consent of others, nor do they need approval. Pontius Pilate asked Jesus during the trial 'what is truth?' (John 18:

38) as he had no idea, being the governor, he knew about power and the exercise of power over others. He was a ruthless, and much-loathed Roman ruler. His question is the question all people in power ask of Christians and they ask because they too have no idea. Sadly, many Christians point to a moral code rather than to the person of Jesus Christ. Jesus nowhere in his ministry upholds a golden rule or a basic principle beyond himself. It is impossible to read the New Testament and see anything other than a radically new way to understand ourselves and God.

Jesus turned his back on political power

At the heart of the Christian faith is the idea of qualification. Jesus, as the eternal Word made flesh, is qualified to act as a candidate to be the atonement for sin, once and for all, as he is both fully divine, and fully human. Jesus was born of a woman under the Law so he might save those under the Law. Jesus is qualified to be the Messiah. His credentials if you like, are the grounds for his qualifications to serve as the sacrifice of God for sin. Therefore, he not only claims to be a truth but the truth, the only truth, as he is the only one qualified. He died, and rose again, proving his credentials and qualifications.

On the other hand, we live in a world surrounded by people in power who neither like us, nor live like us, but many are quick to condemn us, quick to judge, and quick to prosecute us for our failings to live up to the standards they have no intention of keeping. Many claim to be the source of absolute truth, and that they have a monopoly on truth. In these dark days, democratic despots have fragile power and that is why they want to control your thinking, your attitudes, and your beliefs. Otherwise, they would allow us to think for ourselves. We must pass all information by them, ask no questions, present no alternatives, and accept that whatever they do not approve of is misinformation. This censorship is getting worse, and it will soon affect everything we say, everything we do, and everything we believe in. It will end in fire.

What people think of Jesus Christ is the beginning and the end of the Christian faith. Many people online who claim to be Christians say very little about Christ, very little indeed. Covid has been good for many of their careers, but they say little about Jesus Christ. It is because Jesus will get in the way of their vicious, unforgiving political agenda. It is astounding what some fake Christians say online about what Christians should do or support. Jesus cannot be made into a political slogan, nor does he fit in the clothes we expect him to. He is not a member of the Republican Party or the Democrats. He is not conservative or woke. He is not a Liberal nor is he for climate change or against it. He is not left-wing or right-wing. These fake Christians just need the name of Jesus like a brand. He is their ticket to the good life.

Their agenda is not God's agenda, nor is it, nor was it Christ's agenda. Many of these fake Christians want to take over the state and make it a Christian one, once again. They talk about traditional family values or Christian values, long for the good old days when the church was more powerful in society, and say that if we become a Christian nation, we can bring glory to God. We need, they say, to take over the reins of power and have a Christian Party, or a Christian PM, or President, or a society with Christian values. What they mean is they want you to support them and their power grab. They neither love God nor follow him, and they most certainly have departed from the Christian faith because nowhere in the entire Gospels does Jesus seek political power or expect his disciples to.

The Way to the Father is not through political power, it is through Jesus. Political power is irrelevant for the Christian. It always was and always is. Democratic politics is about crafting deceit and Christian Prime Ministers make the worst leaders because their political lives undermine the authenticity of faith and cause many to stumble.

If Jesus was the Son of God and the Son of Man, and the holy one of God, and the Messiah, and if he bypassed Rome itself, he never went there, and he refused to speak to Herod, the puppet king of the Jews, and said to Pilate the Roman governor that his kingdom was not of this world, why do Christians so often try to do the complete opposite? If Jesus did not seek political power to advance his cause, why should we? If Jesus turned his back on political power, why do we not follow him?

Christian Fascism will fail

When Jesus is saying that he is the Way, the Truth, and the Life (John 14: 6) he rejects the idea that he wants us to be the way through political action. The statement that Jesus makes in this sentence makes null and void any power grab, any version of a Christian state, and any purpose behind so-called Christian culture. Jesus is not here to bring about a social reformation, a political revolution, or economic change. He is here to speak to you personally about who you are, and who you are in relation to God.

Jesus presents a radical alternative to those Christians who are in the Culture War. They want the easy road and don't have enough courage to stand with Christ or his people. What Jesus said and who he is, are completely opposed to human power and human ambition. Christians who believe that human power and ambition can be reconciled with the teachings of Christ are people who refuse to read what Christ said, they have their own personal agenda which is of course to promote themselves. Human power and ambition can't be reconciled with the exclusive nature of Christ's claim that he is the way, the truth, and the life. Human power and ambition will always oppose the exclusive nature of Christ's claim.

Those Christians who want to save democracy, good luck – you will fail, because the best thing you could do would be to restore it for a time, only for it to fall again, which it will. Your Culture War will fail. You cannot compare God's salvation with anything, not even political restoration. Only God can bring about personal restoration and reconciliation. Democracy is not worth saving, but you are.

The greatest danger to the faith of a Christian is a church that has lost its way and churches often lose their way. This is not the first time. The church is a threat to faith because it is being recruited by the state to promote a morality that will help to sustain the nation, and the Christian morality language will play its part in that.

One cannot as a Christian abide alongside human power and ambition and remain faithful to Christ. Eventually, the message will change, sooner or later, the exclusive claims of Christ will be removed in favor of human power and ambition. Eventually, Christians who seek human power and ambition betray Christ and become Judas. Judas betrayed Jesus for money. He had been a friend for three years, like the other apostles, but saw an opportunity to advance himself personally and took it. Many do, and it is only a matter of time. Those who see human power and ambition as the way to present the Gospel, know this, it is the path that Judas took. It is the road to apostasy and death.

Christian fascism is the national adaptation and appropriation of Christianity. It is at its worst form when it becomes affiliated with a nation, a national project, history, or identity. Some examples might be the 'Greek' orthodox church, the 'Southern' Baptists, the Church of 'England,' or the 'Ukrainian' orthodox church. Sadly, these churches brought in their nationalistic xenophobia and struggles and are deeply racist. Indeed, many have also struggled with Anti-Semitism over the centuries, which has no place among God's people.

For these reasons, among others, these perversions of the Gospel are the sources of repulsion for many people. This is because they see nationalist religious expressions as out of touch and contrary to contemporary values. Those who are repulsed include many within their respective nations who do not agree that to worship God they must adopt a specific ritualistic affiliation.

The church is a ritual, not a relationship

The saddest thing about going to church is that for many, the church is about a ritual, not a relationship with God. It is distant, not personal. While governments may have perfected propaganda, they are not the only institution employing the techniques and methods. Freedom Matters Today is more interested in freeing people from fascism in the Church.

Desmet's Mass Formation theory is that there is a point in a mass delusion where people are entranced. Interestingly, the Bible agrees that it is possible to cast a spell on the entire world through 'sorcery.' I firmly believe that most people live with various delusions their entire lives. We see this in Covid Hysteria and the bizarre reactions to one localized war in Eastern Europe. I mean the demonization of Putin and Russia in the civil war in Ukraine that has been on for the last 8 years.

Revelation 18: 23 says that Babylon the Great deceived all the nations of the world through sorcery. While Covid Hysteria is important, it is far more important to trace the rise of Christian Fascism in the church. Christians everywhere need to overcome Christian Fascism in every place. This is because we are dealing with eternity, not the rise and fall of nations. Nations come and go, and God does not promise much about any of them. Most of his promises have to do with Jesus Christ.

Applying it to the Church, hypnotic points do exist, and it is clear even from a casual perspective where they are found. We can divide Christendom into the traditional and the contemporary. The point of hypnosis for the traditional church is the Mass, Eucharist, Holy Communion, and Lord's Supper. The point of indoctrination in the contemporary is the Sermon. The saddest thing about going to church is that these rituals are a distraction from the person and work of Jesus Christ.

These rituals act as a point of hypnotic indoctrination. For many, it is their Gideon's ephod, their snare, and the source of their spiritual ruin. For others, it means nothing at all. Many people go to church for reasons other than religion; some for their spouse or parents, some for friends, and some for their job or employment. The ritual of church attendance is not Christianity. One is simply a Christian or not a Christian. It is as simple as that, and yet, as profound. Rich and poor, of all colors and creeds, Christians find fellowship because of their faith in a living Savior who died and rose again.

The church is one hour a week. Sadly, for most who attend these services, this event is the heart and the soul of their religion. It means they do not know God for God is not a thing but a person. He can be known. God is not present in any ritual, but participates in our lives, informs our minds, and gives us breath. The saddest thing about going to church is that, for many, a ritualistic encounter with a being they neither know nor understand. They leave at the end of the service without being any the wiser that they can know God any day at any time.

If one has Jesus, no one needs any intermediary or any special blessing, or any ritual. Christians need not wait for Sunday to meet God and those seeking God do not need to go to church to find him. He is not waiting for them. He is everywhere. He is God. Everyone could know him personally the whole week wherever they go. God is big. He is much bigger than I can even put into words. Even the best of my words fails to adequately describe the wonder, majesty, and power of God. God is present everywhere and he is calling all of us to a relationship with him wherever we are and whomever we are. Anyone can know God and that is why Jesus came into the world so God might be known.

What is the deadliest virus in the church today?

What is the deadliest virus in the church today? They are people who go to church to discourage, tear down, pull apart, undermine, and corrupt. Churches are often like clay on a potter's wheel that has been left alone for a while in the hot sun. It is not fired, only dried. As a result, the clay hardens and is useless. Christian meetings are simply gatherings of people in whom God dwells by his Spirit. If the Spirit is not there, they do not know God, the Spirit is not there to help the group grow. God will not change a person's outward life if their inner life is closed to God.

How do Christians get infected with a virus? Their genuine gatherings become a church, a place rather than a people, and the newness of life becomes stale with the ritual of repetition. For this virus to work, it does not take very long. It can take only a few years, even less. What we often see are national churches. Nationalist or Fascist churches are the worst things Christian people ever created. It is better for them that they never found God, for their institution, by definition, is a repudiation of the oneness in Christ proclaimed in the New Testament.

Christian fascists are venomous, deceitful, spiritually corrupt, and malevolent people. Like Judas, they are there for blood, for payback, rolling their lips over the latest gossip and slander, and wreaking havoc. They follow their true Master, the Devil. Christian fascism is the fast train to Hell and many jump on board. There is no harder heart than a Christian fascist. You will have more luck with converting a piece of granite or a donkey. The greatest enemy in the Western Church is the Christian fascist in the church and churches that allow them to flourish. Christian culture is a curse on faith and an obstacle to the gospel. Christian fascists cannot tell the difference between their national allegiance and their Christian faith.

National churches in the West made up most of their traditions or built them on violence. The Mass is fictional. The church corrupted the Passover due to their intense hatred of Jews, trying to strip Jesus of his authenticity and make him European. They failed. God is not European, and he points people back to the Bible, not to esoteric nonsense, or dead rituals, because Jesus is alive, not dead. He died once, and he remains a whole Savior, not a dismembered sacrifice. He said, 'it is finished,' not 'it has just begun.' Our Savior accomplished his task of saving us. All we need to do is believe.

What ritual has caused more wars than America?

What church ritual has caused more wars than America? It is the Mass, the Magic Show. This ritual allows anyone to participate without confessing any personal devotion to Christ. It is for show, about church membership and identity, and sectarian loyalty.

Where does religious hypnosis occur in the Mass? Anyone watching the Eucharist or Mass can easily see when the focal point of hypnosis occurs. During the ritual, it is the deification and elevation of the cup or chalice, and the wafers of bread on the saucer. The rest is theatre, a performance, and pageantry involving the robes, the incense, the chanting, and the prayers. They all point to the central part of a church service in all the traditional national churches where they each make a partisan claim that God belongs to them, and only to them.

This ritual has caused more wars than America. It divides more Christians than anything alive or dead. In the West, it is the heart of an unspoken narrative celebrating Anti-Semitism. It strips the Last Supper of Jesus from its Jewish roots and disavows Christian witness for the first few centuries before Christianity became the church.

The Mass is unapologetically, unreservedly pagan, and the fact that this ritual has caused more wars than America, is proof that it is utterly Satanic in design and effect. It has divided more families, more marriages, and more communities than anything Jesus ever said, and it was all for nothing because it is entirely fake.

The idolatry (what some call it), the point of hypnosis is the lifting of the chalice and the saucer. I have watched the eyes of the people gaze upwards following the two elements of the Mass, their hopeful eyes, their expectant eyes, their eyes of worship and adoration. These created things do not transform into God and do not change into God. Wishing that it does, does not make it happen, no matter how gorgeous the clothes, how beautiful the chanting, and how humble the worshippers. It is heart-wrenching because they are being so deliberately deceived.

The ritual that is one of the greatest lies in the church. I have said that people in power have lied about Covid. They did, and still do, but the worse thing is lying about God and the Bible. Despite the incantations, and the magic spells, the elements stay as bread and wine, and there is no mystery. They are drunk and eaten, and it is theatre, it is a Magic Show, and it is spiritual abuse. It is a sin, one of the greatest lies in Christendom.

The Magic Show is the heart of Christian fascism and has directly caused the deaths of millions of innocent people. The Church's differences over this ritual have caused dozens of horrific wars, more wars than even America! Almost all religious wars were caused by differences in thought over the Eucharist. As I have said, the function of the Mass is hypnotic indoctrination, designed to consolidate the power of the priesthood and the church, to keep the money flowing in, and to keep you in guilt and shame wallowing in your sin, living in fear of an angry God who is always displeased. You gaze at the priest who performs the rituals and chants the prayers, ancient prayers that invoke the Holy Spirit, bringing him out of heaven and down to earth.

What part of Jesus do they eat in the Mass? Is it the ear, the foot, the thigh, or the chest? Which cut is the best? Only Satan could invent such a monstrous, abusive, twisted, and sick view of God. Jesus died once and he died for sin, and all who have faith in him have eternal life. It is as simple as that. Jesus died on the cross two thousand years ago. He died once. Once was enough to purchase salvation for all who believe. He does not get up into the cross again. As Jesus said on the cross 'It is finished.' Jesus is whole after the resurrection. When you place your faith and trust in him, you are whole too, you do not have a dismembered Savior but a whole Lord.

If Jesus is still dying, then not even the Savior found freedom. If Jesus is still experiencing the pain of death, then God keeps him in torment and how is that love? Only the church would invent something as wicked and evil as the Mass. The Son came to set us free so we can be truly free.

5 WHAT IS CHRISTIAN FASCISM?

The Virus of Christian Fascism

Political fascism in the West is a nasty, virulent political disease. It has been expressed through the War on Terror, Covid Hysteria, and now WW3 against Russia and China. There is in the church today, a worse disease than Covid. It is religious fascism, or what I call 'Christian Fascism,' because it exists in many churches. Christian Fascism is a temptation for all Christians everywhere, especially in nations that pretend to be Christian. There are a lot of discussions these days on the nature of a Christian Fascist. Many assume it to be a right-wing Trump-loving, flag-waving American patriot, but they would be wrong. The roots of Christian Fascism run deep, and you may be one too. A Christian Fascist is not defined by their political affiliation and can be anyone. Christian nationalism, the more popular term, is too stained by the politics of the Culture War, so we need to take a step back and indeed out of the whirlwind that is the madness as to whether America will be great again, or not. Who cares?

No nation can be a Christian nation. Indeed, it is a convenient myth invented by nominal Christians who cannot tell the difference between faith and religion, or Christ and culture. Their version of a Christian nation is a form of slavery, a world Jesus came to deliver us from. Religious Fascism or Christian Fascism hates freedom more than secular fascists and they despise the Savior more because he is a threat to their power and money. Christian Fascists want public morality, not a transformed life.

Jesus is the Way, the Truth, and the Life (John 14: 6). This is the heart of faith for all Christians everywhere, regardless of whether they are Trump or Biden supporters. As a result, this truth is a person, not a set of rules, regulations, traditions, and rituals. We live in a post-democratic, post-Western world. People in power want a new public morality and have recruited many in the Christian Church for this last crusade. Jesus, once again, is on a collision course with what is left of the Western Church. Will America prevail over the Son of God? You tell me. Many cannot tell the difference these days and that is the problem.

These days, most churches see Jesus as a footnote to faith, a symbol, or an icon. In many old buildings, there is a dusty picture of Her Majesty Queen Elizabeth when she was in her twenties. It was a sign of disrespect that her portrait was not cared for. Out the front of many homes, flags fly that are left there overnight. Once again, flags need to be cared for, and not left in tatters. Many Christians see Christianity as an extension of Western culture, an icon, a symbol, something that reminds them of who they are, and what values they hold.

If you grow up in the West, you may think that the only way you can worship God is in the 'Western way.' God is Anglican, Catholic, or Orthodox, and one must adopt certain clothes, styles, traditions, and liturgies. Many believe that Christianity is Western, that the language of the church must be English, and the traditions of the reformation and counter-reformation are the only ones that define our encounters with the Divine. This is a huge problem. This has been a problem for the Gospel. Early Catholic missionaries like Francis Xavier were centuries ahead of Protestants in terms of bridging cultures. Many blunder in and don't know or care about the damage they cause. There were exceptions such as William Carey to India, or Hudson Taylor to China, but most Protestant missionaries could not avoid the temptation of linking Christianity with Western cultural values, ideals, and class structures.

Christianity was appropriated as a form of imperialism, not only for the Protestants of the British Empire but for Portugal and Spain as well. The links between Spain and Rome were the cause of the

Japanese genocide of hundreds of thousands of Christians in the years leading up to the closure of Japan to the West. American missionaries followed the marines into Iraq looking to introduce the people to Christianity, only to find churches that date back to early Christianity. Just look at the global Anglican Church gatherings, all in their antiquated robes, cassocks, and crooks, promoting an English version of a denomination whose persecution led to the flourishing of most Protestant denominations we know today.

Jesus was a Jew, and so was Paul, who was trained as a Pharisee. Augustine of Hippo was a North African, as was Tertullian. The early church flourished in Turkey such as in Ephesus. America or Britain is not even mentioned in the Bible and no disciple ever visited those lands. The church needs to rediscover the real Jesus and take off the Western clothes that they have forced him to wear for centuries. Otherwise, no one will become a Christian once the West turns to dust.

What is the most important choice for Christians today?

One of the lies of Christian Fascism is that nations move from moral to immoral societies. The Bible teaches that people do not change unless God changes their hearts which means societies do not get better or worse. Read Genesis and the story of Jacob and tell me that people are different today, or the story of Judas and his betrayal of Christ. Read the story of Peter in Galatians, who got embarrassed when his mates from Jerusalem turned up and saw him eating like a non-Jew. The human heart is the same. People are the same. God is the same.

Every generation is forced to make a choice about Jesus, who he is, what he did, and who sent him. This is the most important choice people need to make today. Many Christians, however, refuse to allow others to see Jesus because they dress him up like a Westerner, have him speak English, and tell others that he can only be worshipped in the Western style.

There have been some efforts to distance the Gospel from Western values in the last thirty years or so, but that effort has largely failed. Missionaries and Churches cannot help themselves, and nominal Christians who run the churches, don't see any difference. The future of Christianity, ever so desperate to be tied heart and soul to American imperialism is in great and perilous danger of certain extinction.

In some ways, Western Christianity is the greatest obstacle to the proclamation of the good news of Jesus Christ to the non-Western world. Their version of faith is religion, rules, traditions, guilt, and shame, all of which prevent you from encountering God because they stand at the door to the kingdom of God and block it. In addition, many nominals (who run the Culture War), point others away from the Bible to their political agenda, which is reviving their reimagined national past. They use the Bible as a political text, and twist verses to suit a sectarian agenda.

Indeed, much of the Church today in the West is tied to racial, and political objectives, philosophies, or ideologies. Most national churches are deeply racist, and many are explicitly Anti-Semitic, despite the horrors of the Holocaust and generations of enlightened secular education. Most people in the world are not white or European, and Jesus Christ came for all people, not just those who sit comfortably in the West, with the Pacific fleet and America's nuclear arsenal to protect them. Christians trust in God, not people, but they all must make a choice and decide who Jesus is.

You must make a choice about Jesus. One of the goals of *Freedom Matters Today* is to provide people with information to enable them to find freedom from whatever binds them in life. We have identified several things that bind people. One of these is Christian Fascism. I hope that you may escape religion and find faith. Christian Fascism is evil because it involves indoctrination, hypnosis, and delusion. These practices cause spiritual and psychological oppression and social exclusion. Only God can deliver us from the evils of Christian Fascism. A path out of darkness is from religion to faith by leaving the Culture War, state churches, and public morality, and returning to Jesus Christ. My message is simple: give up the politics, give up the Culture War, rediscover who Jesus is, and follow him.

If you do not, you will ruin your faith, you will lead people to destruction, you will be forgotten, and you will fail. God only promises what he promises, and what he does not promise, no prayer or self-effort can guarantee. Indeed, sometimes you may find yourself fighting against God.

If you make politics the vehicle for your faith you will fail. Christians who place their hope in politics or the Culture War are like those who build sandcastles on the beach and the tide is coming in. Don't look back to the fictional reimagined past of a Christian nation. Rather look back and see Jesus Christ on the cross, dying for the sin of the world, and also for you, no matter who you are. All who place their faith in him have eternal life.

Do Christians need to change society or themselves?

What does it mean to follow Jesus? Christians today have a choice: change society or change themselves. Following Jesus requires personal change. Changing society requires ignoring Jesus. If you know God the Father and Jesus Christ whom he sent, you have the Holy Spirit who teaches you all things. If you have Christ and you follow him, why bother with the Culture War? It is not a rhetorical question. Why bother? Why fight it at all?

We have a Savior and Lord who relates to us in the way he came into the world, the way he lived, the way he died, and the way he rose again. Jesus wants to know us personally. Because of knowing us, we can relate to one another in a way that was not possible before.

Following Jesus means we know him, but many do not know him so how can they follow him? The name of Jesus is the Jewish name, Joshua meaning 'God saves.' Jesus lived this out, being Immanuel or 'God with us,' for three years. If God was with us, and we can be with God, what else do we need? God saves us through the work of Jesus on the cross. Consequently, he died for sin and saved us from sin, shame, death, and fear. The saving work of God sustains us through life as we are united to Christ through faith. The Spirit of God dwells within us. We are taught by God all that we need, as we remember what Christ taught. We read the Bible, we pray, and we gather with other Christians.

Religious rituals do not save anyone. They are designed to distract you from thinking about the person of Jesus Christ. They prevent you from making up your mind about him and shaping your life around him. The ritual is an hour on Sunday when you engage in the Magic Show. It is religion, not faith. It is distant and silent.

Faith is personal and active. Jesus lived a real life, and he wants us to live one as well. If you refuse to change, how can you change the world? Many Christians who want to have a Christian society will not change themselves and therefore will fail to change others. Nowhere does Jesus expect political change, but personal change, so we might be his followers, his disciples.

Societies come and go. Do you think you can stop God and his purposes? Read Isaiah, Jeremiah, or Ezekiel for a bit of perspective. Nations are a drop in the bucket on a rainy day. Who remembers what empires lie under the desert sands? If God wants to destroy America, who are you to stop him? If he wishes to elevate China or Iran, who are you to stand in his way? If you are a politician, these problems are your problems, not mine. Who knows the future, but God?

History is full of accidents, surprises, and unpredictable things. Our lives are driven by the latest topic the media throws at us, the latest ruling, or the latest trend. Who cares? Let God deal with it. You are not responsible for the sins or actions of others. Their sins rest on their head. They are accountable. You do not need to have an opinion on every topic. Why should you spend every waking moment, and every breath fighting a Culture War over which you have no control?

We need to start thinking about Christ and following him. We all need to spend more time thinking, reading, and praying about the Lord Jesus Christ. Consider his work, identity, his person, and his life. Contemplate the consequences of knowing him for your life, identity, person, work, and relationships. If you have time over, then fight your beloved Culture War if you must. You need to fail at something. It should be something useless like that.

But once you find Jesus, you cannot stop talking about him, celebrating him, or worshipping him. God directs you in life to what is important, relationships, responsibilities, and duties, so you might be productive in this world.

If you have no faith, face that honestly. My feeling is that most who have a robust Political Theology have a superficial theology of God. They have copied Thomas Jefferson. Jefferson didn't like most of the Bible, especially the miracles and the supernatural. He wrote his own Bible cutting out the bits he disliked or loathed. Not surprisingly, he ended up with a slender volume.

Many Christians today have the same attitude. In my own Anglican Church where I grew up, I often heard many priests make fun of the Bible, poke fun at the life of Jesus, and hear them admit that they believed it was all a fairy tale. Why did they remain priests? They liked to be called 'Father,' in the street, they liked the position, the money, and the power, especially over the people who believed. These religious atheists would give them the Mass giggling and scoffing in secret mocking their faith while wearing the best clothes, eating the best food, and devouring the houses of widows. God knows the hearts of all people. Nothing is hidden from him. All he asks is that we believe in the one he sent and follow him, all our days. It is never too late to start, and it is never too late to turn around and begin a new path with Jesus.

Why did Jesus not get involved in politics?

Perhaps the greatest reason why the Culture War is irrelevant is that Jesus did not get involved in politics. Why did Jesus not get involved in politics? This is an important question. For that, let's go back. The longest and most incredible book in the Old Testament was Jeremiah. Jeremiah is one of my favorite Old Testament books. It is a book on the decline of political power, and I see parallels with the decline and fall of America and the West, in general.

But Jeremiah was a man who knew that Jerusalem was going to fall long before it did. He preached national repentance to no avail. He did, however, turn out to be completely right, and Jerusalem fell suddenly and terribly. Jeremiah only had a few words of advice to those who survived that Holocaust and were sent into exile. They were told to seek the peace and prosperity of the city of Babylon. Whatever faults that generation had, they listened to Jeremiah. As a result, 70 years later, the exiles returned with great wealth to rebuild the wall, and then later, begin work on the Temple. Paul the apostle tells the early followers of Jesus to do the same. He said as far as possible, live at peace with others, and avoid crime, for that reason the state held the sword (Romans 12: 18; 13: 4).

Do Christians have to be 'socially conservative'? Why? Where is this in the scriptures? Jesus doesn't have anything to say about people in politics. He does not expect you to be socially conservative, liberal, or socialist. Yes, a Christian can be a socialist, and even a free-market neo-liberal. I am sick to death of hearing Christians linking Jesus Christ with a socially conservative political agenda and saying that if you are truly a Christian you must be one too. Stop it. It is a sin. It is without any basis in the Bible. If you believe that Christianity is a synonym with any political philosophy, you are a fascist.

You are on dangerous ground because Jesus aligned himself with everyone by not turning anyone away. Of course, there was Nathaniel, a man in whom there was no guile, and a good Israelite, and some of the disciples were originally with John the Baptist and so they might be seen as devout. However, look at some of the men Jesus recruited. Jesus was a true leader. If you aspire to lead, then follow Christ. I dare you. Jesus recruited the worst possible candidates from our perspective.

One of them, Simon was called Simon the Zealot. Many believe that he may have been one of the dreaded assassins who hunted Romans and stabbed them in the back, literally. He was a terrorist. Nonetheless, Christ called him to be a disciple. Then there was Matthew, who worked for the Romans collecting taxes. This was a position widely seen as a vehicle for extortion and personal gain. Tax collectors were despised. Jesus called him as well. Jesus also recruited the traitor Judas Iscariot whom Jesus knew would betray him. Everyone thought Judas was the friend of Christ.

Jesus had at least two secret disciples who were among the men who condemned him to death, Nicodemus, and Joseph of Arimathea. How did they vote? Probably for Jesus, but we don't know. Paul talks of converts in the house of Herod and the House of Caesar, and yet that is all he does. Paul does not condemn them for being in those parties or political coalitions. Therefore, nor should we.

The Culture War is a distraction from the person and work of Jesus Christ. Christians who seek to advance the Gospel through political means are not following the path of Jesus. Jesus did not seek an earthly kingdom and turned his back on politics.

Christian Fascism is the embryo that is born from the egg that is the Culture War. It leads to the melding of church and state. At its heart is nominal religion, people without faith in Christ. Christian Fascism is committed to the rules, regulations, traditions, building, and history of their church and its denomination. Christian Fascism is an albatross around the neck of any good minister, priest, or pastor trying to advance the Gospel. Christian Fascism corrupts the mission of the church by replacing Biblical Theology with Political Theology. The church's agenda aligns with the agenda of the nominal Christians who seek to capture the church for their political purposes.

Many genuine pastors, ministers, and priests, loathe the denominations within which they are forced to work, as well as the ridiculous traditions, for the sake of the Gospel, but why should they? What benefit can be gained if one step forward is met with two steps back? The lives to be saved far outweigh the lives in the church that are dead, stuck in the traditions, and living in the grave of the past. Jesus told his disciples that when faced with opposition, to wipe the dust off their feet, and move on (Matthew 10: 14). That is the Biblical Model.

Let the dead bury the dead. Say goodbye to the albatross, farewell to the loyalty tests, and the efforts to derail your Gospel ministry. If God wants to open a door for you, he will provide it, and you need to step out in faith. The nominal Christians, their dead church, and their rituals will only cause you problems. Those who stay must reconcile themselves with that problem and work it out for themselves but be honest in admitting to themselves the real reasons why they put up with it. I hope, if you stay, it is for a good reason, and not for money, ambition, or fear.

Is it wrong for a Christian to be a politician or soldier?

Is it wrong for a Christian to be a politician or a soldier? First, is the politician. Billy Graham thought President Nixon was an honest man, but he turned out to be a crook. Billy Graham loved going to the White House. It was the place of power and Billy Graham wanted his fill. Nixon wasn't the first or the last politician to trick Christians. Look at the way so many Christian leaders fell for Trump or Biden. It is hard to be a Christian in politics. Many people fall for the charms of a leader who says all the right things but turns out to be quite different. It is easy to be swayed by a charismatic person in the Oval Office or elsewhere.

Christians are free to choose any legitimate profession in society. The problem is when Christians use politics, their job, or their career, as a substitute for their faith. Faith is personal, politics is not, it is about the community, many of whom are not Christians. We have our faith, and we meet someone who does not agree with us. The Christian talks, lives, reasons, and debates. We do not break fellowship with a person over these differences. Many Christians live insular lives, their entire life taking place at the church building and activities associated with that building. They become escapist monasteries where the faithful look inwards and bathe in a baptism of sectarian bigotry.

A Christian is not someone who uses the state to promote their values or punish them for not behaving in a way we do not like. Christianity is about a person's active faith in God, it is not about the behavior of other people in society. That is how so many Christians lose their way these days. They see the Culture War as the vehicle for promoting God's kingdom on earth. They will fail. God nowhere promises the rise of a Christian state or a Christian society, or Christian politics. Whatever God does not promise you cannot claim. History has shown that too, all efforts to build God's kingdom on earth through political means have been a complete failure. I laugh at all the pretenders today in Australia and America and Europe – you will fail. Surely, deep down you know you will too.

Is it wrong for a Christian to be a soldier? Is war wrong? God does not take sides in a war. God does not work for America, nor does Jesus Christ work for Putin. God knows all about war, and he knows the cost of war, and what it means for those people who fight it. God honors all who fight in a war, in the same way, he honors all who take up their chosen profession and seek to be the best they can be in it. There is no dishonor in any gainful employment, nor in following orders, or in soldiering. Being a soldier is a legitimate occupation. Serving one's nation is an honorable profession. Flag-waving is not fascism. There is nothing sinful about loving your nation or serving it in some capacity. It is why I have deep reservations over the use of the term 'Christian nationalism.' There is nothing wrong or sinful about loving your nation, respecting your leaders, or cherishing the soil of your native land. Have the mental capacity to use some sophisticated thought. Call it what it is:

fascism. There is no such thing as 'Christian nationalism.' It is fascism.

As far as war is concerned, the conduct of war, how wars are fought, God knows every thought of all those on a battlefield. God knows the fears and despairs, the doubts, and the anger, the sense of hopelessness, in ways that no one who has not fought can understand. God has seen war, and he fights war and there is no greater warrior than God. Read Revelation if you don't believe me, or Ephesians 6. There is always a war on, in which Jesus fights for his people.

God also knows where all the fallen lay, when they fell, and how, and he knows all their names. Nations may forget, people may forget the battles and the wars, and the sufferings, and move on, but God does not forget. God remembers all the fallen, even when all are forgotten and are shadows of the past and just names on tombs.

God also knows the thoughts and intentions of those people who sent them into battle and why. He knows where these people sit in their places of comfort, often far away from danger and harm, in their plush chairs and nice apartments. God sees them wearing their nice clothes and living their comfortable lives, while the forgotten died on their behalf. God knows all their names too. God will also not forget those who crossed the line from soldiering to murder, genocide, ethnic cleansing, or rape. 'Vengeance is mine,' says God, 'I will repay,' and he will. Being a soldier or a politician does not make you exempt from other people. You may get special privileges in society for being a soldier or representing your nation, but God treats all people the same. That freedom God brings is freedom for all.

Freedom that God brings is freedom from fascism and tyranny, freedom from fear and despair, freedom from sin and death, freedom from guilt and shame, and freedom from past and prejudice. True freedom is found in understanding what Jesus said in that verse or saying of his: I am the Way and the Truth and the Life, no one comes to the Father but through Me. Freedom is from God, it does not come from the state.

The difference between counterfeit freedom bestowed by people in power, and freedom bestowed by God is that people only bestow freedom on an interim, or conditional basis, and the freedom given by God is unconditional, non-discriminatory, and permanent. God does not and will not withdraw the freedom he bestows. Why ask for freedom if it can be taken away? That is what people do, but God never withdraws his favor, once given.

The first fascists were in the church

Who were the first fascists? These days, many people associate fascism with the *'right wing'* and say things like *'right-wing fascists,'* or *'far-right fascists.'* It is a curious association and is often applied inconsistently. The Western media for example decries American white supremacy as 'fascism' but pretends Ukrainian fascists don't exist, even though this tradition stretches back to nationalists like Stepan Bandera and lives on in the Azov Battalion and Right Sector. It is a strange omission from a White House that is obsessed with every document Trump dumped in his garage.

Some people call Christians who long for the good old days Christian 'nationalists,' but this makes little sense to me. The term 'nation' means very little by itself and implying that every Christian who loves their nation is a fascist sound is a sectarian slur to me, and out of place in a modern democracy, at least one that pretends to be.

People should instead be honest and call something for what it is. We are talking about fascism. What is it? Put simply, a fascist society is a former democracy where the people have chosen to transfer power from themselves to one person or a group who will act for them. Fascism arises from democracy. It is a product of democracy, or it cannot be fascism. Fascism occurs when elites give up on democracy, the idea that everyone has equal power and authority. Full-blown fascism existed in Germany, Italy, Japan, Spain, Portugal, and Chile, among other places in the last century, between the 1920s and 1980s. today, it is undeniably the case that the West has embraced a version of fascism with the façade and shell of democracy for exhibition purposes only.

Fascism is a sickness of the state arising from a dysfunctional democracy. Nazi Germany was only one type of fascism. Fascism in a traditional sense began with Italy and the rise to power from democracy of Mussolini. Other versions of fascism included Portugal, under Salazar, and Franco in Spain. Fascist societies are led by a cult-like leader, tend to be warmongers, with a reimagined history of identity, and are often Anti-Semitic.

Surely, the Christian Church opposed fascism? Think again. In secular Fascism, in every case, the national church of that nation fully supported the rise of fascism. The state churches generally supported all forms of tyranny, Hitler, Lenin, the Communists, the Japanese Imperialists, Mussolini, Franco, Salazar, and the list goes on. Google it. In fact, in every example of fascism – Germany, Italy, Spain, Portugal, and Japan, the fascists were supported by many in the church with a few exceptions.

Why did the church support fascism? Many Christian Churches supported the rise of fascism for two reasons. First, many despised democracies because they took away their power over people and they saw the Fascists as a better chance at regaining that power.

Many of these traditional churches were also fascist institutions. What do I mean? Well, in the beginning, the early Christians were equal, all were the same, and all had the Spirit, according to their gifts. The early assemblies resisted hierarchy, power, and money. Imagine that churches were not interested in money, power, or position. Remarkable. Impossible in the West today, where church and corruption are synonyms.

National churches evolved when the state took over Christianity under Constantine. There were popes, priests, patriarchs, and archbishops. None are Biblical terms or titles. Church power was transferred from people to this fascist leadership, from the people to those with political power. This transfer from everyone who had the Spirit to a few or one appointed by the state meant the end of Christianity and the beginning of Christian Fascism. It was the end of Christian communities, where 'all are one in Christ,' to a world where only a few held the reign of power. This included the rise of the monarchies and the perverse theologies of the crown such as the utter nonsense that Queen Elizabeth II was anointed by the Holy Spirit when she was crowned Queen.

Many people in religion crave power. That is why most become priests. Most churches desire the transfer of authority away from themselves to the person at the top. In the Bible, Christ is the head of the 'church,' not the Pope or King Charles. The Bible teaches everyone is a priest, everyone has the Holy Spirit and God sees everyone the same way. Eventually, many churches get rid of the

Bible and create a hierarchy of those in charge and those who obey.

The national churches despise the expression of the Spirit and any movement of the Spirit. This helps to explain why national churches loved to murder dissenters and non-conformists for centuries because they listened to God and not to the Church. Look, for example, at the story of Joan of Arc. She and many other mystics were murdered by the Church because she believed God spoke to her personally, not through the Pope and his edicts and so she had to die.

Who were the first fascists? The Christians, in their church-state marriages. They were unelected, wielding final authority over all people in their territorial domain. The church was the first fascist regime, the inspiration for all fascists. Today, Christian Fascists long for the days when they controlled the state and often believe they are above the law. They are always a threat to any nation because religious people who covet political power tend to forget their faith along the way. History has shown that.

Nonetheless, fascism continues to thrive today in the ruins of representative democracy. No democracy is immune from fascism. Democracies often get sick and so fascism continues to grow, like a sterile flower in a field of wilting roses. Libertarians and Marxists agree that America is a fascist state, especially after 9/11. The War on Terror, Covid Hysteria, and the doctrine of endless war are symptoms of this fascism. Fascism is also arguably present due to Covid Hysteria. The suspension of human rights, vaccine mandates, passports, and lockdowns resembled Europe in the 1920s and 1930s. Many also saw in Trump hints of fascism with his 'Make America Great Again' rhetoric and the cult of personality. Fascism is on the rise in Hungary and Poland, Ukraine, and Australia. Fascism has no place in Christianity, and no Christian can be a fascist. Paul said that all are one in Christ Jesus (Galatians 3: 28). Strange how that verse is so often neglected by many in the church today.

Five characteristics of a Christian Fascist

What are the five characteristics of a Christian Fascist? A Christian Fascist is a person who has the political theology of those in churches loyal to the state. A Christian Fascist holds to an ideology based on cynical nostalgia and sincere hope for a return to the past. It is all about loyalty and showing the government that they are prepared to compromise anything for money or power. The Culture War, Covid Hysteria, and the War in Ukraine are all crises facing society. The Christian Fascists want to piggyback their way back into places of authority. They covet what they lost long ago, true political power and the sword.

The goal of the Christian fascist is not the proclamation of the Gospel. The Christian Fascist hates Jesus Christ and his message that he is the Way, the Truth, and the Life. What is their goal? The last thing Christian Fascists want is for the church to return to Jesus Christ. They recoil in horror at the notion of the Gospel, a transformed life, a life set free by Christ, and personal salvation.

There are five motivations for those who have aligned with Christian Fascism. First, many truly believe the past was better. The present is a disappointment. Christian Fascists are truly convinced that at some point in the past, the nation was better off.

Second, the Church is the place to instill morality, not the Gospel. Christian Fascists do not see the church as the place for the proclamation of the Gospel of Christ. Consequently, they see the church as the place to instill moral order, moral values, and especially public morality. Therefore, the church is not about our relationship with God, but our relationship with others. It is said that the way we love God is the loving of others.

This is religious atheism. There are many religious atheists in the church. They are easy to find, and they don't hide. They say things like *'the way we love God is loving others,'* or *'Jesus taught the golden rule,'* or *'Jesus only wants to obey the two commandments of loving God and one's neighbor.'* Their gospel is one of self-effort, not grace or mercy, and in talking about love, they ignore justice. Christian Fascists preach Moses and not Christ, they mock Paul, ignore Peter, and misquote John. Therefore, like cockroaches in a rancid cellar, they infest many churches, especially the traditional liturgical churches. They believe marriage between the church and state is the definition of a true church, and its function in a nation, shaped by their view of nationalism.

Third, Christian Fascists believe loyalty to the state is the highest Christian virtue, an echo of the Crusades, and monarchy. Both forms of fascism, religious imperialism, and monarchy are irreconcilable with Christianity as only Christ is king. Covid Hysteria was a perfect opportunity for Christian fascists to prove their loyalty to the state. It was a litmus test. They eagerly lapped up vaccine passports and fully supported the demonization of the unvaccinated. Christian Fascists were silent during Covid. They did nothing when the unvaccinated were slandered, locked up, blamed for every death, or called criminals. This new class of people was ostracized, blamed, criticized, condemned, and excluded. Indeed, Christian Fascists gave their assent when the nation was weaponized against this new class, blamed for the pandemic, blamed for the variants, blamed for the lockdowns, and blamed for the deaths, the so-called *'pandemic of the unvaccinated.'*

Fourth, Christian Fascists hate Jesus Christ, and they are doing the opposite of what I am trying to do. I want to place Jesus Christ at the center of faith, they want him removed. The exclusive claims of Jesus are always a threat to their power. For example, they say all this talk of new life in Christ, and the resurrection and reading the Bible is fine, but it dilutes loyalty to the state, the god of the nation. This needs to be stopped, in their view. The church's role is moral reform not spiritual renewal.

Christian Fascists will therefore only tolerate a religion of civic obedience, loyalty to the state, and the new public morality so church doors can be kept open. As a result, so many of those evangelicals who supported Covid Passports did not get the memo. Their church leaders want to cleanse the church of Christ.

Fifth, Christian Fascists agree with the national holiness crusades of the state, to purge the nation of its enemies in search of a nation of better people. First, it was to hate Muslims, then hate Trump, then hate the unvaccinated. Now we are to hate Putin. Christian Fascists want to make themselves useful to the government. They want to prove their loyalty.

The last thing they want you to do is to open your Bible and read it, or God forbid, listen to Jesus. If you want to expose a Christian Fascist, turn to your Bible, read it, and follow Jesus. Pray with them. They will give themselves away quickly. As I said, they don't hide, because they think they have won and Jesus has been purged from the church, like he was in the old days, when the church had the sword.

6 HOW COVID HYSTERIA SPLIT THE CHURCH AND WILL LEAD TO THE GREAT DIVORCE

Six Ways to Identify Christian Fascists

Christian Fascists are everywhere in the church today. They are not wearing MAGA shirts though some of them might be. They did not vote for Trump in 2020, though some of them might have. They do not listen to Alex Jones at Infowars but some of them might. You see, Christian Fascists are not Christian Nationalists. They are not a product of the Culture War. They are not on the far-right. They are not anti-vaxxers, election deniers, or pacifists. This is because Joe Biden is wrong. The Trotskyites are wrong. The media are wrong.

Fascism is not a product of democratic politics, it is not an offspring of party politics, and it is not a type of American politics. Fascism is a system of thought born out of decay. Fascism is a way to describe a political and economic system in a nation where power is concentrated among a few people, a power that has been stolen from everyone else. It is the hierarchy of power that results from the termination of equitable power, the usurpation of the ballot box. American democracy is not a pure elixir of truth being stained by the addition of the poison of far-right fascist, alt-right, Trump-loving, flag-waving, vax-hating, abortion-denying domestic terrorists. It has been dead for years.

The term *'Christian nationalist,'* is itself a product of the Culture War. It is a loaded, subjective, ideological term used as a weapon to besmirch, slander, and denounce one's enemies. It is as useless as an object of study as the term MAGA, Trump's slogan of '*Make America Great Again.*' Not even Trump knows what this means. In a sense, it is a suspicion, it is an accumulation of emotion and sentiment, but it means nothing in practice. It is the way the American Marxists or the American media decry right-wing fascism. It means absolutely nothing beyond rhetoric, sectarianism, and hatred. You cannot see clearly if you are in a whirlwind and the American Culture War is a tornado. Fascism is what happens after democracy is dead, not when democracy is alive. Active, genuine democracy in the West has been dead for years.

Fascism in economics is what happens when competition is dead, not when it is thriving. Fascism in society happens when the past is reimagined and rewritten, not when it is understood. The accusations laid against Trump, that he is a fascist, are a product of lazy and incompetent politics. It is essentially the rise of the Left's fictitious creation of *'fascism'* to counter the Right's fictitious creation of *'socialism.'* For many on the Right in America, any involvement of the government in society is 'socialism,' or 'communism.' This is ideological nonsense of the highest order. It represents either profound intellectual immaturity or profound intellectual deceit for the purposes of ballot box harvesting amongst the ignorant, the naïve, and the stupid.

America cannot exist without the state. America is the state. America is not the Constitution, it is not the Great Experiment, it is not the light on the Hill, it is the state. The American state is one of the most powerful states in the world, and to argue that it is possible to detach the government from the nation in any meaningful way, is a lie. To argue that this monolithic leviathan can be usurped by a small coalition of disgruntled people who for a few hours one January morning vented their anger at the Capitol, got bored, and went home, is fantasy worthy of a poorly written novel, but not reality.

Fascists draw their inspiration from the Christian Church. At the beginning of Christianity, all were equal, all had the Spirit, all had their roles in the local assemblies, and all were one in Christ. There was a sense of all being together with Christ, in a collection of gatherings all over the region. People knew each other, pastors and teachers were regularly exchanged, there was profound freedom. For that first generation or two up until the fall of Jerusalem and the rise of Christianity among the nations, there were no churches, but only Christians.

When Christianity because the church, what was distributed amongst all was concentrated by the few, in a religious hierarchy of invented traditions and rituals all designed to show that the only one close to God was the priest. The desire for religious power corrupted true faith in Christ and the life of the Spirit. This Christian Fascism came complete with blasphemous hagiography, ridiculous and idiotic stories of the martyrs and their death speeches, their fake miracles, and their feats for God. These were in fact, all the people the church murdered. Throughout the history of Christianity, the Spirit of God has moved amongst his people and drawn millions to himself pointing them to the Lord Jesus Christ. At every stage, and every step, the church has been there to persecute them, condemn them, and kill them.

The greatest murderer of the faithful was always the church, which feared Christians who simply followed Christ, and not them. These were people, inspired and motivated to do great things for God, challenge the corruption, and hypocrisy of the church, and change the world they did. Up until the early nineteenth century in parts of Europe and even later in some places, the church was there, with the sword to kill them, and when they could not kill them, they persecuted them in the courts, and now in the arena of public opinion. Even today, many churches believe they are above the law, are a law unto themselves, and are accountable to no one except to a God most do not believe in. Ordinary people following Jesus Christ are not a threat to anyone except the church which hates Christ, despises God, and loves money and power. At least the early Jewish society allowed Jesus to be born and grow to a man of about 30 and even have three years of public ministry. If the church knew Jesus was to be born today, they would force Mary to have an abortion and kill him before he was born, lest he speaks words against them.

In the church today, it is easy to spot a fascist. They are easy to spot if you have an open Bible, follow Jesus Christ, and listen to the Spirit. Covid Hysteria was great for the Gospel. It brought truth to the church and that is a rare thing these days. People were forced to choose Jesus or loyalty to the state. Many priests, pastors, and ministers in the church are what I have called Soul Catchers. They do not want you to know God or Jesus Christ whom he sent. They don't open their Bible, they don't believe Jesus rose from the dead, and they don't follow Jesus.

They want to keep you trapped in guilt and shame, so you do not find true freedom. There are two ways. First, the use of hypnosis in the church, or propaganda, to indoctrinate people and turn their attention away from God. They usually do this by turning our attention towards a ritual such as the Mass or the Sermon. Indeed, both functions to create a false sense of spirituality but they are feelings that come from social interaction not the Spirit of God.

The other way that Soul Catchers trap people is through nationalist versions of Christianity. There is nothing wrong with nationalism or sentimental views of the past, we all have them. We tend to fondly think of events or people we have experienced or encountered. Therefore, we need to be careful when the church starts tampering with nationalism and mixing it with their version of the Gospel. I am not the first to point this out.

In past generations, other Christians spoke of the divide within Christianity using other terms and categories. The English and American Puritans for example spoke of the difference between genuine and counterfeit faith. A common term for this fake Christian was the 'Almost Christian.' Some piety movements in various denominations over the centuries sought to revive personal devotion and piety to God. Protestants in England in the late nineteenth century talked about the difference between the nominal baptized Christian and the person of genuine faith. Christian Fascists attend church, they love the church, they promote the church, they are devoted to the rituals and seek to capture the state to advance their religion. They have no faith in Christ, none whatsoever.

Christian Fascists create a reimagined past, a fictional past, invented for political purposes. Their followers become a socialized weapon to enforce contemporary conformity and rewrite history. They invent a past that never existed. You cannot return to something that never existed in the first place. Christian Fascists believe in public morality, not personal faith. They believe in a twisted vision of Moses and the Law. They do not believe in the grace and mercy of Jesus Christ. They cannot grasp God's forgiveness or understand the death of Christ. They are relentless in excluding people based on their list of unforgivable public sins. Jesus, however, welcomes all to come and find freedom, forgiveness, and hope.

Fifth, Christian Fascists have a religion shaped by their loyalty to the state. Christians have their faith shaped by their loyalty to God. Sixth and finally, these Fascists have created a religion that is shaped by edicts, policies, and whims of political leaders. Christians have a faith shaped by the person and work of Immanuel, God with us. My use of the term 'Christian Fascist' is to replace the antiquated term of a 'nominal' Christian, and the confusing term 'legalist,' and locates the focus of this person of religiosity – their desire to extinguish the Spirit, deny equality, and impose their religion on others in a religion shaped by nationality, not faith.

What was the cost of shutting down churches?

Christian Fascists are loyal followers of the state's intent for social control. Loyalist churches are churches whose loyalty lies with the government of the day, not God, the Ancient of Days. Their loyalty is to the nation and nationalist ideology. Their religion is shaped by national identity, and they have no room for the Gospel in their sacred halls and buildings. They are careful to discern the priorities and goals of the ruling class of the day and tailor their message, their focus, and their resources to promoting government agendas. During Covid Hysteria, many churches, priests, pastors, and ministers, bowed on bended knees to the state. Consequently, they not only closed their churches but condemned anyone who had a point of view that differed now-discredited narrative of public health policy. We saw their true face, and that is that their faith in Christ was only the façade. They made their choice. Now they protest and say that they were forced to obey against their will. Pity they took the money. Were they forced to do that? Now that the lockdowns are over, will the churches repay Job Keeper to the state like so many private organizations? They said they were only *'following the science.'* If so, then ban the Contagion Chalice of the Mass, a vessel for communicable diseases, and keep churches closed while Covid continues to rampage through the community. The reality is that the government handouts have dried up and so the churches have lost their principled position.

What was the 'science' of the church policies? This was the view that vaccines will stop the transmission of Covid. Most people have the injections, and more people are contracting it than ever. I have been told that the reason Covid is being contracted by injected people is that the 'unvaccinated' have not been injected. What does this mean logically? The annual flu shot millions receive each year is therefore completely ineffective unless 100% of people get the flu shot. We know that is not scientifically true. If you take the flu shot, it should protect you from this year's influenza. Why is Covid any different? This bizarre rhetoric is indicative of many of the intellectual contradictions that Covid produced, and yet most people fell for it, and still believe it today. If you are inoculated from a disease, you are protected from that disease, plain and simple. This is called science.

Loyalist churches kowtowed to the state. Many priests brought politics into the pulpit and told their people to get vaccinated. Many openly criticized other Christians who held to different views, ostracized them and many lied about the work of God in the world. What did the loyalists say about Christianity and Covid? Here is a sample.

'God wants you to get vaccinated.'

'God wants us to love others and the proof of this is our vaccination.'

'Christians must obey the government in everything, so get vaccinated.'

'Christians who do not take the vaccine are not following Christ.'

'Getting vaccinated is proof you love others.'

'Get vaccinated and you will stop the spread.'

'Be vaccinated and you will not get Covid.'

These statements and others like them are nonsense. The extent of spiritual abuse in these statements is unparalleled. As a result, never in living memory, have so many Churches been remiss in guarding the deposit entrusted to those who follow Christ. What was going on, what was it all about? On one level, it was about the money, certainly in Australia. Churches need money, and they were happy to keep quiet. They certainly did, overall, except for a few thousand dissenters, who were roundly condemned as far-right domestic terrorists, extremists, and crazies.

Loyalist Churches want the end of Gospel Witness. Covid Hysteria, therefore, saw the revival, not of Christianity, but civic religion, a new state religion. This new state religion has long been the goal of the state, which has sought to extinguish the gospel in the West for a century. They have their reasons, and not all of them are negative. Christianity took a major hit during Covid. That was the goal of people in power: take down the church, capture it, silence it, and weaponize it. Christians believe the ruling class is on their side. It is their most fatal mistake.

Those who remained in the churches will now need to remain on their knees as new directives come down the chain of command including the need to condemn Russia, promote climate change policies, and the new public morality. Some call this the social credit score, which is, in the old-fashioned language, a series of loyalty tests. The new standard for Christians in the West will be their loyalty to the state through a series of public affirmations, statements, and lifestyle choices. Just listen to the hypocrites condemn Putin but ignore America's continual occupation in the Middle East. The Western Church, overall, is aligning its future with American imperialism, the future of America, American values, and the West. I am sorry, but it's all downhill from here. There is no 'new normal,' and no 'return to the good old days.'

Loyalist churches, churches loyal to the state and not to God, do not abide in the Gospel. There is something evil about the last three years. In other words, we do not, as Paul says, wrestle with the World Economic Forum, Bill Gates, or Joe Biden, but with principalities, powers, rulers in the heavenly realms, and spiritual wickedness (Ephesians 6). I am not saying that demons are running the churches, why would they bother, for it is the love of money that kills most faithfulness to God. Money is the great snare for Christian Fascists. Without true faith, they need money to keep their churches open. They chose money instead of the Gospel. Now, in Australia, throughout 2022, Covid is tearing through the community with hundreds dying every day, and these religious hypocrites ignored the science, and opened their churches, not to keep people safe but because the money from the government dried up and they needed more cash from their congregations. The money came before public health safety.

The Australian lockdown madness bankrupted the nation, failed to kill Covid, and drove the nation insane. In this chaos, a true fascist was born, Scott Morrison, the former Prime Minister, who created a secret shadow government, assuming secret control over all strategic portfolios, accumulating power like a dictator in what was effectively a coup against democracy. Apparently, according to the Constitution, the Prime Minister can hold all portfolios of his Cabinet himself and rule by himself, or herself, in an Australian democratic system. What this means is that the Constitutional Monarchy of Australia provides the legal pathway for the rise of a dictator, a fascist leader. The fact that this story is now buried and ignored suggests many in the ruling class of Australia are deeply attracted to fascism. The Australian church, for its part, says nothing.

Every generation is faced with the same choice

Every generation is faced with the same choice. We are no different. There is nothing special about this generation. There is no reason why the same principle that has been at work in every generation ceases to operate because we live in modern America or Australia. The choice facing each generation is clear: bow to Baal or worship God. In every generation, most fail, but a few do not. God does not believe the majority will ever follow him. He expects they will turn away. They always do. Not everyone, however, bows to the national religion or the dictates of the state. It is for their sake that the Great Divorce is coming. It is long overdue and certainly welcome.

In the days of Elijah, the prophet, 7,000 refused to bow to Baal.

When Paul felt alone, God reminded him that he had many people in that city. In the days of Imperial Japan, only the members of the Non-Church Movement and a few other groups or individuals stood up for Christ. The rest bowed to the emperor and gave up their faith.

Uchimura Kanzo, the founder of the Non-Church Movement refused to bow to the Emperor of Japan during the Imperial Edict of Education in 1891. He went to the church expecting to find support, but they told him to bow to the emperor as a living god. All those churches are dead now. Well over a century later, many Japanese people still know the name of Uchimura Kanzo, because he held onto his beliefs and refused to compromise them. The reason the Japanese church is so small is because of the apostasy of the 1930s. In the days of Fascist Germany, members of the Confessing Church stood against Hitler and the Nazi Party while most German Christians supported the fascists.

The Puritans in England suffered terribly at the hands of the Church of England. In 1660, 2000-plus priests and ministers were kicked out of the Church of England because they did not kowtow to the Book of Common Prayer. John Bunyan was one such Puritan, the author of the Pilgrim's Progress. He was put in prison for 12 years for not submitting to the authority of the Church of England.

Every generation has the church making the wrong choice. In every case of mass apostasy, the apostate bishops, priests, archbishops, and pastors have their clever theological arguments, word plays, and semantic obfuscation to defend their every repudiation of the Gospel as they have done during Covid Hysteria.

The Christians who lined up to support vaccine passports were apostates. Like Esau, they were happy to sell out their faith for a bowl of soup, like Judas, for thirty pieces of silver. As I have said before, churches and Christians that closed their doors to the unvaccinated or promoted vaccination policies in the pulpit or wrote Covid Theology betrayed Christ and betrayed God's people. There is nothing special about their betrayal. Every generation is faced with the same choice. Most choose poorly.

Keep in step with the Spirit

Keep in step with the Spirit and step out of the church. Christians who read their Bible, pray, and walk in the Spirit are a threat to power. What does it mean to keep in step with the Spirit? Once you start bowing to the state, there is no getting up again. There will be no end to the loyalty tests. A strong state will not care about loyalty. A strong state knows people will stand up when needed, voluntarily. Australia, New Zealand, and Canada, among others, are not strong states, but easily bend with the winds of empire.

In the last twenty years, we have seen the erosion of the credibility and longevity of the state in the West, the crumbling of legitimacy, brought about through globalization, and the rise of multiethnic societies, the bane of the old white aristocracy.

Check your Bibles about the rise and fall of nations. The future of all nations is dust, and if they are lucky, gradual, but certain decline. Others end in fire. The future will be no different. No nation is under God's special, eternal protection. The way to keep in step with the Spirit is to listen to the Spirit and the Spirit's audio files are the Bible. Each step through life needs to be shaped by your encounter with God's word.

Secular Fascists are astonished some keep in step with the Spirit. During Covid Hysteria, people in power were genuinely surprised at the opposition from many Christians. You could tell it in their faces during the Press Conferences. The government was and is astonished that some people keep in step with the Spirit. For the first time, they encountered genuine Christianity. They had never seen it before. The only people they know are Christian Fascists. After all, the atheists and agnostics in the ruling class went to the same religious schools as the Christian Fascists. They probably never met a real Christian.

Keep in step with the Spirit and bow only to God. Even the apostasy of prominent evangelicals and churches to follow the script of people in power did not stop these people. Their loyalty was to God, not to their priest. What this represented was a rebellion in all major denominations as people realized their pastors, priests, and bishops were fake and spiritually corrupt. These new church-less people want a more personal faith, not bound by to-down laws and rules. The institutional church lost control of many of its people.

True Christians are always a threat to Fascists. Fascism is evil. It is the only form of governance that comes straight from Hell. It is capricious, unstable, and treacherous. The rewards for loyalty are more loyalty tests, more compromises, and there is no integrity. Christians are among the people who make the best citizens, but fascists have no respect for their citizens. Fascism is the last stage of society before the collapse. Fascism is the desperate cry of anguish of a nation falling into the fire.

The appearance of many Christians who refused to bow to the state was a problem for the government. People in power assumed that priests ran the hearts and minds of their people, but that is not true. Covid Hysteria showed that for many Christians, God is the one in charge.

Many people only attend a local church out of convenience, not loyalty to the denomination. This was a shock for both the church and the state. They have faith in Christ, not in the bishop, priest, or pastor. There are many underground churches, home churches, informal churches, and so on. This represents a threat to the state and the power of Christian Fascism. In Australia, New Zealand, America, and Canada, the ruling class is moving against unaffiliated Christians, those who follow Jesus and not the state.

In a secular society, the benefit of established churches is that they can be controlled by the state. That is why they exist. The idea that there are people out in the community, Christians, who are not part of a state-sanctioned religious group, living out their faith in their lives, reading the Bible, and helping others, fills government officials with terror. They are meeting outside of official, state-sanctioned buildings, refusing to identify with denominations and they insist on being called Christians.

Many who now attend churches that bowed to the state do so with a sense of pride that they *'did the right thing'* by the government and are protected by the state in the future. They believe that they proved their loyalty and can go back to *'business as usual.'* They could not be more wrong. Remember what Christ said about loyalty to the world. Christians that are trusted by the government to rubber-stamp every proclamation are not Christians at all. Christians are always labeled by Fascists as extremists or conspiracy theorists. True Christians are strong, they are Spirit-filled. No priest or bishop controls them. They follow Jesus, even when their churches tell them not to. Many Christians who refused to toe the line were sick of the lies, sick of the double standards, and the restrictions. They were not alone. Their cries went up to God and he is never silent.

Our God is a God who acts, and His Spirit is always on the move.

The Great Divorce is Coming

Covid split the Christian Church in the West down the middle. At the smallest hint of the possibility of persecution, many bold and fearless Christians lost their nerve and gave up their faith. It is easy to be a Christian when the government is on your side, but it was incredible to watch, in real-time, churches, seminaries, and ministries fall from faith and become echo chambers for what were catastrophic government policies. Many evangelical and so-called Bible-based seminaries demanded vaccine passports and turned students away arguing they only wanted to keep people safe, only to open them again not based on science, but politics.

Many of the biggest names in the Western Church gave up their faith in Christ and fell in line. After all, what would happen to their vast financial empires if they went up against the state? The complicity and involvement of the church in giving legitimacy to these appalling social policies will not be forgotten. Churches closed their doors not to keep people safe, but to avoid suffering the consequences, such as fines, or imprisonment. The imposition of vaccine passports on church members was clear apostasy. The Western Christian church will never be the same again. This is because, finally, thank God, the Great Divorce is coming.

Covid Hysteria also brought apocalypse, which means a revelation of many things kept secret. Covid was certainly God's doing, or at least, God was weaving his purposes through Covid, as he does through everything. Certain men meant it for evil, but God meant it for good. Covid Hysteria and the loyalties it produced answered a curious question that I have been pondering for some time. Churches aligned with the state showed their true colors and their true loyalty. In Australia, for example, the greatest ambiguity has been the fake bastion of evangelicalism in the Australian Anglican Church, a strange mix of ritualism and evangelical fervor.

The high point of Sydney's brief flourish of faith was the 1959 Billy Graham Crusade, led by the controversial successor to Billy Sunday. Graham was, like Billy Sunday, a fascist. His message was popular as an antidote to communism and the importance of personal faith. His simple message of giving your life to Jesus filled the churches and the seminaries. Many Christian leaders in Australia today were converted under his ministry, and there has never been anyone like Billy Graham. He saved a dying, corrupt, nepotistic, racist church from extinction, at least for a while. Many of these converts ended up in the established church, the Anglican church, the church of the ruling class. It began as a mission from India, not Britain, and has long been associated with the landed aristocracy. It has a disgraceful and scandal-ridden history, but it is the church of money. It is not surprising that many of the converts of the capitalist-preacher Billy Graham ended up in the church of old money. Anglicans in Australia get some of the best salaries and tax-free benefits.

The Anglican church, for its part, was completely committed, wholesale and spirited, in dedicated obedience to vaccine passports, mandates, and the preaching of vaccines from the pulpit. Now that Covid is rampaging through the Australian community, all these churches are now completely open.

Billy Graham was not the only influence on the church. Following their role when the church held the sword, established churches play a critical role in informing and dictating public morality. Underneath the veneer of the gospel, the established churches have monied interests and social control as their overall ambitions. If it ever came to a choice between the gospel on one side and money and power on the other, it is obvious that the latter would be chosen.

Few in the ruling class in Australia are naïve enough to believe that the established churches are driven by faith. People are polite about it, as most observe social niceties. Everyone knows it is about money and political power. One mediocre but popular Christian leader once proposed the goal of having ten percent of Sydney go to church through traditional evangelism. He failed. That was in the 1990s, before 9/11. Curiously, in the last twenty years, established churches are engaged in a very successful pro-state counterattack to revive public morality, loyalty to the state, and the removal of the Gospel, following the pattern in other countries. The Anglican Church of Australia, which used to be the heart of evangelicalism, has fallen. It has struggled for years between the Gospel and Christian Fascism, but the Fascists have prevailed. This denomination will not rise again because is too busy proving its loyalty to the government and it is consumed by the Culture War such as their criminally negligent war on gay marriage and transgender children.

Gay marriage is now legal in Australia. Churches that refuse to celebrate gay marriage on church property are breaking the law of the land, in fact, the only law of the land. The state does not recognize 'church law' and never has. If the churches refuse to obey the law, then why should they receive financial benefits from the state? Why should they continue to receive charity status? If they have the 'right to break the law,' then why not introduce Sharia Law for the Muslim faithful who seek it? It is only fair. Furthermore, is not obedience to the state mandatory for all Christians? Is that not what we were told during Covid Hysteria? The Anglican Church is Australia's de-facto establishment church, in other words, they run most of the private (religious) schools where most of the rich parents send their children.

The Great Divorce is coming. It should have happened centuries ago when the church and state nominally divorced and went their separate ways, but religious people in power could not give up their seats of power and have continued to meddle and interfere for centuries. Nations have lingered for centuries in this limbo, this quasi-world where societies are not quite secular, and not quite sacred. Liberal Democracy has been the sanctuary for the continual survival of the old, aristocratic, fascist church, but now democracy is faltering, what will become of the old regime?

The churches are rotting because they ignore the cornerstone, Christ. The Great Divorce is the separation of church and state, and the final, long-awaited death of national churches, their surrogates and operatives, disciples, and propaganda. Some are in advanced states of decay such as the Lutheran Church in Sweden and Germany, and the Italian Church. As it says in Proverbs, *'The memory of the righteous is a blessing, but the name of the wicked will rot'* (Proverbs 10:7). The churches are rotting. There is decay everywhere. This is the hand of God. He does not need to squash churches, they are simply falling because they neglect the foundation, which is Christ. The final demise of the national church, the church of the establishment, national religion, institutional religion, whatever name you like is a blessing to be embraced.

Three strategies of Christian Fascists

There are three Strategies of Christian Fascists. Covid Hysteria brought Christian Fascism into the light. The Culture War is a temptation for many well-meaning, but mistaken Christians who think they are advancing the Gospel by forcing others to conform. Faith in Jesus cannot be forced, it must be a decision of the will, the heart, the mind, the soul, and this can only be genuine if it is one's own decision, not the decision of others. Living a life based on duty, without true faith by honoring the ancestors, parents, or spouse will not be sufficient for the trials and difficulties of life. Sadly, many walk in the clothes of a Christian in the Culture War but are far from being genuine. They see a constituency that might advance their personal power-grab. They claim to be Christian, then ignore the Gospel.

Christians involved in the Culture War want to force belief on others. It is the opposite of what Jesus does. Christian Fascists do this by creating a fictional past to justify their contemporary political agenda which is to force belief. This reimagined past is entirely fictitious.

These Christian Fascists use one of three strategies. First, they like to talk about the Christian past in a positive light. As a result, they say things like *'in the old days, more people went to church, and it is a shame that people don't go anymore.'*

Second, they like to talk about moral decline. In other words, in the past, people were moral and Christian, but now, they are immoral.' For example, they talk of Christian *'values,'* or *'traditional values,'* that are being undermined by new groups of people or minorities. Their targets are usually children. Christian Fascists love going after the children, just look at their fascination with infant baptism, youth groups, and kid's programs. These days they want gay and transgender children and teachers expelled from their schools.

Third, they like to talk about Christian heritage, but rarely beyond generalities as if there ever was such a thing as a Christian heritage. It has only been in the last generation that the denominations have stopped hating each other. In the past, most churches despised each other, so which heritage are we trying to protect?

It is easy to see, therefore, that these three strategies of Christian Fascists have everything to do with a reimagined national past and nothing to do with Jesus Christ. Jesus is a footnote to their ambitions. They crave his name only, which is useful only as a slogan. They are not interested in the person of Jesus or his work for us. Christian Fascists come in all shapes and sizes, and there are different factions. However, while they may wear different suits, they were all made by the same tailor.

When was Australia a Christian Nation?

One of the most appalling examples of religious revisionism in Australia has been the fake history that Australia was a Christian nation. When was Australia a Christian Nation? Christian Fascism is not Christianity because our relationship with God is a personal one, not a collective one. Nations concern people while God is concerned with the individual. Read Proverbs, Psalms, and Ecclesiastes. These books were for all of Israel, but they were addressed to individuals. Individuals are encouraged to make choices in their lives in the paths God has presented them with. God's communal concern is never at the expense of the personal. If it was, then he would not be a personal God, but a distant one. The goal of Christian Fascists is that they want to turn the Gospel away from a personal relationship with God. They want to focus on a distant, national relationship with something God-shaped, their ancestors, their lives, and their relationship with God.

Christian Fascists deny the individual nature of faith. The Culture War is not a personal relationship with God but a collective relationship between the nation and its citizens. Christian Fascists insist their nation has a Christian character rooted in the past. They argue that the present situation is worse than the past.

This Christian Fascism, I repeat, is not Christian, because Christianity is a personal relationship with God, not a collective one. A person cannot inherit the Christian faith. It is not about national identity, blood, or language. It depends on a personal decision to believe in Jesus Christ or not. You are either a Christian or you are not. It is as simple as that. The strategy of the Christian Fascist will fail. People do not go backward; they live in the present.

Like the Nazis who invented Germanic myths to prop up the Holocaust, Christian Fascists have invented a fake past. This reimagined past never existed. Take any Western nation and ask yourself when the glory days were when the nation was Christian, or at least lived according to its Judeo-Christian legal system. When was America living out the kingdom of the risen Lord Jesus Christ? Was it during the genocide of the First Nation's peoples or the celebration of the slave plantations in the Old South, or was it during segregation when African Americans were denied their humanity?

In Australia, can we say that the good old days were when Sydney was a prison colony, and convicts were handed out to the landed gentry like slaves to work the land, or sent to Tasmania to endure terrible cruelty and suffering? Maybe it was during the time the landed gentry and their friends in the church went out and slaughtered the Indigenous people, men, women, and children, were they the good old days? Were the good old days during the time of the 'Yellow Peril' when people have been turned away because of the color of their skin, or the White Australia Policy when people were excluded because of their race? Or was it during the days of sectarianism in Australia, from the middle of the nineteenth century until now, when Catholics and Protestants hated each other?

When was this magical time when Christian values existed, and everyone went to church and loved their brother? People do not change. God does not change. No generation is better than another. We live in the present and our choices matter, and we are responsible for them.

7 CHRISTIANITY IS A COMPLETE FAITH

Religion leads to the church, faith leads to Jesus Christ

Jesus Christ brings faith to completion. This completeness is found in the person and work of Jesus Christ. Jesus is the full, sufficient, and perfect salvation for all who believe (John 3:16). The best the church can do is a ritual they invented. The slogan of the ritual says: 'your guilt can only be dealt with as long as you participate in the ritual.' This, therefore, is a far cry from the words of Jesus on the cross: 'it is finished,' (John 19:30). Not surprisingly, many people are astonished to hear about the truth concerning the Church. They are interested in how far the Church diverges from Christianity and Jesus Christ. From the days of Jesus walking on the earth until now, there is a vast gulf between those who follow Christ and those who follow the church.

It is very important to make the distinction clear so there is no misunderstanding. This is because most people today cannot tell the difference. There is much misinformation or fake news about Jesus Christ. The greatest critics of the life, the person, and the work of Jesus do not come from pagans, Muslims, Jews, or even atheists but from the church itself.

Christianity is a complete faith because Jesus is the Way, the Truth, and the Life. Religion leads to the church, while faith leads to Jesus Christ. Christianity is not about attending a church building on Sunday. It is a living, daily, real relationship with God the Father, and Jesus Christ whom he sent, being led by the Holy Spirit. Christianity is a personal relationship with God. This relationship stems from a decision that you need to make concerning what you think of Jesus Christ. That decision can be sudden or gradual, or a series of decisions. This decision can happen at any time in your life, even when you are a young child. But faith is about your decision to follow Christ. There needs, therefore, to be a turning to God, an acceptance of him, and a decision to follow Jesus.

Faith is not about religion, rituals, tradition, liturgy, factions, or buildings. Indeed, faith is a relationship with the God revealed in the Bible, who died for sin, once for all, on the cross. Since Christianity is a complete faith, Jesus finished what he set out to do. Therefore, it is this Son of God who stands at the right hand of God. He is a whole God so we might be whole. God is not dismembered each time you have the Mass.

God is no Magic Pudding from which you eat a slice of God that only lasts you a few days until you need to feast again on his flesh and blood. This cannibalistic Magic Show is a ritual the church invented to distract you from knowing God. After all, knowing God is the goal of faith. To know God is why Jesus came. Jesus knew God, testified about God, pointed to God, and paved the way to God through his life and work.

Jesus is alive. He is living. He does not die again, nor is he hanging on the cross. He died, was buried, and rose again. He is present with all who gather in his name, even two or three. Jesus is present in all believers. He sits at the right hand of the Father, in heaven. In addition, he is constantly at work praying for us to the Father. He is not on the slab, being cut up by the priest every Mass to be nibbled, chewed, and eaten.

The purpose of the Magic Show of the Mass is simple. It is about power and money. The Mass entrenches church power and the power of the priesthood. Consequently, the priesthood can control you, your minds, hearts, and soul, preventing you from knowing God. The Magic Show is a wicked creation. John in his gospel never talks about the Mass. He doesn't even mention the Lord's Supper in his Gospel. Luke, in his gospel, emphasizes that the meal is the Passover, not a new ritual initiated by Christ. Two cups are passed around. James, the writer of the Hebrews, and the Gospel writers do not mention the Mass beyond the last Passover of Jesus. Paul ignores the Lord's Supper at the Passover. When he does mention it, he does so once, and he is referring to an actual meal the early assemblies of Christians enjoyed together, not the Passover. He tells them that the meal they are enjoying together 'is not the Passover.' At this hospitality meal, the rich ignored the poor, disgracing the person of Christ by their lack of love. In that way, they were guilty of the body and the blood of Christ because they ate the meal without love. Paul is not insisting on self-reflection before the Mass (1 Corinthians 11). He is chastising them for their lack of hospitality which represented an awful lapse of integrity.

If the Magic Show was so important, why is it absent in the New Testament? The same with infant baptism. The New Testament does not mention either of them. It follows quite naturally, therefore, that they were not commonly taking place. These rituals were created and promoted much later, well after the creation of the New Testament as we know it today. Tragically, Paul's brief allusions to the Passover in 1 Corinthians are the basis for the church's distortion to create the monstrosity and evil of the Mass. This ritual has caused all religious wars and divided nations. It has destroyed more lives than any form of imperialism, even America or Assyria, or Babylon. Even today, Rome teaches that no non-Catholic will enter heaven because they do not accept the infallibility of the Pope and the supremacy of Rome. Rome teaches that only those who have the Mass are forgiven by God. Rome insists that anyone who does not show loyalty only to Rome is a heretic. So much for ecumenicalism.

The Mass is to Christianity what Covid Hysteria is to democracy. It is an exercise in mass formation, indoctrination, or propaganda. It is an exercise in hypnotic delusion. This ritual keeps most bound in their sins, caught up in their guilt, and shame. Rome refuses to preach the Gospel and holds back the offer of full and free forgiveness of sins found in Jesus Christ. For Roman Catholics, there is no forgiveness, and a dozen ways one can fall from grace. As a result, people have a sense of inferiority before a mean-spirited God who refuses to embrace them or love them. The God of the Mass is always distant, always suffering, always on the cross, always dying, and never accomplishing anything.

Christianity is a complete faith because ours is a faith of finality, ours is a faith of accomplishment and ours is a faith of completeness, found in the Lord Jesus Christ. Jesus is the Savior. He is our Savior. He can be your Savior and if he didn't save us from sin, then no one can. No matter if you attend Mass every day for all eternity. Only the death of Jesus on the cross paid for our sin.

All who have turned to God in faith have received the spirit of Sonship because the Spirit of Christ is poured into their hearts. This Spirit cries *'Abba Father,'* so that there is no condemnation for those who are in Christ Jesus (Romans 8: 1). The pagan lords who run the Mass hate the freedom that Christ brings, they hate the personal relationship that God offers, and they hate the Spirit whom Christ sends for the Spirit is the Lord and with the Spirit, there is freedom (2 Corinthians 3: 17).

A religion with Jesus always dying means his death counts for nothing. No wonder they invented the Mass, in all the idiocy and hocus pocus and crazy rituals and incantations. It is drowning in ancient Antisemitic paganism as they follow the spirit of the world, the spirit that is now at work in the sons of disobedience (Ephesians 2:2). The Mass is a pagan ritual. Only Satan, in all his cleverness, could invent the monstrous evil that is the Mass, which has enslaved billions over the years, in a spirit of bondage to fear, guilt and shame. Guilt and shame have no place in a Christian. The death of Jesus on the cross 2,000 years ago destroyed the power of guilt and shame. That is why Jesus is the good news because he brings good news.

If you want to see fascism at work, don't read about it in history books, it is alive and living today, in every town, go to church, sit in the pews, take the Mass, and believe the lies. Sit at the feet of the priests, who hate you almost as much as they hate God, whom they hope you never know, and whom they hope you will never find in church. You can find fascism in both the church and the state. The Church however is the model for fascists everywhere. The Christian Church is the source, the origin, and the model for fascism and inspired fascists to do the same in their respective nations during the last century. The road to the Holocaust was through the Church. In Germany, the national churches appeased and applauded the Nazis. German Christianity had bathed in centuries of Anti-Semitism.

The last thing the Church wants is for you to open your Bible, rediscover Jesus, turn to him in faith, and follow him. Christianity is a complete faith while the Church is an incomplete ritual. The Church invented the Mass, the Sermon, and other tricks to prevent these things from happening. Christian Fascists fear faith and they fear the power of a transformed life, a person transformed by the Spirit of God. Christian Fascists fear a person who relies upon God, trusts God, and listens to God, and not them.

A true Christian leader wants his people to know God and to know Christ so they can be set free, and they can grow in their knowledge and love of God. All Christians share that desire. God can be known because God became one of us and lived among us. That is Jesus, who calls us to follow him.

Freedom by itself is not freedom

Jesus brings true liberty. Freedom by itself is not freedom. The Lord Jesus Christ brings true liberty to us from all the things that bind us. The end of lockdowns meant the end of restrictions imposed by the state who denied them in the first place. A more accurate explanation might be *'restoration of civil rights suspended by the state.'* Most people think, however, that freedom is something from the government. This is not true. Freedom is from God who is the only one qualified to give us true liberty.

Freedom is hollow and meaningless unless it relates to that thing or person from which we are set free. There is no such thing as something called *'freedom'* that exists independent of something. Freedom is the result of an action. For the Christian, Jesus came to set us free. What does this mean, however? Freedom is not simply a state of being. It is the end of our relationship with something or someone that prevents our freedom in the first place.

The liberty of Jesus is complete. Jesus came to set us free from sin, the power of sin, the guilt of sin, and the penalty of sin. In addition, Jesus came to set us free from fascism and religion, from our past and our prejudice, and from all that binds us. Indeed, Jesus' death on the cross accomplished this. On the cross, he cried out *'it is finished,'* meaning the work of salvation is accomplished. It is done (John 19:30).

In Australia for example, the end of the lockdowns was prefaced as being *'Freedom Day,'* in an obscene way to justify the gross violations of human rights abuses of the state under lockdowns. Lockdowns did not stop the spread, nor did they achieve anything in terms of public health outcomes. Lockdowns were not scientific; they were bureaucratic and political decisions. Some of the major proponents of Covid Hysteria, including the former Prime Minister who introduced martial law, have been mired in allegations of corruption and undemocratic political activities. Even today, those responsible refuse to release the actual public health advice given to them during the pandemic.

Across the West, there was public health fascism, inspired by the fraudulent methodology stemming from the discredited World Health Organization (WHO) and other fascists at home and abroad, who define political action as unaccountable thuggery. This fascism was widely accepted in all the nations known for a long history of political fascism, such as Italy, Germany, France, and even Australia. In Australia, lockdown insanity was supported by mediocre local politicians who saw Covid as the excuse to attack democratic institutions and foundations. Australia entered two years of martial law which suspended parliaments and banned elected officials who were not vaccinated from entering Parliament, armored personnel vehicles were rolling around deserted city streets, soldiers in black running around the streets shooting rubber bullets at unarmed protestors with gleeful enthusiasm, arresting people for not wearing masks.

The fascist media celebrated these measures as essential to protect democracy. Even the unions, now an integral part of the ruling class, condemned working class people from marching or protesting the social and economic deprivations of an economic policy that had no economic, social, or public health legitimacy. Australia, as in other nations, walked proudly back to the bosom of fascism that would make the Old Guard and New Guard proud. From day 1, the language of the state was the language of deceit. Governments knew about the lab leak and covered it up. Many ordinary people supported the end of democratic freedoms, including many in the church, who revealed that their true loyalty was to the state and not to God.

Human *'freedoms'* never make any sense, but they are predictable. Throughout 2022, thousands continue to contract various strains of Covid even though they are so-called *'fully vaccinated,'* or *'triple boosted,'* or *'quadruple boosted.'* People continue to transmit the virus and continue to be hospitalized. For the last few months, the fascists have refused to publicize the death rates according to vaccination status, which is odd, probably because it might show that vaccinated people are continuing to die from Covid. No one calls this the *'pandemic of the unvaccinated'* anymore. It is more likely the pandemic of the vaccinated.

If these *'Freedom Days'* had meaning, what were we free from? It could not be Covid, since Mr. Covid is still with us, and he is not going anywhere. Since he was created in a lab in China, he has been busy doing his thing around the world. Whether he was concocted by rogue scientists or not, he wants his place in the sun and will be around for a long time. It was not freedom from transmission, sickness, fear, hospitalization, and death, because they are still with us. With us also are the social, economic, and mental costs of lockdowns that have ruined our society. Most people today also live with a litany of manufactured fears.

Only the rich were immune from these effects of Covid Hysteria. We now see, much more clearly, the class distinctions in society, especially the existence of a small, clearly identifiable ruling class. They are completely out of touch with the lives of most people. The future will be unsustainable since it is the failure of the ruling class to understand or sympathize with the population that leads to social collapse. Every time ordinary person expresses their true feelings and frustrations, the ruling class, their operatives, and disciples, condemn them as extremists and conspiracy theorists. They scoff, cough, and go back to their chardonnay and cheese and talk about equality and freedom, which they have no intention of bestowing on others.

I see no evidence that the political class or ruling class even cares and this is not surprising. In Australia, the fascist media condemned ordinary Australians for protesting lockdowns. But when the public sector unions went on strike for higher wages in nursing, teaching, and transportation, under martial law, however, the media were very sympathetic. These middle-class, well-paid professionals had a right to strike during martial law whereas ordinary people did not. In a fascist society, unions and other state-approved bodies are part of the state and act against the people. Since the 1980s, the old labor unions have become part of the corporate establishment in the West, fragmenting the social ties with ordinary working-class populations.

This behavior is more proof of Western Fascism, so it is not surprising. Incidentally, Donald Trump was able to connect with these millions disenfranchised by capitalism, those who were sold out by free trade, globalization, and NAFTA. His political crucifixion, even after leaving office is indicative of a ruling class on the precipice of social chaos, unrest, and financial ruin. The ruling class will need violence and force to keep their *'democracy'* from falling into the abyss.

In the West, these disparities are getting worse and worse, and no one is listening. It was like this last time too. Fascism grew out of a discredited democratic system in Italy and Germany. The freedom the government offered was freedom from the restrictions the government imposed on the people. It was freedom from government, fascism, and failed government policies. These policies failed to achieve even the most basic objectives. If the lockdowns were successful, why are people still getting Covid?

The reaction of most people however was bizarre. Many people thanked the government for restoring *'freedoms,'* the ones the government took away in the first place. These policies could not possibly work. They were not designed to work. People thanked the government for abusing, lying, controlling, and manipulating them. Most Westerners are victims of this mass formation, this indoctrination. Listen to how people talk about Covid Hysteria. They are simply rehashing the same statements from the government, the same talking points, the same arguments.

Covid Hysteria led to nothing new about humanity. It only confirmed what we knew already; that vaccine mandates are loyalty tests for failed states, and that democracy is no better than any authoritarian regime in modern Asia. Democracy has its greatest support from people in power and the political class. This class runs the nation and is the heart of economic and political power. Democracy or not, this political class is remarkably predictable, and all countries tend to behave in the same fashion. They make it up as they go along. People in power are simply the blind leading the blind. They call it *'science,'* but it is political science, they call it *'economics'* but it is pork barreling, they call it *'social justice,'* but it is cronyism. The Bible is very clear on this. Only a fool would trust in the government. If you do, then you are a fool and you only have yourself to blame.

Do not trust in man but God. The Psalmist writes in Psalm 146:

3-6:

'Do not put your trust in princes, nor in a son of man, in whom there is no help. His spirit departs, and he returns to the earth; in that very day, his plans perish. Happy is he who has the God of Jacob for his help, whose hope is in the Lord his God, who made heaven and earth.'

True freedom has nothing to do with government. True liberty comes from God. When God gives you freedom it is not removed. God's freedom is complete and finished. It is full and unconditional to all who seek it. God is not like governments, he is impartial. He treats everyone the same, and money means nothing to him.

In other words, all people stand on equal footing before God. Freedom by itself is not liberty. Freedom that is from God found in the Lord Jesus Christ is true freedom. It is life-transforming freedom and freedom from all the things that bind us. If Christ sets us free, then we are free indeed (John 8: 36). The liberty of Jesus Christ transforms everything, and nothing is the same again.

We need to rediscover the real Jesus even if it costs everything

The truth is a person, not a set of ideas, doctrines, or beliefs. Christian Fascists and people outside the Christian faith share at least one belief, that Jesus doesn't matter. He is a footnote to faith, whereas the religious experience of the Mass, the ritual, the church, the sermon is the centerpiece. This is what most people believe. They also hold onto a few sayings of Jesus that fit with their worldview. Beyond that, at church, Jesus doesn't matter.

The starting point is to recognize his identity – he is the truth. The truth is a person. Much about Jesus has been censored by Christian Fascists in the Church. When you read the Bible, you are often surprised by the life of Jesus Christ. The picture presented to us in the Gospels and the letters are often the opposite of our perceptions or cultural assumptions. The real Jesus of scripture is not the Jesus of popular culture.

When Jesus claimed to be the Way, the Truth, and the Life, it was an outrageous statement. Our immediate reaction is 'that is not possible, he cannot be.' The church usually censors this verse. There are several common responses. First, some say that Jesus didn't say it, but that the early church added it to justify sectarian control. Second, some try to explain it away by saying that Jesus is using cultural, linguistic, or semantic wordplay. Third, some don't believe it or understand it and so brush over it. This one is a common response. A fourth response is to use the verse in a way that we call *'proof-texting.'* This is the selective use of a Bible verse to suit whatever political agenda we have at the time. None of these are ways to discover the real Jesus.

What Jesus is saying is that truth, way, and life are wrapped up in his identity. They find completion in who he is and why he came. This is not the belief today. It is a belief that will meet problems and indeed, strong, and formidable opposition. Yet, it is the only Christian message. Paul writes that *'for no matter how many promises God has made, they are "Yes" in Christ. And so, through him, the "Amen" is spoken by us to the glory of God'* (2 Corinthians 1: 20).

Christian Fascism does not use Jesus as their starting point, but the Culture War. There is always a Culture War. Other terms might be *'the spirit of the age,'* the *'conventional wisdom,'* the *'norms of the day,'* or *'polite civil society.'* Every nation has a culture war. They wax and wane according to the way a nation has been organized. In the 1970s, following the rise of the environmental movement, Christian environmentalism sprung up as well, trying to give a Christian spin to the Bible and creation. Most of those books are dated now.

When the Western world began to be concerned about the problem of poverty in the then developing world, Christians started writing about these issues. They wrote with a Christian spin such as Ron Sider's *Rich Christians in an Age of Hunger*. Why don't we see books on the environment from a Christian perspective in the 1920s? Or on feminism in the 1930s? Or gender equality in the 1850s? Christian people were not thinking about it.

We need to rediscover the real Jesus in each generation. The real Jesus speaks to us in every generation. It is the same message: I am the Way, the Truth, and the Life, no one comes to the Father except through me (John 14: 6). Christian fascism is the product of the world, it is not the product of new ideas. In each generation, many faithfully follow Jesus, while most are stuck with distractions, side issues, and alternative visions of the kingdom of God. Every generation needs to rediscover Jesus for themselves. The fascists are wrong. God does not speak through their traditions, liturgies, or rituals, he speaks to us through his word the Bible. It is a living word about the living Savior who brings life to the world.

It is interesting what Christians of previous generations were concerned about. I have an antique book series on Christianity and faith written in the nineteenth century edited by Hastings. Things that we think about today hardly rate a mention or are passed over scantily. However, there are pages and pages of information on one subject: werewolves. This was a subject of great importance in that generation. In the 1920s and 1930s in America, alcohol was the heart of the Culture War. In the first generation of Christianity, the issue of circumcision was significant. Later, as the Gospel spread to Greek and Roman circles, the issue of food sacrificed to idols.

Even so, the Church is usually reactive, not proactive. These movements for social reform originate in society, as people grapple with the problems around them. Christian Fascists try to link those social issues with their version of the Christian religion. They crave relevance to the whims and sentiments of the times. One of the great lies of Christian Fascism is that Christians were responsible for the welfare state. The church was not at the forefront of social welfare reform. The Church was at the forefront of opposition to social reform. Look at the writings of Rev. Thomas Malthus and his opposition to the reform of the poor law in England. Malthus and his ilk opposed all forms of social reform. This all changed after the Russian Revolution in 1917 which showed that nations that ignore the poor will be destroyed. True social reform came about through genuine fear of the masses and social collapse, not Christian compassion.

Faithful Christian teachers are all disciples of Christ. We need to rediscover the real Jesus, even if it costs everything. May God bless the memory of those faithful Christians who through the ages have preached the truth about Jesus Christ. These people have one thing in common. They all talk about Jesus Christ, the Gospel, knowing God, the death and resurrection of Christ, and a transformed life. Christian Fascists usually don't write books, they are too busy counting their money. All faithful disciples of Christ have been pebbles in the shoe of the church, a thorn in the side, ostracized and maligned. They point to Christ, they rejoice in Christ, and they speak about the power of God to transform lives as we follow Jesus. I think of people like J.C. Ryle, A.W. Tozer, Oswald Chambers, Uchimura Kanzo, R.A. Torrey, Horatius Bonar, and Watchman Nee. There are many others. All the paths to God lead to Christ. Jesus is the Way, the Truth, and the Life.

Christian Fascists do not follow Jesus

Christian Fascists do not follow Jesus Christ. The old Fascists focus on self-effort. The new Fascists blame the problems of society on minorities. Both factions exclude the grace and mercy of God found in Jesus Christ. They are not a genuine Christian movement. Christian Fascists are a mirror of the various political philosophies of the day. In society, there are different political groups such as left and right-wing. The Christian Church has simply adopted these visions for society. The Church has become a home for the expression of these views. The Church has become a political office.

I have said before that God presents Jesus to us on an unconditional basis, faith being the only prerequisite. There is no point in claiming that we find salvation by faith if there is no faith to begin with. God does not give us salvation anonymously or without our knowledge. God doesn't trick us into faith. Our faith is not a mystery to ponder, but a reality to cherish. God does not bring us into faith without our awareness or knowledge. There is no mystery to faith. The mystery is the love and mercy of God.

When we do come to faith, we follow Jesus, regardless of who we are. It is our common calling. Rich and poor, Jew or non-Jew, slave or free, all are called to follow Jesus. Politics among Christians must converge in the wonderful reality of faith. Regardless of one's political views or affiliations, we are bound together in Christ. Christian fellowship, love, and faith draw us together. The Spirit of God brings fellowship across cultures, ethnicities, and backgrounds, regardless of politics. The rest is irrelevant.

These days, there is enmity between the government of Ukraine and Russia. There is a civil war, a blood feud if you like, that has history, those kinds of conflicts always do. There need not be enmity between Ukrainian Christians and Russian Christians. If there is,

Christ is not present in the lives of those people. I don't care how many times you go to Church or how many sermons you give, or how important you are. The tragedy today is that Christians are not calling for peace, but for war, they do not want settlement but the expulsion of Russia, and they do so alone, for as Jesus said if you live by the sword, you will die by the sword. The path of peace is the only path for the follower of Christ. If you fight, you fight alone, and God is not on your side.

In the Pacific War, Japanese Christians suffered in the West. During the China-Japan War (1937-45), Christians on both sides suffered. Many Australian Christians still hate the Japanese people for what the Imperial Army did in the 1940s. This enmity is a sin. You cannot hold everyone in a nation responsible for the actions of their government, army, or past generations. Christian Fascists do not follow Jesus by allowing war to divide the faithful. They are deeply partisan when it comes to war. In Australia, the church is weaponized to take sides on ANZAC Day, the day for the glorification of the war dead and recruitment for the next conflict.

Sadly, Christian Fascists do not follow Jesus. There are two approaches to Christian Fascism in the Church today. I would call it the traditional and the reformist movements. You could also call it the liberal or evangelical movements. They hate each other and fight among themselves for power and money. These groups are the same. Both are loyal to the state and fight over their vision for the church.

The traditional faction is dying out. Many old fascists are too tired and weary. Their faces are wrinkled, and their arms frail. They need money for kneelers and soft cushions, and legacies so the next generation can praise the long dead. That is what self-effort does – it kills you slowly. People die with a smile on their faces as they did their best. Their influence is waning through decay.

The traditional Christian Fascist places an emphasis on what we need to do to meet God's moral standards of perfection. This is the heart of religion: self-effort. We make ourselves right with God. They emphasize us doing the work of salvation and trying our best. No one attains perfection. They shoot their wounded, condemn the doubters, and expel the critics. The ten commandments or variations of it, are at the heart of this form of Christian Fascism. The moral code or versions of it are the grounds for our becoming right with God. This version of Christian Fascism is not Christianity. People listening to Jesus once asked him what they needed to do to inherit eternal life. Jesus said that the only work required was to believe or to trust in the one the Father sent into the world (John 6: 29).

Paul says that when we turn to God in faith, the veil of Moses is lifted (2 Corinthians 3: 16). When the veil is lifted, we see Moses and the Law in an entirely different light. We realize that the law leads to death and the Spirit leads to life. Most people think that obedience to the Law brings life, but it is the ministry of death. The Law leads to death, but the Spirit brings life. That life is the righteousness of Christ that we receive by faith.

Jesus makes no preconditions for coming to faith. Anyone can, and anyone is accepted. At the beginning of his friendship with Peter, Jesus said to him *'Follow me,'* and when Jesus met Peter after the resurrection, on the beach, after their breakfast of fish and bread, did Jesus have a new role for Peter? No, he simply said *'follow me.'* Those whom he knows, he also asks the same of us, nothing more. If you follow Jesus, then you know him, because it is not possible to follow him if you do not. For them, Jesus brought a new law, a new Moses, where reputation before God is based on obedience to the laws of the church, and the ones with authority to curate moral priorities, the clergy.

The new *'evangelical'* fascists want to shape national morality. The evangelicals who are Christian Fascists are the same as their liberal counterparts except they are engaged in the Culture War including abortion, family values, and gender identity. These days, the target for Christian Fascists are those people who are in minorities, who approach gender differently and so this verse is sometimes used to condemn them and their gender identity.

I would like to talk about their approach to gendered minorities. These Christian Fascists say that only certain genders can find faith in Christ and that certain people are excluded by their self-described identity. In other words, gay, transgender, and other minorities are excluded from the grace and mercy of God, they are to repent of all their ways as a precondition of faith. That is how it is presented.

There are two things to say here. First, it is a strange way to approach the grace and mercy of God, placing preconditions on faith. It would have been a strange choice for Jesus too. He believed that there were no preconditions for faith among any of his disciples or anyone he encountered in the world, simply to believe in the one the Father had sent into the world. All that is required is to place one's trust in Jesus that he is who he said he is, and that he was in fact from God.

John 14: 6 is about the identity of Jesus, not our identity. Christianity is not about our identity at all, it is about the identity of Jesus Christ and our identification with him, his person, his work, and his presence. To all people who come to faith, regardless of gender, Jesus says to them, and us, come follow me. We are to follow Jesus and be his disciples.

Second, some of the staunchest opponents of gay and transgender people are themselves amongst the minorities they so convincingly condemn for being outside the grace and love of God. They fear that they must, in other to cover up their own gender identity. If they do not condemn, they might out themselves. There are many hidden gay people in the Christian Church, often living in fear. In the Christian church, the strongest voices against sexual minorities are often from a place of fear that they are also among the ranks of the very people they condemn.

The real Jesus, the one we need to rediscover, is the one who is the way, the truth, and the life. Jesus says to all who believe in him, *'Follow me.'* Remember, our following of Jesus is our individual journey with him. It is not someone else's. It is not our parents or our friends, but it is our own. Peter, after the resurrection, was upset that Jesus didn't explain to him what John the apostle was supposed to do. Jesus rebuked Peter and said basically: *'John's journey is not yours; it is his and it is quite frankly, not your concern. As for you, follow me.'* As Christians, we follow Jesus. We do so as the Spirit leads us on the paths God has set out for us. All our paths are different, but we follow the same Lord who lived and died for us.

The world rejects Jesus completely

The world will not accept Christ except on their terms, thus they will never understand him. If the church is uncomfortable with this statement by Christ, that he is the Way, the Truth, and the Life, then imagine how the world feels.

I can confidently say that most people today will reject the claims of Christ outright. They do not believe Jesus is the Way, the Truth, or the Life. It is offensive to them. They have their truth, and it is their truth, and they believe they have a right to their truth. This is a common belief today. People say: *'if I believe it is true, then it is true.'* It is not that they don't like Jesus. Most do, they simply do not like what he says when he contradicts their point of view. I will let you in on a secret, so you are in no state of being misinformed. Jesus doesn't care about your truth.

Jesus claimed to be the Way, the Truth, and the Life just before his death, making the statement with the full assurance that he would live. He proved his statement by his subsequent action. You are still alive. If you die and come back from the dead, then I suppose you have some credibility as well.

That is certainly how the Gospel of John portrays it. John only tells us what Jesus said because of his firm conviction that Christ rose from the dead. It makes no sense to John that any of the sayings of Christ would be worth preserving if Jesus did not accomplish what he set out to do. Jesus was not Confucius. He didn't have a series of pithy sayings to be used to shape filial relationships. His message was not words about love but actions and his dying on the cross for sin was the way he put his words into action.

The words of Jesus recorded by John are completely dependent on his belief that Jesus did rise from the dead and enjoyed breakfast on the beach with John and his friends a few days later, the risen Jesus, eating with his mates. John knew those who hated Jesus personally and he saw the crucified Jesus and spoke with him in his last moments, and had he known the High Priest at the time, he would most certainly have known the men who buried Jesus. Jesus was crucified. He died, and he rose again.

Jesus, in this verse, repudiates every value in our society that privileges personal self-validation, self-approval, and self-justification. Jesus is saying that it doesn't matter what you think. It does not matter whether you agree with him or not. He is still the Way. Jesus does not become real if you believe in him. He is real even if you reject him. He is the Way, even when you refuse to believe it. This is the fact of faith, that faith is real regardless of what you think. Faith does not make Christ real. Faith links you to the promises of God made to his people.

Some Christian Fascists say that if you believe that Jesus rose from the dead, then to you he did and that is all that matters. They say it is only true if you claim it by faith. Christian Fascists do not believe in Jesus. We have seen that. Jesus is a distraction from their moral crusade. They are too busy counting the money from their congregation to worry about the historicity of the resurrection.

Ponder the radical nature of Christ's exclusive claim. It is true even when you reject it. Christ's claims are like the Chinese flower that blooms yearly for only one night. It always does, even if there is no one to see it. This flower can bloom in the dark, it can bloom in the house, it can bloom with people ignoring or admiring it, it does not matter. Jesus is the Way, even when you deny his existence.

The West is at war over truth. It is relativism versus absolutism. The West has convinced itself that something is only true if I say it is, and that opposite truth can coexist side by side, so that we all have our own truth, and live in our own reality. Our nation says: find your truth, find your way, live your life. Once we have discovered our truth, then we can live it, free from the truth of others, who have no right to tell us what to do.

This is certainly the truth of the individual and what people believe, though I am unsure how long this 'relative truth' will last in a world of mass formation psychosis. We are seeing the rise of state propaganda, loyalty tests, and the new public morality, so this new wave of censorship is gutting and filleting the old relativism.

I believe in a risen Christ and this event of history; It is true. It happened. Jesus rose from the dead. I believe the Bible is God's revealed word to us, and that God's word, his promises, can be trusted because we have a God who keeps his word. I am not surprised by the relativism of the age, because this is the last hurrah of a decaying society. A society that believes in nothing comes to nothing. The world rejects Jesus completely by refusing to accept the reality of the resurrection of Christ.

The West displays astounding hypocrisy. The West rejects Jesus completely because they have substituted themselves as the Way, the Truth, and the Life. Even so, The West refuses to make a stand on anything but interests and ambition, and that is tragic. It is always political morality, calculated, and cynical. Its moral stance is always circumscribed and limited. We see this in the stance of Ukraine but the complete disregard for Yemen and Ethiopia. We see this in the continued imprisonment of Julian Assange. The West stands for imperial interests and strategic ambition, not principles.

Now Russia allegedly committed war crimes in Ukraine. That is terrible. Julian Assange exposed war crimes allegedly committed by America in the Middle East. He is in prison because the West refuses to see itself as anything less than completely righteous and beyond criticism. This is one example among dozens. The world rejects Jesus completely. I see no evidence to the contrary. We are told that America makes no mistakes and every decision they make in Washington has God's approval since God has a special relationship with America. God blesses them. This is nonsense. The West doesn't need Christianity anymore, they have all they need in themselves: their self-importance and pride.

The West doesn't even need God because they have their truth. To understand him, they need to have room for Jesus as the truth, but there is too much self-righteousness for there to be any room for another, least of all, God, whose name they so wretchedly invoke every time their President speaks. They talk about a generic 'God,' but few mention Jesus Christ or his claims. Therefore, I can say with confidence that they reject Jesus completely because they dare not mention his name. If you are going to invoke God's name, get his permission first. I find no evidence in the Bible that God is America's God. He is the God of Heaven and Earth, and he treats all people the same.

People in power have no room for Jesus

People in power have no room for Jesus Christ. This is obvious in the world we live in as the state, in the pursuit of its new truth, pushes Christianity aside. Christian Fascists are desperate to retain political influence. They will sell their souls for a piece of the action. They do, quite readily.

Relativism is dead, replaced by a single truth. This is the new post-relativist view of truth, post-Covid, post 9/11. The only ones we can trust, in this view, is the state. We must obey and they are the only ones with the truth. But what is this truth? Most people would say that Jesus is not the way, the truth, or the life. They would say that Jesus is a crazy fundamentalist for assuming to be all truth.

In the same breath, they would tell you that there is something that is called 'truth' and they possess it. It used to be Covid Hysteria.

If any questioned the official narrative, they were pure evil, almost as bad, if not as bad as Hitler.

Hitler modeled his nightmare on the Church. He was inspired by the pogroms, the Spanish Inquisition, and other precursors to the extermination of the Jews. Hitler is dead. His spirit lives on in eugenics, Anti-Semitism, and fascism, all of which the West loves and adores. The West has followed all three with varying degrees of devotion these eighty years or so.

Covid Hysteria is rooted in eugenics and fascism, so that is two out of three is not bad. Thank God for the state of Israel. If the Jews needed to trust the West, they would all be dead. Thank God for the Exodus. Those of you who know what I mean, take note. Whatever problems there are in the Middle East, the Jews needed their homeland. Now they have it. This is God's blessing. Everyone needs a home. Everyone needs a family.

WW2 did not extinguish Anti-Semitism forever. There is enough Anti-Semitism in the West for another Holocaust. The spirit of the Nazis did not die. It simply changed form. We see this specter rising across Europe and America in recent years. It is a deeply worrying development. Few are talking about it. Anti-Semitism is deeply rooted in European DNA dating back to before Jesus Christ. The Church did its best to purge Israel from the Bible. From the middle of the second century until today, the Jewish origins and character of the Messiah have sat uncomfortably in a church determined to have a Western Christ. In the Anglican Church, Jesus is a rich white man with blonde hair who speaks perfect English. In America, Jesus believes that might is right, wealth is good, and Mexicans can go home. Thankfully, the last few generations have seen renewal and reconsideration of the Jewish roots of the Christian faith and the identity of Jesus Christ. The last relic of Anti-Semitism remains the Mass and its other variations, so there is still a long way to go.

People in power have no room for Jesus because they believe they embody the truth. The old relativism I spoke about recently, the 'live and let live' approach – 'you have your truth, I have mine,' is being challenged by the new public morality of state-led morality and truth. In the last decade, truth is changing faster than fashion. Yet people who do not keep up, are condemned for being conspiracy theorists or purveyors of fake news.

Part of the new censorship is the selective revision of American and British history. Some even condemn the dead, the long-gone, the people of the past who cannot speak for themselves. They condemn old dead white men for supporting slavery. They smash their statues, take their names off the street, and rip up their books. The reality is, however, that our entire economic system is based on slavery. Our prosperity depends entirely upon the suffering of others. Who do you think makes the cheap clothes you wear, or the shoes, or the white goods? Our votes support that system, our politics defend that system, and our self-worship celebrates that system.

This new public morality panders to the senses of the middle class, which is not surprising. Freedom for many after Covid was freedom to indulge the senses, freedom to drink, freedom to gorge, etc. Most happily got vaccinated and will do so repeatedly. They don't care about the unvaccinated or their loss of income or their loss of social standing. It does not affect them personally. The middle class only cares about the middle class: *'It doesn't affect me personally. I only care about what affects me personally.'* That is the philosophy of our world today, especially for many in the middle class. I take issue with the idea of people being sheep or lemmings. Animals are not stupid. Sheep are intelligent animals; they have survived thousands of years. Many people are also not *'sheep without a shepherd,'* they simply don't care about others. Many do care, but many do not.

The suffering of others is awful if it upsets our evening meal or our appetites. We are selective in what issues we care about; we make sure our caring satisfies our selfish interests. In addition, we give money to the poor because it benefits us. We help Ukraine because it benefits us. Economists call this self-interest, acting out of a sense of utility. Even our altruism is self-centered. We have become our own truth, and God celebrates our narcissism. The consequence of this new recycled truth is that more are slipping through to poverty.

It is hard to keep up with the intolerance of this ever-changing truth in the West. In the post-9/11 world, the West continues its journey through a series of new truths that simply become redundant once they have served their purpose. The West will leave no lasting positive legacy except deep-seated resentment from the rest of the world. First, it was the War on Terror, then the war on Trump, then the war on the unvaccinated, then the War on Putin, and soon the war on climate change and the war against China. These are elite conflicts, conflicts within the political class and the rest of society endures the fallout.

It is hardly the right way to run a society, but we often hear the statement from our political leaders: 'this is the best country in the history of the world,' so what can you expect? These leaders have no room for Jesus in their world because only they exist in their world. The West loves to promote truths about things over which they have no control. When Covid Hysteria began, the conventional wisdom was that the church was non-essential and could offer nothing to help us through this crisis. The Christian Fascists agreed, and shut up, while genuine Christians protested and were condemned.

As Covid Hysteria falls apart due to a lack of evidence and evidence to the contrary, the West has moved on to the Ukraine Civil War. Even now, this distraction from Covid is faltering. War is difficult to manage as a PR exercise as it involves lots of chaos and death. The war has been catastrophic, and this is what war looks like. It is not surprising. It could easily have been prevented and it is not the War America wanted as it cannot be controlled. Some in the American ruling class are now provoking Russia into further conflict, trying to repeat a strategy they used against Japan in 1941. The origins of the war in Ukraine are not in nationalist Ukraine or the Kremlin, but in Washington.

The civil war in Ukraine is remarkable only in the extent of the massive propaganda war that has accompanied it. There is so much fake news. One myth is that this is the first war in Europe since WW2. This is a lie. The collapse of former Yugoslavia was in Europe. During that terrible conflict, America and the West did nothing. They stood on the sidelines, watching genocide and ethnic cleansing take place. The world did nothing.

The West is now a machine for recycling truth. People in power have no room for Jesus because they spend all their time reimagining truth. The absolutism of the West today is terrifying. It is secular fundamentalism, a greater threat to freedom than anything the Caliphate presented. The insanity of the War on Terror ushered in American Fascism. That has morphed into something more terrible, a machine for recycling truth. This recycled truth washes out alternative opinions. Loyalty is the highest virtue of citizenship, and the West is the goal of all civilization. Instead of pointing people to Jesus, Christian fascists wave their flags and build their kingdoms on earth.

Behind this is a wealth that has never been seen before and which gives life to this secular fundamentalism. It is the wealth of the West that has conceived the pride, which has given birth to arrogance and is drowning in self-righteousness. People in power can wax lyrical about truth because of a good salary, comfortable lifestyle, streaming services, and coffee shops on every street corner. This recycled truth machine churns out regardless of the unhappiness, despair, and sadness of most people's ordinary lives.

Despite the new *'truth,'* most people are miserable and full of fear. Therefore, the West is doomed, it is the way all nations fall apart and have through history – from within. To use an analogy, the canary in the coal mine is not only dead, but it has also become a skeleton. People in power simply don't care, their heads are in the trough. They are eating their fill. While they are stuffing their faces, they are ordering the rest of us to obey them. The latest truth must be accepted without question until that is discarded for another truth. Only a fool could think this system will last forever. Jesus said in three Gospels these words: *'heaven and earth will pass away, but my words will never pass away,'* (Matt 24: 35; Mark 13:31; Luke 21: 33).

People in power have no room for Jesus. Time to take away our eyes from the world that is perishing to God and his word which never perishes. As Peter wrote in his first letter: *'for you have been born again not of seed which is perishable but imperishable, that is, through the living and enduring word of God. For, "All flesh is like grass, and all its glory like the flower of grass. The grass withers, and the flower falls off. But the word of the Lord endures forever." And this is the word which was preached to you.'* (1 Peter 1: 23-5).

Only God can transform your heart

Faith is not about you at all, it is about God and who he is. In the past, Christians were called bigots for being fundamentalists, but now the secular West has become fundamentalist. This has been the case since 9/11. While Christian Fascism has flourished, church attendance has collapsed as people are leaving in their droves. It is not surprising. People do not go to church because they know the people who do and cannot stomach the hypocrisy.

People in power have also become what they hated. Society used to be governed by the principle of 'live and let live,' which allowed for a diversity of views, all in the marketplace. Those days are gone. Covid, Ukraine, 9/11, and climate change are all shaped by truth and misinformation.

There is only one truth, and the rest is fake news. Families are broken, and relationships fracture because one is divided by these political debates. This is worse than the Taliban or ISIS at their height or any form of religious fundamentalism. This is because one never knows what the truth is until they inadvertently utter fake news or espouse misinformation and thus incur the wrath of the censors.

The current insanity in the West is rejuvenated by middle-class prosperity. It is also, however, sustained by self-worship, a secular narcissism, that we are gods, that we are the most important people in the world, that my opinions, my thoughts, my beliefs are all that matter, and that hell can freeze over before we listen to others.

But this is not God's problem or my problem, but your problem. Faith is not a prop to hold up the choices you have made. Faith is not a red pill or a blue pill to take to gain God's approval of your politics.

Jesus is not here to rubber stamp your truth, to bless the decisions you have already made for yourself, or to pat you on the back and say, keep up the good work, nor is he a vitamin supplement you can add to your diet in a life centered around yourself. So many Christians today see Jesus as an additive to allow them to keep doing what they want to do when they want to do it. Jesus is only relevant when he is approving me to do what I want. A Jesus who wants us to change, or go in a different direction, or challenge our narcissism, then that Jesus is shown the door.

Only the Spirit can change a hardened heart. Some say they cannot believe in God and that they cannot believe in anything about Jesus Christ. I am not surprised because that is what the Bible says too. It is impossible to believe in the revealed Son of God by oneself, that knowledge is hidden, veiled to those who do not believe.

Otherwise, the truth about God is not revelation. Only God can reveal himself at his timing and in his way.

Transforming a heart is impossible. Only God can change a person's heart. One cannot come to faith through education or weighing up the evidence or working it out for themselves but through the power, agency, and personality of God. It is God's Spirit at work in their lives, who takes the words of the Gospel and applies them to someone's heart.

The Spirit is not involved in inane babbling and the idiocy of speaking indecipherable nonsense. Only the Spirit can transform your heart. He is here to point people to Jesus Christ and to convict the world regarding sin, righteousness, and judgment. In other words, he is here to remind people of the words of Christ and point people to the cross and the empty tomb. That is Christianity and that is the work of the Spirit in this age.

The way is to introduce them to Jesus Christ, who he is, and what he has done. Sometimes, it is instant. Other times, it takes time. There is no shortcut. Christians are not called to change society by forcing others to abide by a moral code. Christians are called to give a reason for the hope that they have in Christ. The transforming power of God's grace is the momentum for transforming our lives into the image of Christ. Christians do not preach morality; they speak of the good news of God's grace for it is only God who can change a person and bring them out of darkness into the kingdom of the Son.

Christian Fascism is the graveyard for religious people who have given up on God's promises. Their only way forward is a better society. They have corrupted the church and are purging the Gospel from it, so they can align with social and moral change. It is a fool's errand and history has shown that whenever the Church engages in social change, it is disastrous. Just look at the Church's involvement with Indigenous people, children's homes, or poor houses, the abstinence movement leading to Prohibition, or the current involvement in Covid Hysteria. People cannot change their ways if their hearts remain unchanged.

If we need to trust God to change a person's heart, then we should trust him with that heart and that person from that day on. God knows what he is doing. We should trust him and his methods to change the world and usher in his kingdom, one person at a time.

Only God can transform your heart. It is to those days we are returning where Jesus is a footnote to our moral crusade, and churches are too busy forcing people to change their behavior, condemning them for breaking a select group of curated sins distilled by our prejudice. Instead, churches should be telling people their hearts can be changed and they can become new men and new women through faith in Christ.

8 MASS FORMATION PSYCHOSIS AND REVENGE

Who is to blame for the evil today?

As the West continues to crumble in a world of mass formation psychosis, the language of society is betrayal. Betrayal has become the diet of our age. It is driven by the politics of suspicion, mistrust, enmity, and division. As the Culture War tears America apart, and war with Russia expands to Iran and China, propaganda will become more important to enforce loyalty. The Covid injections and the *'politics of vaccination'* were nothing more than loyalty tests by failed states. The level of hysteria directed towards the minority of people who refused to take injections that were proven to be ineffective was unbelievable in terms of the social exclusion they demanded, the legal segregation they enforced, and the vitriol they engendered. After two years of complete political insanity, fake science, and corruption, we are expected to *'shut up and move on.'* Nations need to prove loyalty amongst the population and root out those who have alternative opinions. They will need to be canceled, de-platformed, unfriended, and excluded. Cancel culture, de-platforming, unfriending, and exclusion, are all new virtues in our society.

It was not Covid Hysteria that introduced propaganda to our *'perfect society.'* For six years, the mention of the last President, a single-term leader continues to divide families, friends, and marriages. His flaws were highlighted, while similar flaws in his opponents were, and continue to be ignored by the media. This way of thinking was the result of the propaganda of course. It was, therefore, very careful, manipulative, and coordinated. Trump challenged the military that runs America, and a culture of lifelong political operatives who saw him as an outsider.

Those over 25 might remember 9/11 and the resulting nightmare of America's neo-con fascism. Few Muslim leaders were able to stand against the tsunami of hatred. 9/11 was all about American foreign policy, not about religion. Most people, however, saw Islam as a great evil. Many still do because of the lies of the War on Terror. This Twenty-Years War was even more pointless than Vietnam. This again was propaganda, careful, manipulative, and coordinated. Even after defeating America, the Taliban are still treated as pariahs in their nation. Curiously, American bombs and weapons could drive the Russian army back to the borders of the Russian Federation in less than a month but could not drive the Taliban out of Afghanistan for twenty years.

Covid Hysteria saw the flowering of betrayal as an art form, a cultural reflex, and an intuitive statement of loyalty to the state. The new leaders were those select few, unelected, unknown, and unremarkable people who run what is left of democracy. For example, people in Australia were encouraged to report their friends and family to the police if they knew of breaches in Covid public health policies. They were asked to report participation in illegal protests. More broadly, Covid Hysteria reduced a person's character down to whether they had an injection of a chemical that cannot protect them.

But there is nothing new under the sun. Who is to blame for the evil today? Do not think for a moment that society is getting worse and that we are living in more terrible days than the days of the past. The Christian Fascist would like you to think so, so they can lead you to despair as if the entire world is falling. They want to lead you into a dark room, keep you trapped in there, locked away in their church. They reimagine a past that never existed, except in their twisted minds.

Know this, if the world is a cesspool today, then know that it has always been one. The anonymous author of the book of Ecclesiastes, for example, wrote thousands of years ago. He said, *'there is nothing new under the sun'* (Ecclesiastes 1:9). The writer of the shortest letter in the New Testament, Jude, could have been writing of today. He said of those who undermine faith: *'These people are grumblers and faultfinders; they follow their own evil desires; they boast about themselves and flatter others for their own advantage' (Jude 16)*.

The Christian Fascist will counter and ask how we can make sense of what is happening today. What about all the evil, all the wickedness? They make up some stories about how wonderful the past was. Perhaps you are blind to the world for some reason, or you keep your Bible closed and you do not pray. Maybe you do not recognize your own failings and your need for grace and mercy. We are all in the same boat. Consequently, we are all responsible before God. All have fallen short of the glory of God. All need a Savior and God's merciful embrace thanks to the work of the Lord Jesus Christ. Christians will always point to their own failings and their need for God's forgiveness. The fascist will always point to someone else as the one to blame for the sins of the world.

Christian Fascists love to judge. Evil is always in someone else. There is always evil around them- in other people. They quickly point out the wicked in their midst. The Bible is different. The heart of man says Jeremiah, is desperately wicked and beyond understanding. I agree with what some people say: *'there but for the grace of God go I.'* Jesus tells us that by the same standard we judge others, God will also judge us (Matthew 7: 2). This suggests we need to be careful in passing moral judgment on the moral failings of others without first considering our own hearts.

Today is the same evil, just organized differently. Recently I discovered some new recipes. They were using the same ingredients I have used for years, only I organized them in a different way to bring out new flavors, tastes, and textures. The world and evil are the same. Paul writing 2,000 years ago said:

'They have become filled with every kind of wickedness, evil, greed, and depravity. These people are full of envy, murder, strife, deceit, and malice. They are gossips, slanderers, God-haters, insolent, arrogant, and boastful; they invent ways of doing evil, disobey their parents, and have no understanding, no fidelity, no love, no mercy.' (Romans 1: 29-31).

As Paul says, people, today simply invent new ways of doing

evil. Nothing has changed. People are always the same. Jesus says that our society will embrace betrayal as a norm. *'Brother will betray brother to death, and a father his child; children will rise against their parents and have them put to death.'* (Matthew 10:21). In addition, Jesus also says: *'From now on, five in one household will be divided, three against two and two against three.'* (Luke 12: 52)?

Betrayal is in our blood. We cannot change our hearts. Only God can. Beware where you sit, in judgment or in the docks. Who is to blame for the evil today? Christian Fascists see an opportunity to judge others in the Ukraine War. They blame Russia and all Russians. In addition, they condemn all Russians everywhere and say they are all responsible. They apparently have the eye of God and can see perfectly into the hearts of all men. How remarkable. How clearly, they must see the world. Did they provide the same clarity on the war in Afghanistan? Will they also condemn America for invading Afghanistan, a sovereign nation, Iraq, Libya, or Syria? Of course not.

The war in Ukraine has become a propaganda war. The West shut down any news outlets sympathetic to Moscow and so all the news is filtered through propaganda channels in the same way the West shut down criticism of the Twenty-Years War. The truth will not be found for years. Remember Julian Assange, the Australian journalist who brought the attention of the world to alleged human rights abuses committed by American troops? He is still languishing in prison while America and the West prepare human rights tribunals against Russia, for the same type of crimes Assange revealed in Wikileaks.

Remember, Jesus never promised world peace. Wars and rumors of war will mark the Last Days (Matthew 24: 6). Humans will never get along by themselves. The reality is that people cannot stand each other.

Whom does Jesus hold responsible for all the evil in the world? It is for this evil, this wickedness that Christ came. Who is to blame for the evil today? Everyone who has lived. We are all responsible. But Jesus came not to judge. He came to take the blame for all the evil in the world. He let the blame for it, fall on him. We bear responsibility for our own choices, our own mistakes, and our own problems. Christian Fascists will sit in the judgment seat. Christ stood in the docks and became sin for us (2 Corinthians 5: 21). He died so we might live (2 Corinthians 5: 15). Where do you sit? In the judgment of others, or in grateful thanks for the love, mercy, and grace of God found in the Lord Jesus Christ?

Have you ever been betrayed?

Have you ever been stabbed in the back? In your life, have you ever been betrayed? In your life, have you ever been misrepresented, slandered, libeled, gossiped about, ostracized, or victimized? The answer is probably yes if you live in this world for any length of time. It is difficult to walk through life without one or more of these things happening to you.

None of these things are pleasant, none are satisfying, and none leave without making their mark. It could be professional, personal, or political. It is poisonous, whatever form it takes, whether it is in a word, an action, or an envelope. Betrayal strikes you when are weak, makes you speechless, and stops you in your tracks. The sin of betrayal can destroy your life, your family, your marriage, your reputation, and your entire reason for living. People who betray others are friends, allies, mates, spouses, or neighbors.

If you have been betrayed, then you are in good company. Jesus was betrayed by his friend, a man by the name of Judas Iscariot. The Church has been trying to excuse Judas for centuries, but it is a fool's errand. Judas was a traitor. He knew what he was doing. He knew what he did would get Jesus killed and he did it anyway.

Jesus claimed to be the Way, the Truth, and the Life. If he was betrayed, does it mean that Jesus' plan was brought to a halt by the heartlessness of his friend? This is a good question. Many have asked it and many still ask it today. The fact is that Jesus knew he was going to be crucified. It was only a matter of time. Jesus was not stupid. He could have run, but he chose not. Jesus could have escaped, but he chose to stay. He could have disappeared, but he needed to be true to himself and honest to his Father in heaven. He gave up his life voluntarily.

Jesus did not have an easy life. If you go to church, you can see the buildings, the money, the power, your priest in a nice house, and kids at a good school. This is so different from the life of Jesus

Christ. When we look at his life, we see a life of suffering, denial, and death. Yet in all of that, you see a life worth living, a life that is true life. The true life of Jesus is in the real world, the same world you inhabit, but a world many completely ignore. Maybe you do.

Jesus had a real life, and he experienced real things, with real people. He experienced all the depths of human suffering, neglect, starvation, embarrassment, anger, and loneliness. Even so, he could say a few hours before his trial that he is the Way the Truth and the Life. This is a remarkable thing. He knew he was going to die. Yet, he said those words. He believed these words would sustain his disciples. He believed he would rise again. The coming of Jesus had a purpose. He did not arrive by chance, nor was he a product of circumstance or context. Jesus arose because of his own purposeful choice and decision to stand in our place. He came into our life so he would know us.

Jesus would be able to say that he knows how we feel because he was there himself. It is easy to be a God if you do not bleed, but Jesus bled. Jesus bled for us, his hands and his feet were nailed to the tree. He died a painful, horrific death for our sin. Yes, he knows about life. If you read the Gospels, you read about everything we experience and more. That was the life of Jesus. We see him in his sadness, and joy, we see him in his anger and his peace. We also see him being popular and we see him being left alone. The life of Jesus was real life.

It was a difficult life. It was a short life. He was killed only after about 3 years of public ministry. No one has made more of an impact on the world in such a brief time as Jesus Christ. He knew he was going to die. He knew Judas had gone to betray him. He knew that his enemies were gathering, and he knew that was soon to be arrested. Yet in all of this, John records the statement that He is the Way, the Truth, and the Life.

John does not record that he was the Way, and he tried his best. Nor did Jesus say that he was the truth and he tried to point that out. Jesus did not say that he was the life, but it was going to end. Jesus was convinced that his Father would raise him to life. He was confident that death could not keep him in the grave. He could say moments before his trial that he was the Way, the Truth, and the Life.

The Christian faith is the belief that Jesus died for the sins of the world and rose again three days later. This is the belief in the impossible. If you don't believe in the resurrection of Christ, then you stand in good company. Many church leaders don't either. During Covid Hysteria, they outed themselves when they said: *'we must follow the science.'* What they were admitting to was that they don't believe in the resurrection. Science tells us that the dead can't be raised. There must, at some point be the parting of the ways between Western science and the Christian faith over the question of miracles and the resurrection. If it is scientifically possible, then it cannot be miraculous.

I have said it before. Christian Fascists tolerate the supernatural for the sake of some in their congregation. Otherwise, the coffers will dry up and no one will give them any money. But they do not believe a word of it. Their focus is morality, a Christ-less code of behavior. Have you ever been betrayed? Do you know someone who has been betrayed? Go to churches run by Christian Fascists. They will betray you every day by not telling you the truth about God. Christian Fascists say that the Bible is a set of dubious morality plays written by Jews in the past to explain human behavior and pose questions that science now resolves. This means Jesus did not rise from the dead and means that there is no such person as God. Few in the church say it openly though most are lying through their teeth. I know of many priests in Australia for example who do not believe in God, the resurrection, the Bible, or the existence of Jesus Christ. This means that there is no such thing as a miracle. Have you ever been betrayed? Any person who claims to be a Christian and yet denies the supernatural power of God is not one.

Modern Western science, a product of North America and Britain, which began in the late nineteenth century, and led to two world wars and maybe a third, is now facing a credibility crisis through Covid Hysteria. Modern science was the door for religious atheism, and many walked through it. They are happy to still take the money and wear the robes of religion even though they do not believe in God. Yet this science led us to fascism, communism, and the Holocaust. Despite all this, the hypocrites still believe in a science that can stand apart from politics or greed, even in a world of corporate capitalism.

This is remarkable faith. This is astounding faith. Despite their faith in science, many cower like dogs in the kennel afraid to go outside in fear of Covid despite being quadruple vaccinated. Their confidence in science leads to an atheism of fear and despair.

Christians will only point you to Christ. Christians are far more tolerant of others than Christian Fascists. I am not telling you to go to church, or what to do with your money, or your time. Christian Fascists will never take no for an answer. They demand church attendance, obedience, and money. They will tell you what to do, and they will make the standards high. Maybe you can meet them. I don't know. Many play along. If that is the cost for you, then pay it, if not, then don't. Let us distill their thinking about all of this:

You have, after all, the government, in whom you can place your trust. Let us examine this way of thinking:

'They never lie to us. They only tell us the truth and never engage in propaganda. Governments always give us the information we need to make up our own minds. It is the same with the media. The media can always be trusted. They are always impartial. The media never engage in propaganda. As the government and media tell us all the time, the only misinformation comes from people who challenge the facts. We know what the truth is now because we can trust the government and real media. They look after us.'

This is the language of betrayal. This is the cup of betrayal that many drink daily. This trust in authority leads to death because people turn off their moral compass and their ability to discern facts and information for themselves. Only a fool refuses to question, reflect, ponder, and criticize. Authorities are human and humans are weak and unreliable.

Some people believe and others do not, that is the way it is. Paul says that the gospel is the aroma of life to some and the stench of death to others (2 Corinthians 2: 16). If you reject the Christian gospel, there are still many blessings in life you will receive. The rain falls on the righteous and the unrighteous (Matthew 5: 45). You are not, in this life, excluded from all good things that come from the God you do not believe in. Nowhere in the Bible does it say that God withdraws his favor from people simply because of unbelief. Read the Psalms if you doubt me, or Job. Some Christian fascists say that if you give money to the church, then God will return blessings to you. This fake principle is found nowhere in the Bible. The only return you will receive is a diminishing bank balance.

All I can do is try to persuade you to believe in the Lord Jesus

Christ. If you choose not to, then that is your decision. Don't blame God for it, or me. I am innocent of your blood because I have proclaimed to you Jesus Christ. (Acts 20: 26).

Jesus didn't come to teach us morality

Why did Jesus come? Jesus didn't come to teach us morality. The only acceptable version of Christianity for the state has Jesus promoting morality. They will not tolerate anything else. They often tell us that Jesus came to teach the Golden Rule, which is what we all need to follow: do unto others as you would have them do unto you. Most people think Jesus invented the saying. *He didn't.*

He also didn't tell us to follow the Golden Rule. I cannot find it anywhere in the New Testament. I struggle to reconcile this expectation of Jesus and his personality. Jesus taught many things and he affirmed many things. This included the teachings of Moses and the Sinai covenant made between the people of Israel and the LORD God. He approved of the Law for he lived under it and obeyed it. This covenant includes the ten commandments. But can we say that Jesus came to teach us morality?

Jesus didn't come to teach morality, or how to live a good life. He came to point to himself and embody the truth, the way, and the life. Jesus did not point away from himself and expect others to follow his gaze. He expected them to look at him, follow him, obey him, and worship him.

In the Gospel of John, chapter 14, his disciples ask him *'where are you going and why can we not follow you?'* Jesus is of course talking of his impending death, burial, and resurrection. The disciples had been told this, even Peter. But for some reason, it had not sunk in. Perhaps they did not think it possible. You don't appreciate something until it is gone. When it goes, it is far too late. Maybe there was a bit of this in their thinking. When Jesus speaks of himself as the 'way' or the path or road, he is not speaking of some moral code to follow. He is not saying that he is introducing a code, a principle, or a method. Jesus is the path. He is the Way. Christ is the road.

Jesus did not say to love others or love God. Moses said that. The so-called Golden Rule exchanges in the Gospels are simply recounting what Moses taught, which was to love God and others. Jesus in all cases affirms this and declares that this is a summary of the contract at Sinai. Jesus lived under the Law and obeyed it. Many of his disputes with others in the Gospels are issues to do with the Sinai covenant and the laws stemming from those documents found in the first five books of the Hebrew Bible. Jesus affirms the Law because he lives under it, as a Jew, in first-century Israel, and lives as Paul says, under the Law.

He is not going to deny that which he sought to fulfill. Jesus must live under the Law to obey the Law, and there is no reason in the Gospels to expect that Jesus did not do that. He was scrupulous in his obedience to the Law. Jesus didn't come to teach us morality. He came to live the perfect life under the Law we could not. Jesus disputed with other teachers the interpretation of the Law. His radical teachings on the Law were on the side of mercy to those in need. Much of the conflict was sectarian between the sects that existed at the time, namely the Pharisees, who created the synagogues, and the Sadducees.

These men had produced their own interpretations of Mosaic Law, their own versions of the Law, and were the dominant views of the time. If we wish to use a contemporary analogy, Jesus was the purveyor of misinformation and fake news because he stood alone against men who had hedged the Law, by creating additional rules around the Law in its various forms. Nowhere does Jesus hate these men. Many became believers in Jesus after the resurrection, including Paul.

Christian Fascists simply could not help themselves and twisted these encounters for their own political ends. They say that Jesus tells us to follow Moses and that he and Moses are saying the same thing. The liturgy of the Church of England places these legal exchanges at its heart, and ignores the Gospel, not that they care much about that. Their Book of Common Prayer is remarkable in that it speaks more about Moses than Jesus.

The Golden Rule is as low as you can get. The Law of Moses said to love others according to the standard you expect others to accord you. If you hate yourself, then you must hate others. You determine the extent of the love. You are the standard-bearer. This is a low standard. The height of love is only measured by your estimation of self-worth. Jesus gives his disciples a new commandment. Jesus goes well beyond the Golden Rule and says that he was giving a new commandment, and this was to love others as his disciples as he loved them (John 13: 34). They were to love as he loved them. The words of Jesus were profound, but they meant nothing without his actions. There is a difference between the words of Moses and the commandment of Jesus.

How did Jesus love them? Jesus lay down his life for his friends. Jesus gave up everything for others – that is the standard. The Son of Man came not to be served but to serve and to give his life a ransom for many (Mark 10: 45). What does it mean to love others as Christ loved us? Paul says in Ephesians that the husband is to love the wife as Christ loved the assembly and gave himself for her. This means (Ephesians 5: 25) that the husband is to die daily for his wife. The moral code, if there is one, is to live a life like the one Jesus lived, looking out for the interests of others, serving others, and laying down your life for others (Philippians 2: 4). That is what love looks like.

Being the 'way' meant that he was the way. The path to the Father was through him. Throughout his life, Jesus said that he came from the Father. He said that he would return to his Father. John's Gospel places Jesus as both existing before his birth and existing beyond his death. Jesus didn't come to teach us morality. He came to restore that which was lost, an intimate relationship with the Father. This was lost by sin, it was frustrated by sin, and the only one capable of overcoming, defeating, and destroying sin was Christ. This is the Christian message. The restoration of life with God through Christ is the greatest gift to humanity. One could spend one's entire life pondering the wonder of the forgiveness of God, and it would not be a wasted life.

This is radical, this is subversive, and chances are, many of your church-going friends don't believe a word of it. Many Christian Fascists today do not believe Jesus is the Son of God, or even that he rose from the dead. That is too much for them. They would accept that Jesus was a good man, who said lots of nice things. He simply wants us to love each other, and live good lives. Their religion is Moses and the ten commandments.

The beliefs of Christian Fascists align with the beliefs of ordinary people. Most people believe that we are all morally good, we are not criminals or murderers. We don't understand why we need a Savior because we don't need saving. After all, we do our best, and make the best of the situation in life, always making excuses for our lives, our actions, and decisions. Christian Fascists, therefore, need a theology of God since they reject the salvation of God. They don't believe in God, but they need to say something. This is Love Theology. What they say is *'God is a God of love, we are all God's children, we are all forgiven, we are all in God's family, and it is all about love.'* This is hippy love. *'Get on the Love Train brothers, look at those mushrooms and breathe in that smoke. Amen, brother!'*

The problem for traditional Christian Fascists is that people do not believe in love. Quite the opposite. They believe in revenge. People believe in payback. They believe in betrayal. The War in Ukraine for example is fostering dynamics of revenge and payback and hatred that will continue for generations between Russians and Ukrainians. No amount of soppy Love Theology will be able to assuage the anger, the hatred, and the desire for blood. God help them, for he is the only one who can. There is no hope in vacuous Love Theology in a society driven mad with hate.

I believe however that a world that holds to revenge is a harvest for the gospel. The Gospel is that the Father demanded the death of the Son to pay for sin and that Jesus died on behalf of his people as the lamb of God. It was bloody, it was brutal, it was for you and me and on that dark day on the cross, Jesus bought our salvation from sin, from death, from shame, from guilt, and from evil. Jesus satisfied the wrath of God for sin, and he also took away the need for revenge.

A true Christian cannot take revenge on anyone, because of the cross, because he or she sees Jesus dying for them. The liberal Christian Fascists can smoke pot till the cows come home. Their Love Theology means nothing in a world that demands justice. Christian Fascists don't care, but God does.

Can there be forgiveness without blood?

How can we be forgiven if justice is ignored? Can there be forgiveness without blood? Jesus Christ is the only one who understands true forgiveness. He is the one who became sin for us. Jesus took upon his body on the cross, the sins of the world, dying not only his death but in our place.

I believe he is the only one who could understand forgiveness, certainly one born of a woman, under the Law, as he was. I stand with him on this, and I don't care what people think. The alternative is a cult of death and revenge, payback without end. Just look at our world today. Unfolding in Ukraine is not a war, not a civil war, not even an invasion. It is a recipe for centuries of bloodletting, and payback. This has already been a family dispute for over a decade. Enough blood has now been spilled for generations of hatred, family division and enmity, anger, discrimination, and exclusions. There are martyrs, victims, casualties, and war heroes.

The only ones who will benefit will be the foreign death merchants, the arms dealers, the analysts, and the experts. They make their living picking through the corpses of nations and write books and academic papers in their ivory towers. They all live far from the warzone, wearing their designer suits and drinking the best champagne. The ordinary people will continue to suffer. Can there be forgiveness without blood? Without Christ, there will never be forgiveness in Ukraine or any theatre of war. There will be a war without end, until the return of Christ.

Without death, there is no true forgiveness. Just look at American foreign policy. Look at Hiroshima and Nagasaki, and the carpet bombing of civilian targets in Tokyo and Osaka. All the Western imperialist powers acted in the same manner. They have the same assumptions, expectations, and beliefs. These nations laid waste to the world, trying to build it in their image and they expect to get away with it.

If history is any indication, nations do not forget. Nations always plot revenge. Blood will be required. It was not only the Law of Moses that required the shedding of blood. Can there be forgiveness without blood? What do you think? Look at the burnt cities in the Middle East, or the lament over Hiroshima, or the graveyards of the Killing Fields. Payment in kind is universal, it is common logic. The writer to the Hebrews, about the Law of Moses, writes, *'In fact, the law requires that nearly everything be cleansed with blood, and without the shedding of blood there is no forgiveness.'* (Hebrews 9:22). James reminds us that war is simply hatred on a national level. People are always the same. He writes in chapter 4, verses 1 to 3:

'What causes fights and quarrels among you? Don't they come

from your desires that battle within you? You desire but do not have, so you kill; you covet but you cannot get what you want, so you quarrel, and fight and you do not have because you do not ask God. When you ask, you do not receive, because you ask with wrong motives.'

There is often a disconnect between the rich and the rest in terms of vengeance and payback. Some people cannot be bought off. Some things cannot be forgotten. Often, there needs to be blood. I have often said that people do not change, and the world does not get better or worse. People do not want to forgive others. They want justice. This is an ancient belief. Most believe it today. Only a fool would ignore the power of this logic. Any plan of salvation must resolve the problem of vengeance.

Forgiveness without justice is fake. Can there be forgiveness without blood? As I have said before, the liberal, traditional Fascists in the Church are dying out because people do not believe in their Hippy Love Train version of God. People believe in punishment for sinners, and justice for the oppressed. They believe that forgiveness without justice is false. Those Christian Fascists who cast aside the atonement of Jesus, the cross, and the Old Testament, have guaranteed the extinction of their religious movement. Good riddance.

If God can simply declare the forgiveness of the whole world, then why was there any reason for Jesus to turn up in the first place? Why bother being a Christian anyway if all the matters are simply living a good life and trying your best? In fact, why bother going to church and paying the salary of the Christian Fascists? They say that God is love and all are forgiven and that Jesus' death on the cross was not in payment for sin. They say Jesus just offers us an example of kindness and there is no need for an atonement. All God must do is make it happen, at no cost to him and no cost to us. This means Jesus died for nothing. It means that Jesus did not even need to come.

If all we need is love, why are so many churches full of gold? I once heard a priest, dripping in gold-leafed embroidered cloaks, stand up. He was in a pulpit made from Italian marble imported from Europe. His church cost tens of millions of dollars. He said all we needed was love. If that was so, then he didn't need the gold-leafed embroidered cloak, or the Italian marble, or the expensive church, did he?

Most people talk about forgiveness but want revenge. I believe that most people believe in revenge, even if Christian Fascists do not. They want punishment for sinners. They want penalties for those who commit crimes. In addition, they don't want forgiveness for anyone. Even the smallest mistake is unforgivable. Can there be forgiveness without blood? I don't think so. Sit in any cafe and wait for the prejudice to spill over. Someone is usually to blame, someone is usually needing destruction, death, or imprisonment. The idea of forgiveness revolts most people. One mistake is enough to destroy a person. There is no going back, no second chance, and no forgiveness.

People believe a 'sinner' is someone else. The old Christian Fascists preach that Jesus did not have to die. They say that God is a God of love, that we are all God's children, and that all is forgiven. It is all about love, love, love. The problem is that no one outside the church believes it. It is this old Hippy version of Christian Fascism that is dying out faster than the supply of magic mushrooms, and long-haired hippies. It is replaced with the new stricter Christian Fascism that goes to the opposite extreme. For the new Christian Fascists, there is forgiveness only for the morally upright and a list of unforgivable sins for others. The list changes from place to place. The basic message is that a sinner is someone else. We are righteous and it is only others who are the sinners. This is what the new fascists believe. As the West continues to 'purify' democracy and embrace fascism, religious fascists will reign supreme in the church with new pogroms, crusades, moral campaigns, and inquisitions. God help us all.

It is not love that makes the world go around, it is blood. Vengeance, payback, revenge, the vendetta. It is the heart and soul of the culture, and it resonates deeply in many cultures around the world. During Covid Hysteria, this was clear. The unvaccinated were promoted as the worst sinners in the world. They were putting people in harm, being selfish, and not looking out for others. At other times, Muslims received the blame for women, minorities, or people of different ethnic backgrounds.

What does God think of vengeance? The old Christian Fascists don't believe in God, so they see talk of revenge in the Bible as primitive, pre-Western superstition. The new Fascists rejoice that

God will destroy those who do not conform to the new righteousness and loyalty tests. But what does the Bible say? God will take revenge. He tells us not to.

Paul says in Romans 12: 19: *'Do not take revenge, my dear friends, but leave room for God's wrath, for it is written: 'It is mine to avenge; I will repay,' says the Lord.'* God tells us to think about the death of Jesus and the payment for sin paid for on the cross. It is very interesting.

What is the greatest evil in the world? The greatest evil in the world is rejecting the Son of God. Even a murderer can find grace and mercy from God if he or she believes Christ is Lord. No one will receive mercy if they reject the Savior God has appointed. That is Christianity. Christian Fascists will have a heart attack if they read this. They will lie to you about the Christian faith till they are blue in the face. They want your money, your support, and your devotion. Indeed, they dismiss the Bible and don't believe in God, so why do you tolerate them?

The writer to the Hebrews says: *'How much more severely do you think someone deserves to be punished who has trampled the Son of God underfoot, who has treated as an unholy thing the blood of the covenant that sanctified them, and who has insulted the Spirit of grace? For we know him who said, "It is mine to avenge; I will repay," and again, "The Lord will judge his people." It is a dreadful thing to fall into the hands of the living God. (Hebrews 10: 29-31).*

Whom did Jesus blame for his death?

Who betrayed Jesus? Whom did Jesus blame for his death? It was Judas, his friend, and his disciple, who knew exactly what he was doing and what would happen and did it anyway. Whom did Jesus hold responsible or accountable for his death? This is perhaps one of the most controversial questions in the last 2,000 years. The story of the death of Jesus is a complicated one. There were lots of moving parts. There was, as is often the case in political assassinations, factions, confusion, and uncertainties.

I am not talking about the deeper question of who put Jesus on the cross, or why, or theological questions about our responsibility or the role of the Father in the atonement. I am talking about the actual events leading up to the cross, the human elements, and the human relationships. Jesus was fully God but he was also fully human and so he felt pain and rejection and betrayal. He was not superman. He felt the sting of betrayal and the pain of denial. What we know of the mind of Jesus is only found in the Gospels, the four accounts of the life and ministry of Jesus, written by men who knew him, such as John, his best friend. Jesus did not write a book, and what we have is only recorded by others.

As a result, we do not know the mind of Christ except in the recorded testimonies about his life. There are other accounts of the life of Jesus written much later than the period of the first generation or two of the life of Christ. We can easily discount these as fairy tales and make-believe. The Church, typically, ignores the Gospels but loves these fairy tales and many popular church traditions stem from these fictional accounts.

For Jesus, there was only one candidate. It was Judas. Judas was responsible for betraying Jesus. Therefore, he was the one Jesus blamed. Indeed, he was the only one. Maybe this is not the answer you were expecting. Most people think that the Bible teaches that the Jews were responsible for the death of Jesus. Many believe that the Gospels begin the 2,000 years of tradition for the persecution of the Jews. This is wrong. Jesus did not believe this. He did not blame the Jews. Jesus was a Jew. Paul was a Jew. The disciples were all Jewish. Most of the early Christians up until the end of the century were also Jews. More importantly, Jesus did not blame the Jews, nor did he hold them responsible.

Jesus did not forgive Judas. Judas was a traitor. Jesus had already made up his mind about Judas. He said in John's Gospel, *'While I was with them, I protected them and kept them safe by that name you gave me. None has been lost except the one doomed to destruction so that Scripture would be fulfilled.'* (John 17: 12). What Jesus is saying in his prayer to the Father is that the only disciple that was lost was the one who was doomed to destruction.' This was Judas. Judas betrayed Jesus.

During the kangaroo court before Pilate, the Roman Procurator, Jesus held only one guilty of what he called the *'greater sin,'* the one who delivered him over to Pilate (John 19: 11). He did not hold the high priest or the Jewish Sanhedrin responsible, or he would have said so, but he held Judas responsible. Perhaps the greatest proof of my argument comes from the words of Jesus from the cross, as he lay dying. He said *'Father, forgive them, for they do not know what they are doing.'* (Luke 23: 34).

Who were the ones he forgave? It was the Jews, his fellow people, the Sanhedrin, full of rage, the people who had become a mob, and even the Romans who executed him. While he was dying, Jesus pleaded with his Father in heaven that they might be forgiven. Why? Because they did not know what they were doing. In a real sense, they did not. Events had their momentum, driven by hatred, prejudice, and fear. The Sanhedrin pushed the prosecution quickly under the cover of darkness, which is never a good idea. Covert decisions often cultivate the darker side of human nature. They are unaccountable before the light of day and the scrutiny of others. Events ran away from them.

There is also evidence in the Book of Acts that following the death of Jesus, there was some angst, and sadness over what happened amongst the men who were part of the mob. This is often the case with mobs. They get heated and commit acts of violence, but later, feel guilty about it all. The aftertaste of communal violence is shame. The legacy is forgetfulness.

Peter told the people of Jerusalem what had happened in the crucifixion. Peter makes a broader statement of responsibility towards the mob, the politics, and the role of the Father's purpose. The response of his audience was remarkable. Luke records 'When the people heard this, they were cut to the heart and said to Peter and the other apostles, "Brothers, what shall we do?" (Acts 2: 37).

The Church may hate Jews, but Jesus never did. I am not going to defend the Church. Their history of hatred for Jews is a fact. They like to use Jesus and say that it was the Jews who were to blame for the death of Jesus. Judas is forgotten or he is seen as misunderstood. What could be misunderstood about betrayal? It is simple. Anti-Jewish sentiment existed long before the arrival of Jesus. Pilate hated Jews. He would have hated Jesus as much as any Jew. People like Pilate already hated the Jews long before the coming of Christ. It is deeply ingrained in European cultural DNA. Just look at the rise of fascism in Europe again or remember the Holocaust.

We see this anti-Jewish belief in a simple question by Pilate to Jesus during the kangaroo court when he asks Jesus 'Am I a Jew?' (John 18: 35). It is a strange question. Pilate was a Roman, but he had asked Jesus whether he was King of the Jews. Jesus replied with a question of his own: *'do you ask this on your own or did others tell you about me?'*

Pilate was offended and asked, *'Am I a Jew?'* in other words, *'it would be a cold day in hell when you would see me, Pilate, conversing with Jews, the 'others' you refer to in your question.'* In other words, *'you would never see me in a conversation with Jewish people, or anywhere near them for that matter.'* Jesus, for his part, didn't even condemn Pilate, or the Jewish people. But he did single out Judas because he betrayed him. We see in this, the humanity of Jesus coming through clearly. This is the sting of human relationships that are broken and cannot be mended. This is a line that people dare not cross.

Judas knew exactly what he was doing. He knew what the consequences would have been, and he knew that he was selling Jesus for money. Judas knew the trouble he was stirring and the results of his actions. He had been with Jesus he has tasted heavenly things. Iscariot had seen the miracles; he had been there when Lazarus was raised from the dead and bore witness to the confession of Peter that Jesus was the Messiah. Judas enjoyed the company of the man humanity loves, Jesus the teacher, Jesus the wise man, Jesus, the teller of sayings, and the doing of good. Yet with all this backstory, he still sold him out, for money. He did not hesitate to turn up that night knowing full well that he had betrayed Jesus. Judas would signal his love of money with a kiss of friendship. Jesus held Judas responsible because he knew what he was doing. He was responsible.

The Bible records the tragic, awful story of Judas and his betrayal of Jesus. Jesus asked the Father to forgive the Jews because they didn't know what they were doing. Jesus was going to die anyway, that was why he came into the world, to be the one who would bear upon himself the sins of the world. But, humanly speaking, the actions of Judas cut Jesus to his heart. His friend stabbed him in the back. If you have ever had that happen to you, then you are in good company. Jesus has been there too. He understands what it feels like. He knows what it means.

It is another reason to follow him.

Christian Fascists have a forgiveness problem

Christian Fascists have a problem with forgiveness. The old Fascists say *'Love, love, love, get on the Love Train,'* while the new Fascists say: *'God only forgives the morally upright.'* For all the criticisms against the apostle Paul, he made sense in terms of what we might call modern counseling or psychology. Many of his reflections and recommendations in the Bible make good sense and were good advice. Interestingly, they were advice from 2,000 years ago.

Take, for example, the limits he places on forgiveness. Many experts would agree with his thinking here. Forgiveness is one thing but placing oneself in the same situation for further abuse is another thing entirely. Paul recounts an awful experience he once had with a man by the name of Alexander, who was a coppersmith by trade. Paul, in his journeys, encouraged people to turn to God in faith and trust in the Lord Jesus Christ instead of idols made by human hands. Many people relied upon the crafting of these idols, such as Alexander. Not surprisingly, these men lost some business because people turned to faith in God. Paul said in 2 Timothy 4: 14: *'Alexander the metalworker did me a great deal of harm. The Lord will repay him for what he has done.'*

Interestingly, he doesn't seek revenge. He simply commits it to God that he will take care of it. It is a common Christian response. Leave revenge to God. It is hard to do. We like to take responsibility, but it is a dangerous path to be on. It is better to leave it to God.

But Paul goes further. He tells Timothy, the intended recipient of the letter, that: *'You too should be on your guard against him because he strongly opposed our message.'* (2 Timothy 4: 15). In other words, don't place yourself in a situation like I was. Avoid him. Have nothing to do with him. This is not what Liberal Christian Fascists would say. They would say: *'forgive him, embrace him, forgive him, love him.'* Paul didn't. He was a realist, and he was not stupid. He found this Alexander to be trouble and warned Timothy about him. That is wisdom.

Paul goes further. It was not only Alexander. I guess Paul had a list of people who tried to kill him, people who stoned him, people who beat him, and people who betrayed him. He makes a list of his experiences in the New Testament in a few places, such as 2 Corinthians 11: 16-29. At some point, names didn't matter. What mattered were principles people could apply in their own experiences.

In 2 Timothy 3: 1-7, he said:

'But understand this: In the last days terrible times will come. For men will be lovers of themselves, lovers of money, boastful, arrogant, abusive, disobedient to their parents, ungrateful, unholy, unloving, unforgiving, slanderous, without self-control, brutal, without the love of good, traitorous, reckless, conceited, lovers of pleasure rather than lovers of God, having a form of godliness but denying its power. Turn away from such as these!'

It is no surprise that the heyday of Liberal Christian Fascism after the end of the Second World War was the time of the worst forms of child sexual abuse in the Church. The theology of the time was *'Forgive, forgive, forgive.'* So, they did, and generations of children were abused, often by men who were known abusers. This history is now, mostly in the open.

This profligate apostasy from the truth, this blanket forgiveness was forgiveness without question. Even today, in these churches, all you hear is love, love, love, get on the Love Train. This is where God smiles at you when you do what you want. He lets you abuse people all the time with no consequence. Many churches today are toxic factories of gossip, slander, bitterness, and factions. Is it any wonder the state churches were crawling with more child molesters than cockroaches behind a takeaway?

The new Christian Fascists focus on a new public morality code that must be obeyed. They are always telling people how to live, what to do, and who is to blame for the problems in society. As old Christian Fascism is discredited, these new Fascists are piggybacking on whatever social values are being pushed by the ruling class. Christian Fascists have a forgiveness problem because they are simply parroting the world. These days, if the church says it, they were not the first to say it. They didn't invent these ideas. They do not come from the Bible. They come from misogyny and bigotry, the values of white supremacy, and the old regime, where white men are in charge, white women are oppressed, and foreigners are out (apologies to General Ismay).

This new fascism is about integrity, good character, the traits of a good person, the identity of a good citizen, and the importance of ethics and values. Christian Fascism is a mirror of social values and beliefs. These social values are created by the ruling class for their own reasons, and the Church is a mirror of that, largely because of social overlap.

New Christian Fascists do not make it easy for themselves. They believe they share with society certain values, but this is increasingly blurring. Christian Fascists have a problem with women. They have a problem with sexual minorities. I know of many pastors and teachers who teach their women to submit all the time to every decision of their husbands, even in the situation of abuse, domestic violence, and suffering. This is not Christianity. This is Christian Fascism. Just as the abstinence movement had supporters outside the church, the new war on homosexuality and other gendered minorities does too, but Christians forget that the gospel is for all people, not just the majority.

If you are in an abusive relationship where your spouse is threatening you or your children, get out, flee, run away, whatever you need to do. If you go to church and your priest tells you to forgive, to submit as a good wife, and put up with the blows, the violence, the psychological abuse, and the threats, then leave immediately. He or she is not a Christian minister. They are fake.

Christian Fascists have a forgiveness problem. These new Christian Fascists are just another version of Billy Sunday. Billy Sunday was the former alcoholic who led a revival a century ago in America. He helped promote the end of alcohol and said that all Christians needed to stop drinking. He was a Christian Fascist. Perhaps one of the best. He confused Christ with America, the flag with faith. Christian Fascists always do.

His disciples today say the same thing, except they have their own crusades. They do not want to hear about a transformed life, sin, death, or Hell, or the Devil. These people want their ears tickled and they want their prejudices affirmed. They want to keep their churches closed to all the usual suspects. They will teach the Law, they will teach morality, and an unforgiving God, who never sent Christ. If he did, then it doesn't include you. But God doesn't have a problem with forgiveness because that is why Jesus came. God came to forgive you, even if the Church will not. In Christ, there is no condemnation even though the Church throws you out. In Jesus, we find peace with God, even though the Church tells us that our guilt and shame remain.

Faith and revenge

Faith and revenge. These are the fault lines for today. For Western people, at the end of the Covid Hysteria, we are amid the Culture War, and the new purity drives for national morality. We had the vaccine mandates and passports, now we must denounce Putin, soon we will have to agree to a spate of climate control policies and support war with China. There is only one choice, one truth, and no room for error. We now live in a new Puritanism with a set of morals and virtues and a set of sins and deviations. All the language of this new morality has been stolen from Christianity.

People talk about public health 'morality,' or vaccine 'truth,' and this morality is defined by the state, which is run by the ruling class. Fact-checkers run by the ruling class corporate interests is an oxymoron. The new morality is about revenge. Morality crusades always are. They are driven by a hatred of faith, a hatred of those who believe in something or someone that is not shaped by revenge.

Western nations are now on a purity drive, a holiness crusade. The West has rediscovered morality, but it is a selective view of morality. Instead of turning to God in faith, seeking a Savior, and accepting the need for a new creation, the West sees only goodness in its reflection. Evil is synonymous with its enemies. There is nothing more revolting that the amoral promoting morality. There is nothing more repulsive than those with no morality pushing it on others. Faith and revenge are at war in our world.

We see this in the vaccine mandates, the selective censorship of alternative views, the book burning, and cancel culture. This war about faith and revenge will see lives destroyed as well as nations. The West will tear itself apart. It already is. There is worse to come. All nations that are dying go the same way. It is the way of things. The people of America, Australia, Canada, and New Zealand, have nothing in common except these new loyalty tests. The white supremacists that run the West are horrified by a world run by Asians and Africans. They want to control the world. This crusade will end in a society that will cannibalize itself while the rest of the world watches in complete surprise and astonishment. We are seeing this right now. America wants to rule the world, like the Babylon of old. To do that, many want a nuclear war with Russia or China. They don't care about the consequences. There is insanity lurking beneath American imperialism, the wickedness that will stain everything, a failure to age gracefully, a temptation to be No. 1 forever, a design that will end in fire, death, and destruction, and because many American Christians love America more than they love Christ, their churches will fall into the depths of hell.

Jesus deals with our sin because we cannot see through the anger. Before the coming of Christ, there was no reason to end the bloodletting. there was no reason to stop the killing. There was no reason to put an end to revenge. What are all the wars today but about revenge, what are most of our problems but about grudges and unforgiving hearts, and what are most crimes today but expressions of the sense of being excluded, forgotten, ignored, and punished? Our cultures are defined by revenge and payback, and the need for blood.

Jesus died for our sin so that our punishment might fall on him. Christian Fascists always see the problem as external. Christians see the problem as the heart. The Christian message is the good news that Jesus died for sin, once for all. All who place their trust in him, have eternal life. This is to know God the Father and Jesus Christ whom he sent. It is that simple. A gospel message is good news if Jesus died for our sin. It is good news because Jesus died for us. We needed a Savior because our sin separates us from God, from whom we are estranged. The gospel is good news that Jesus came into the world to die for sin, once for all, and reconcile us to God. A Gospel without the death of Christ is not good news. If the death of Jesus accomplished nothing, then God must simply forgive us. If so, then what happens to sin? What happens to wrongdoing? What happens to punishment for evil? The Christian Fascist says it doesn't matter. But it does.

For sin, there must be blood. For evil, there must be restitution. Christianity says that there is one who did that, who stood in our place and died in our stead, and he died for all so that all might live. Forgiveness without the cross means no one is forgiven.

There is no one beyond the grace of our Lord Jesus Christ. No one. There is no one beyond the love and mercy of God. The penalty for sin has been paid. Jesus paid it, with his blood, with his death, his bloody and brutal death, for all those who hated him, and for all those who look to him in faith. Christianity is not about morality, but it is about God and what God has done. It is about who God is, and what God came to do. Christianity is not about me, but about Jesus. He is the Way, the Truth, and the Life, not just for me, but for all people.

The Cross is for all my days, not just my past. If Christ died for me, the battle is done. It does not depend on me, because I cannot do it. I am too tired. I am too weary of life. My sins drag me down, looking back, I can see my mistakes which I cannot take back.

I cannot go forward in my own strength. Therefore, I rely entirely upon the grace and mercy of God found in the death of Christ, the Son of God who died for me and took my sins upon him on the tree. As a result, I feel the greatest burden lifted and sigh a great sigh because I could not do it.

Each day I am reminded that I could not do it. The best days are wrecked by the wrong words or the hasty decision, the lack of prayer, or the burst of anger. My mistakes and personal catastrophes are forever on my mind, but I live by the grace of God. My strength is made perfect in my weakness. I can do anything through God who gives me strength.

I daily live at the cross of Christ, where my truth was laid bare before God. Therefore, I cannot walk in my own strength or survive without God's sustaining power. I celebrate that Jesus is the Way the Truth and the Life. I thank God for his many blessings, the most important being that I know him and that he knows me.

9 WHY ARE THE CHURCHES LYING ABOUT TAXATION?

. Why does the Church look like the world?'

The Church today hardly resembles a gathering of people who follow Jesus Christ. The Church looks, smells, acts, and resembles something earthly, worldly, and temporal. Jesus cautioned his disciples against allying themselves with the world. He stressed the need to be different, to show, by their love that they were his disciples (John 13:35). Jesus said that a true Christian will always be at enmity with the world, will always have trouble, and will always face persecution of some form (John 16:33). This is the cost of discipleship (Luke 14: 25-34). Christian Fascists deny all of this. They, after all, love the world. Just go to some of the Churches. Why does the church look like the world? Well, to avoid following Jesus.

The author of James in 4:4, tells his readers a truism that *'friendship with the world means enmity against God.'* He also says that *'anyone who chooses to be a friend of the world becomes an enemy of God.'* These are strong, but clear words. Jesus sums up the relationship of Christians with the world in John's Gospel, chapter 15: 18-20: *'If the world hates you, keep in mind that it hated me first. If you belonged to the world, it would love you as its own. As it is, you do not belong to the world, but I have chosen you out of the world. That is why the world hates you. Remember what I told you:*

'A servant is not greater than his master.' If they persecuted me, they will also persecute you.'

Christ does not believe that any of his followers can escape the world unscathed. He was a realist. He expects they will face persecution. He expects continual difficulties with the world. During Covid Hysteria, Christian Fascists were quick to argue that the lockdowns, church closures, and vaccine passports were not forms of persecution. Of course, they were. The government engaged in intense Christian persecution for two years. The Church's failing is their faith in the West, not in God, their faith in capitalism, not in Christ, their faith in democracy, not in the Ancient of Days. The world is always at war with God's people in some way, either brute force, or callous indifference.

The apostle John goes further, arguing that the world is not impartial, but under the control of the Devil (1 John 5: 19). He writes in 1 John 4: 4: *'he who is in you is greater than he who is in the world, therefore they speak of the world, and the world hears them.'* You will not hear this in Church, or at least not openly. I know many Christian Fascists in Australia who will have a heart attack if they read this. They don't believe in the Devil as they are religious atheists.

Why follow Jesus when you can have political power? This was and is a great temptation for Christians. It tempted Billy Sunday and Billy Graham, it tempts the Christians who love political circles and fawn over the latest 'Christian' party. Christian Fascists don't bother following Jesus became they crave a kingdom on this earth that centers on political power. Their craving for power is insatiable. The Churches ignore the Bible in favor of alliances with temporal authorities, the government. They fawn after political operatives that pay them even the scantiest attention. They claim anyone a brother even if they entertain the vaguest notions of the existence of God.

Christian Fascists have created for themselves in Western nations a spaghetti structure of interlinking institutions that go well beyond the local church building. Many are heavily invested in education and social policy. These networks provide political support and economic patronage for Christian Fascism. Out of misguided loyalty, many graduates who have no faith in Christ support Christian Fascism, its values, and its beliefs. Where the church ends, and the state begins is a matter of conjecture now. Marx was wrong.

The old feudal, fascist, and medieval structures of the church, the old regime survived into capitalism, shapes it, and controls it in many ways. It is aristocratic, class-based, xenophobic, and powerful.

Christian Fascism is the attempt of fake Christians to align with or capture the state for political and economic power to revive or revisit the old regime. The result is a religious disease that has wreaked havoc in our world, much like other political movements such as Communism or secular Fascism. Christian Fascism is not new. The Church looks like the world in every age. Jude could have been writing of Christian Fascists when he said: *'These people are...shepherds who feed only themselves. They are clouds without rain, blown along by the wind; autumn trees, without fruit and uprooted—twice dead.' (Jude 12)*.

That sums up Christian Fascists. They are not Christians. Yet they have shaped, or deformed Christianity for centuries. Theirs are the wars, the pogroms, the witch trials, the sectarianism, the enmities. They inhabit most Christian assemblies, have their own sordid agenda, and spend every waking moment opposing the Gospel of Jesus Christ. Anyone in their churches who seeks to promote the Gospel is thwarted, undermined, expelled, or destroyed. Christian Fascists are a law unto themselves and obey no law other than their own. They are a blight on the stability of the nation. They are a source of division, entranced by corruption, they undermine political authority, and confuse the population.

As I have said, and have continued to say, the greatest threat to the Gospel, the work of Christianity is not the government, but the church. The government is essential for maintaining law and order and while it may exceed authority or lapse in duties over the centuries, every society needs stability. It is easier to force people to change their behavior than to let God change their hearts. God changes whom he wills. It is his decision. Often the ones changed by God do not dance to the tunes expected of them by the church. They read the Bible, and find the words of Christ that say, 'love your enemies,' or 'Christ is the head of the church,' or 'all are one in Christ,' and many of these converts are cast out as filth.

I have called these people Christian Fascists. I believe the title suits them. They are the first fascists, long before Hitler, the Gestapo, Hitler Youth, the SS, and long before the Duce, Benito

Mussolini. Even today, the supporters of Hitler and Mussolini still march to his tune from Ukraine to Italy, from America to Germany, but Christian Fascism is a 'church'-religion, and they are in their millions. The idea that God speaks through his Spirit to people who believe means an alternative source of authority for life. This the church cannot tolerate and so they created the church from the assemblies, priests, and bishops from the elders and denominations from the fellowship of the Spirit. God calls each of us to faith, he gives us His Spirit, he teaches us from his word, guides us, and loves us. This Spirit-led source of personal authority is always the target for Christian Fascists. They envy our faith, despise our personal relationship with God, scoff at the resurrection and the truth of the Bible, and mock God. Their religion is about morality, and ritual, and laws and rules, a love of legalism and conventions.

Through experience, I have discovered an awful truth. There are two kinds of those who seek intimacy with God. The first are those who genuinely seek to know God or to know release from whatever binds them. Many go to churches to seek release, liberation, hope, and freedom. Often, they never find it, but they keep attending, hoping that they might find what they so earnestly seek.

The second group is like, for want of a better term, 'spiritual vampires,' they crave to be around people of faith, they like to bathe in their aura, and they feast on the energy that comes out of those who know God. There is powerful spiritual energy to people of faith, joy, happiness, and excitement. This excitement can be intoxicating. We see this psychological condition in many situations.

They want a little bit of God, a little bit of faith, a little bit of holiness, a little bit of spirituality. They don't want to change. They don't want to know God personally or don't want to get too involved. They like their life the way it is, a religion without faith, a walk without difficulty, a life without suffering, salvation without the cross, a God without the new creation, on their terms. The churches are full of these people. They hang around people of faith like bees to honey or flies to a coleslaw. Many Christians cannot tell the difference between spiritual change and psychological manipulation.

Sadly, many Christians often appoint Christian Fascists to positions of authority, and before long, the devastation ensures, lives are wreaked, and people are destroyed. Churches become the playthings for these power-hungry, abusive religious frauds. They can wield incredible power over people for generations. I have seen it. So have many. These people are Christian Fascists, the nominals, the spiritual vampires, and the enemies of faith and of God. These people use their positions of power in churches for their own personal gratification and abuse. They can destroy the Christian witness of entire churches, towns, and even cities.

Why does the Church look like the world? Because Christians have fallen asleep. Christians need to wake up before it is too late. In the 1920s and 1930s, Christianity was derailed in America by the temperance movement. In the 1980s it was derailed by the so-called 'moral majority movement.' Now it is being derailed by Christian Fascism, a political movement deadlier than Covid.

Christian Fascism is a disease in Christian assemblies, especially in the West. There is so much nominal Christianity in the Culture War. Many Americans have no idea what Christianity is about. Many Westerners have no idea what Jesus said. Most people think Christianity is the church and that being a Christian means attending Mass or turning up on Sunday. Not everyone in Christianity who claims to be a Christian is one. Not everything 'Christian' is in fact, Christian. Jesus is not an American. He does not vote Republican or vote for Trump. Jesus didn't vote for Biden. He doesn't support the American wars abroad. He is not an imperialist, nor is he a capitalist.

Many Christians are asleep today because of laziness, the Culture War, and the love of money. If you are going to stand up for something, rest on the promises of God. Remember, God does not promise what he does not promise, but all his promises are sure. As Paul writes, *'For no matter how many promises God has made, they are "Yes" in Christ. And so, through him the "Amen" is spoken by us to the glory of God'* (2 Corinthians 1: 20). Beyond these promises, we walk alone.

How can we put the fear of God back in the church?

The last person the Churches fear is God. Proverbs teaches us that the fear of the Lord is the beginning of knowledge, but fools despise wisdom and instruction (Proverbs 1:7). The Psalmist asks that God may 'teach us to number our days, that we may gain a heart of wisdom (Psalm 90: 12). The Churches believe their days are both secure and guaranteed. Their wealth is safe, and their power is preserved. This is false confidence.

It is time to give the churches something to worry about. No, I am not speaking of persecution. They avoid that by being like the world. The churches are like the man who follows you into the revolving door only to exit ahead of you. I am not talking about calamity. I would not wish that on anyone. It is time to go straight to the thing they love the most, their most sacred treasure and source of power. No, I am not talking about God, faith, Jesus, or the Spirit. I am talking about money, their money, or money they have accumulated.

Have you worked out the Church's greatest deception yet? Did you know the churches have been lying to the government for at least a century? This is large-scale deception. Forget the World Economic Forum and the so-called 'Great Reset.' Forget the CIA and global espionage. Forget the military-industrial complex. All these things are distractions for middle-class intellectuals with too much time on their hands. There is always something going on, somewhere. There are always forces in the shadows. There are always alliances, schemes, projects, and conspiracies. Forget Bill Gates Elon Musk and George Soros. They are wealthy guys, and they have every right to use their wealth to promote their ideas. It is perfectly natural. If you had a trillion dollars, you might want to say a few things as well.

The name of God is blasphemed among the nations because of the church, not because of Bill Gates. This lie of the Church is more important because it concerns the reputation of Christians in our world. As Paul says in Romans 2: 24: *'As it is written: "God's name is blasphemed among the Gentiles because of you."'* It concerns the name of God, in whose name Christians like to walk. Christian assemblies like to talk about walking worthy of the Gospel (Colossians 1: 10, Ephesians 4:1, 1 Thessalonians 2: 12). The problem is that they don't because they are guilty of something they have been hiding for at least a century.

This deceit is the cause of most of their problems. It is why Christian Fascism flourishes and why faith dies, it's why attendance in the church has collapsed. It explains the problems in the West. This deception will lead to the downfall of Christian Fascism once and for all. It may break the church. If it was exposed, it would lead to the biggest reform in Christendom since the days of Luther. It is time for the church to come clean before they are forced to.

How they put the fear of God back in the Church: expose this lie. It is about taxation. Churches prefer to lie than follow God. The Bible teaches the church must pay taxes to the state. This is not just for individuals, but churches themselves, the assemblies are required by God, to pay tax. This is indisputable. It is impossible to argue against it. It is plain as day. God wants churches to pay taxes.

It is in the Bible. I did not make it up. These commands are clear. The payment of taxes by the church is unavoidable. The Bible teaches the payment of tax from the church to the state is unavoidable. It is inescapable. Paul mentions it twice in Romans. He is emphatic: the church must pay tax to the government. The fact that they do not, means the churches are sinning against God. Governments are failing in their duty to follow God, which means they too are in trouble.

How to put the fear of God back in the Church? Remind them to perform the act of love Paul speaks of in Romans. Just pay tax. In the letter to the Romans, Paul is writing to the assembly of Christians or assemblies of Christians in Rome, the 'church' of Rome. His letter is not to an individual, but a group of people. The words he uses are interesting. He does not use the term ecclesia which is done in other letters such as 1 Corinthians 1: 2, or Galatians 1: 2, the assemblies in Galatia.

Paul however also uses other phrases as synonyms in his description of Christian assemblies, so to qualify what he means. The word 'assembly' in Greek is generic. It does not mean 'Christian.' It could refer to anything. Paul needs to add additional information, so his readers are clear as to whom he is writing. In 1 Corinthians Paul says he is writing to the assembly of God in Corinth, *'to those sanctified in Christ Jesus and called to be his holy people'* (1: 2). In other words, he is writing to the gathering of saints, Christians who have been called out, or made holy, set apart by Christ, or by Christ.

Why does this matter? Well, because Paul uses the same terminology in Romans. He is writing to the holy ones, those called to be saints, as a group, *'to all in Rome who are loved by God and called to be his holy people'* (Romans 1: 7). In Romans, Paul speaks to the assembly, to the gathered multitude of the faithful, not to individuals.

Payment of tax is a corporate Christian duty. If Paul is speaking only to individuals, and there is no corporate responsibility, this interpretation would do linguistic violence to Paul's entire letter. Paul is speaking to two groups, Jews, and Gentiles, or as I prefer, 'to the nations, as Israel was, and always is, a nation. To say that Paul suddenly addresses individuals only in these few verses introduces a virus into Paul's understanding of both the body of Christ and union with Christ.

The Church will say that I am wrong, that Paul is addressing only individuals and not the assembly or church itself. Who cares what they say? I am interested in the truth, not in material power parading as a virtue. Christian virtue signaling is all about lying about our relationship with God and our relationship with others. While Paul emphasizes the personal nature of salvation, he does not promote the idea that Christians are disconnected from one another by faith in Christ. Indeed, we are united to Christ by faith. We are part of the body of Christ. We have the fellowship of the Spirit.

If the Church is to obey the government, then it must pay tax. You might remember this passage from heretical Covid Theology: Romans 13. During Covid Hysteria, Christian Fascists used Romans to promote the obedience of the church to the state's public health policies. The argument was that the churches needed to shut down to obey the government. The churches needed to introduce vaccine passports to obey the government. The churches need to cease commenting on public policy to obey the government.

In the same breath, Paul says that the church must pay taxation. He says it twice. Paul writes in Romans 13, from verses 5 to 7 that:

'Therefore, it is necessary to submit to the authorities, not only because of possible punishment but also as a matter of conscience. This is also why you pay taxes, for the authorities are God's servants, who give their full time to governing. Give to everyone what you owe them: If you owe taxes, pay taxes; if revenue, then revenue, if respect, then respect, if honor, then honor.'

Therefore, he repeats it twice, in verses 6 and 7, the necessity to pay tax. Next time your priest tells you to pay tax, ask why he doesn't. Churches certainly demand that their members pay individual taxes to the state, and they demand tithing. They do not however want to pay taxes themselves. Indeed, the last 150 years have seen established churches escape further into a labyrinth of tax-free loopholes, schemes, exemptions, and arrangements at the same time individual and corporate taxation have flourished.

In other words, while ordinary people and businesses in a nation pay higher taxes, the churches have managed to secure deeper exemptions for themselves. This is a disgraceful, sinful, abomination. While the poor, vulnerable, and the unemployed struggle for higher wages, and unions and sectors negotiate incremental rises in living conditions, the churches sit pretty and are laughing all the way to the bank.

How to put the fear of God back into the Church? End the Church's love affair with easy money. Paul insists that Christian assemblies pay tax to the authorities. He tells them twice in the same passage. For Paul, it is no big deal. Paul is like most of us. We all pay tax. We do it. Taxes go to help society. It is no big deal. Paul addresses it in passing. His thinking is that it is quite normal to pay tax. After all, there was the Temple tax, and he possibly has this in mind as a model for Christian assemblies.

Many assemblies met in someone's house, but not always such as the assembly in Corinth which may have met in a public space. Paul also couches his discussion in terms of love: Christians are to pay taxes out of love for the nation, out of fulfilling a debt. Do churches love their nation? If so, then pay tax, and express that love in actions. Give up some of that money for the sake of love, for the sake of following Jesus.

Churches should pay tax as a gift of love to the nation they pretend to support. Paul says in verse 8, immediately following the verse on taxation: 'let no debt remain outstanding, except the continuing debt to love one another, for whoever loves others has fulfilled the law.' In other words, assemblies ought to pay taxes to fulfill debts and act in love. Is this not what the Christian Fascists are always talking about anyway? It is a pity they do not bother to do what they preach.

Churches should pay tax. I don't see why it is such a big deal. Imagine the impact on the Gospel of Jesus Christ if the churches voluntarily set up taxation arrangements with the state and said, 'we will pay tax on our properties, on our income, and we will end the special treatment we have enjoyed. We will now be treated as a service provider, for that is what we are, and we wish to make a valuable contribution to the nation.' Imagine that? Can you imagine that ever happening? Eventually, the state will come for the wealth of Christian Fascism and wrench it out of their hands by force. Is it not better to give it up voluntarily? After all, you corrupt religious hypocrites, God demands it. How to put the fear of God back into the Church? Introduce some taxing times for an institution that believes itself to be above the law.

Is the Church a place or a group of people?

Is the Church a place or a group of people? This is a question that has caused a lot of trouble in the history of Western Christianity. The phrase *'My family and I go to church'* is a common way of speaking. It is not a Biblical statement, however. All Christians are brothers and sisters in Christ. Their identity is in Jesus. This bond is not inferior to blood. It is superior because it is eternal. The church is a place because that is what church means in English. But the Biblical term assembly or gathering simply means a gathering of people who meet to encourage one another in prayer and testimony.

Forget Big Pharma, the Churches are involved in regulatory capture. Their position in politics is secure thanks to cronies in party structures, and decades of neglect within the state. In America, Canada, New Zealand, and Australia, the Christian Church has managed to effectively capture the state in terms of undue and disproportionate political and economic clout. The last 150 years have seen a dramatic decline in church membership and religious affiliation and yet, the growth of Church power and money, especially in America and Australia.

This mirrors the power and influence of say, the alleged behavior of pharmaceutical companies in recent years, or the entrenched power of the military-industrial complex. Call it rent-seeking, regulatory capture, or simply old-fashioned political cronyism, the Christian Church behaves in an entitled, arrogant fashion, expecting special treatment, a blind eye to its many failings, as well as massive economic privileges. Church privileges are out of touch with a secular society. Christian churches continue to enjoy privileged positions in society. But these positions also sit more uncomfortably with societies that are ostensibly multiethnic and multi-religious.

The status of the Christian Church is also more precarious due to economic pressures. With the 1970s came the economic crisis, to be followed by the boom of the 1980s to be followed by more crises and then financial crises and then global financial crisis, and now the Covid crisis. The high growth period of the post-war boom is over. Now is the time for nations to be careful with their spending and have a greater awareness of inflation and the cost of living. The churches pay little or next to nothing and are always begging for more assistance as well as pleading special exemptions for their positions in society.

The Great Church Tax Dodge is a form of Mass Formation Psychosis or propaganda. As I have established, the Church run by Christian Fascists has functioned in much the same way as the secular state. Indeed, given its longevity and history, it was the model for fascists everywhere on how to run a nation. It was simply a case of applying the principles left behind by Christian Fascism when nations were formed in the nineteenth century and early twentieth century. The recent discussion of Mass Formation Psychosis is simply another way of considering the power and influence of propaganda in modern society. Propaganda is ubiquitous and pervasive. This mass formation is certainly seen in Covid Hysteria and the Ukraine War, as well as the War on Terror.

But these examples are insignificant compared to the power of the Christian Mass to delude billions over the centuries. It is entirely without any Biblical basis, being invented by the churches centuries after the New Testament to enshrine political and clerical power. It is deeply anti-Jewish; in fact, it is a ritual to mock the Passover. The Mass is the heart of Religious Mass Formation Psychosis for Christians. The Mass is the central mechanism or ritual for mass formation psychosis in Christian Churches, especially traditional Churches. It is a point of hypnosis, namely the elevation of the elements. People are entranced. There is mass delusion about the fictitious 'mystery' of faith and the fictitious transformation of the bread and wine into the body and blood of a man whom the Bible says, lives at the right hand of God. The ritual distracts from Jesus Christ, his death on the cross, what it achieved, and why it was significant. The cross and the empty tomb are at the heart of the Christian message. More importantly, the Bible remains closed, because the Mass is not found anywhere in the scriptures. The Mass has deluded people of faith for centuries. It still does.

The interesting thing about religious rituals that distract from Jesus Christ and Christianity is that many people have noticed. Several popular movements have spread over the years in response to the hideous delusion that this ritual has engendered. These movements emphasize personal piety and faith, the Christian walk, personal devotion to prayer and Bible reading, acts of real charity to others, and a careful, considered life. Christian bookshops are usually full of books written by these people, whose lives inspire others, and have done through centuries. They also have another thing in common. Almost all these people have been persecuted by the church. Many have been murdered, tortured, imprisoned, or silenced.

The Mass is not the only deceptive delusion in the church. There are many. These are not the conspiracies of fiction, like monkeys in the Vatican, or ancient, mystical orders. There are lots of conspiracies around secret books of the Bible or hidden messages. They are all rather sensational and boring at the same time. They make for good reading in novels or exciting plots in movies, and most of them are intuitively nonsensical.

These ridiculous stories enable the Christian Church to deflect criticism away from the things it wants to keep quiet. The main one is taxation. The tax issue is in plain sight. Most priests, ministers, or pastors preach about the importance of their congregations paying taxes. They even invoke scripture to prove their case. They, however, pay no tax and hide behind the Church tax wall. Why is that? Why preach to others what they themselves do not do? This is what the Bible calls hypocrisy.

Priests could encourage their congregations to minimize their taxes or create arrangements in the law to ensure lower tax rates or get a good accountant. I have never heard a sermon telling me these practical details. I have often heard sermons however on Jesus saying to give to Caesar what belongs to him and the importance of obeying the law and paying taxes. Churches boast about their tax status regularly and laugh all the way to the bank.

The Christian Churches like to claim that they are the modern version of the Synagogue. The Christian Fascists who run the Churches, like the Pharisees of the New Testament, have created their own system that corrupts God's Word. The Law of Moses was good. It served a function. It was God-ordained. Some of the Pharisees in the days of Jesus added to the law of Moses. They burdened people with thousands of regulations and extra rules. The Pharisees created the synagogues which were allegedly the places where the Law was discussed in the towns. The proper place was in the home, and at the Temple. Nowhere in the Hebrew Bible were the synagogues proposed or suggested or mandated. People think they are part of the Old Testament. They are not. They are probably a product of Jewish nationalism concerned with the Hellenization of Israel, in other words, the growing impact of Greek culture, ideas, and values. They functioned in a similar way to ethnic schools in the West eager to ensure children retain their original language, but also cultural values.

Christian Fascists in the Churches today behave in the same way. The word 'church' as it is linguistically understood, is not found in the New Testament. It is a mistranslation, but not in the usual usage, but it is applying to the Bible a meaning that is not found in the scriptures. Christian Fascists also use the Greek word presbyter to mean priest. It does not. There is no possible connection between the presbyter and the priest. The Greek word priest is found in the New Testament and that means, not surprisingly priest in every use of the word. All Christians are priests (1 Peter 2: 9, 5). This means that all the priests in the Church are fake. They are not priests, certainly not in any Biblical sense of the New Testament. The Bible speaks of Jesus Christ as the Great High Priest (see the *letter to the Hebrews*).

Church, in the English language, means a place, a House of God. The only 'House of God' in the Bible is the Temple in the Old Testament. Jesus overturned the Temple through his death and resurrection. The Temple was made null and void in terms of its efficacy to bring about repentance and salvation. The writer of the Hebrews makes the point that those who reject the atonement of Christ and seek to find solace in the temple once more after the atonement will find no forgiveness there, only a curse (See Hebrews 6). Indeed, Hebrews places the strongest condemnation of the Temple cult than in any other book of the New Testament.

Is the Church a place? The word church means a house, or a place, but the Biblical word assembly means a group of people. The confusion is that strictly speaking the church is a place, a house, an actual building, but this word is not found in the New Testament. The words to describe 'churches' are usually assemblies or assembly, meaning a group of people gathered. There is no evidence that there were any 'churches' in the New Testament, that is, church buildings, but they may have been places Christians gathered to pray and encourage each other. Acts 2: 46 records *'Every day they (the disciples) continued to meet together in the temple courts. They broke bread in their homes and ate together with glad and sincere hearts.'* Do you notice immediately that it was not once a week, but every day and that it included hospitality? This was a lifestyle, an extended family experience, not a ritual.

The English word for 'church' is difficult to ascertain, but it seems to come from the medieval Greek word which means *'House of God'* or a building. That Greek word is not used at all in the New Testament. This means that translators have mistranslated the word for the church for centuries. The reason they have done that is obvious. It is about power, money, and control.

The common Greek word for 'church' is ecclesia which does not mean church or building, but simply 'assembly.' This is the meaning of the way the word is used in the New Testament. Another word in Greek comes from the word synagogue which means, not surprisingly, to gather. The New Testament is very clear. The early gatherings and assemblies of Christians were simply people meeting together to pray, study the scriptures, and encourage one another. Meeting together to encourage one another was central (1 Thessalonians 5:11; Acts 11:23; 15:32; 16: 40, 20: 2; Romans 1: 12; 15:4-5; 2 Corinthians 13:11; Colossians 2:2). The association of Christianity with the physical 'church' was much later once the state began to control Christianity and bend it to its political will. The rest, they say, is history.

Why does Jesus need our money?

Church as a place is a cultural relic, not a home for faith. Why does Jesus need our money? He doesn't, the church does and that's the problem. We need to stop supporting a system that doesn't work. If the Bible does not support Church as a place, why do we? If the

Bible sees Christianity as a gathering of people, an assembly, not as a building, why do we? The church is seen as a place for cultural relics, identity, and memory. This is fine, but it is not Christianity. Christianity in the West looks remarkably like national identity and national politics.

Churches are tolerated simply because of cultural traditions, and the political support of those cultural groups. Churches, the physical, and institutional structures reflect national or sub-national cultural identities and are rooted in the history of the nations. The Scottish have their Presbyterian Church, the English, the Church of England, the Germans, the Lutheran Church, and the Italians, the Roman Catholic Church. These churches are relics of cultural identity. Churches are museums of the past. They embody ideas or values of yesteryear and contain images, documents, and ideas that used to resonate in the nation.

There is nothing wrong with museums. I love to visit them, and I see the values of the past and can learn about people, places, and memories. I also am aware of the historical and cultural traditions of many Churches in society. They are the same – relics, stuck in the past. Churches live in the past. They resonate with values that most no longer hold.

The Church of England in Australia, for example, especially in rural areas, resonates with the values of a White Australia. It struggles with racism and xenophobia, which includes deep distrust of city people. You only must look at those in leadership. They are, overall, white people, in a multiethnic society. The church leadership in most churches more broadly does not reflect the cultural norms of society. If you want to see the White Australia Policy and the values of the 1950s go to church in the rural areas. You will see it. These churches cannot survive without money, and lots of it, but are their values worth preserving?

If we are not changing, then we are already dead. We can learn from the past and for much we can give thanks. But we also move on, not only in our lives but in our national experiences. Many past ideas and values are out of place, many are astounding and reactionary, and some are now illegal, and it is important to ask whether they are worth preserving.

Cultures and societies move on. People move on. Culture in a nation that refuses to change inhibits national growth and development. There is a place for relics and museums, but increasingly, Christian Churches are finding that they are more of a financial burden than a blessing in society. Many buildings are heritage listed, many are built the wrong way, and according to out-of-date standards, many are a money pit, needing constant repairs. There are serious questions facing the viability of all denominations in the nation now.

The only house of God in the New Testament is the Christian individual. It is the person who has come to faith in Christ. He or she is the temple of the Holy Spirit. If there is a 'house of God' in the New Testament, it is not made with bricks and mortar, but with people. Your bodies are the temple of the Holy Spirit Paul reminds us (1 Corinthians 6: 19-20). This is a radical and incredible statement to make. Every Christian has the presence of God dwelling in them and God is present with them.

It is no wonder the Christian Fascists sought to destroy this and twist it to transfer the presence of God from the person or persons of faith to an external structure. It was within this external structure, the fascists sought to distance the believer from God, from the presence of God, from intimacy with God, and from a relationship with God. Why does Jesus need our money? He doesn't and he never asked for it. He wants our hearts to be in tune with him and our feet to follow him. You cannot buy favor with God.

Christian Fascists brought into the church all the rituals and relics of the temple including the altar or the so-called Holy Table, as well as incense, pews, seating arrangements, and candles. All these relics and items were used in the Temple in Jerusalem before the Romans burnt it to the ground in AD 70. No Christian assembly used any of these rituals or relics for generations.

This desire to recreate the temple at Jerusalem is deeply problematic for many reasons. It is Anti-Semitic for one. Jesus nowhere talked about recreating the Temple. He spoke of the Temple as being torn down and rebuilt three days later. He meant that just as Jews went to the Temple to meet God through the sacrifices, Jesus was the sacrifice through which all could meet God through faith (see John 2: 19). Jesus spoke of his death as opening the way to the Father for both Jews and non-Jews.

I have always believed that the church building was just bricks and mortar. It is of no importance. If the building matters to you, then I am sorry because there is nothing in the Bible to support your devotion. It sounds more like the building is an idol to you. It is an idol. I have seen people stroke the walls like one does their pet or kiss the brick like one does a lover. Church buildings do not contain God. He is not waiting there for you to turn up. He is not present in the space you have created for him. This thinking is all vanity.

In addition, many of your cultural churches alienate people for whom Christ came. You want them to worship God not in spirit and truth, but in your way, in your words, and in your style. You impose burdens on people that should not exist because the burdens are to do with culture and history and the past, which is of no relevance to people today. People need to make their own culture, their own traditions, and find their own way, not just rake the gardens of the dead. If you want people to know God, then get rid of all the obstacles that cause stumbling blocks. Sell your church buildings and meet in a public place. Why keep something that is a burden to you and others?

The reason Christians gather is not to meet in a place, but to meet each other. We gather not to worship God because we worship God all the time. The reason we gather is not to perform or participate in the liturgy. Once again, these liturgies are cultural relics, not affirmations of faith. We gather to encourage one another and pray. The rest is not Christianity, it is Church, and that is the problem. Does Jesus need our money? No, the church does because they have never been able to run their buildings properly.

This is more than a lie because most people are under a delusion about it. Indeed, this delusion is like the effects of propaganda. People are often completely unaware that there is no basis for the collection of monies to sustain the church in the New Testament. The Western Church says *'yes, Jesus needs your money.'* No denomination or church organization has been immune from the love affair with money. Churches have grown in power, and influence in the West for centuries. Much of this power and wealth has come from the relationship of the church with the state.

This wealth has come from various tax exemptions that have allowed churches to accumulate funds privately away from the scrutiny of tax officials. This love affair with money is deeply entrenched in church culture. Without money and wealth, the Christian Church in the West would not be the power center that it is today. It is also highly likely that the wealth and power of the church are the main attraction for most of its leaders. The American church boasts of a strict separation of church and state and yet it is the state that has bankrolled the church for the last century or so. Tax credits, tax exemptions, and other tax arrangements are tax benefits and special treatment. The true safety net for Christians is Christ, not the IRS. It is the same in other Western nations.

During the New Testament times, most assemblies (churches) met in homes or the public square, or even in the Temple in Jerusalem. The 'church' had no real cost. There were no upkeep costs or rent, or mortgage to pay, nor were loans required, or the necessity for large administrative systems like many churches today. In the letters, Paul, John, Peter, and James address the assemblies of Christians gathered in various places or cities. These were perhaps groups that met in various places or one central location regularly.

The early Christians were characterized by genuine compassion for the work of the Gospel in other places. They were also moved by the suffering of others. Paul was involved for example in the collection of funds to assist assemblies in need in various places. The verses in the New Testament about collecting money were principally concerned with the provision of funds for the needy gatherings in cities experiencing financial hardships due to the problems of the time (see for example 1 Corinthians 16:1-2). Paul is not talking about raising funds to pay for the priest or the priest's home or his salary, but to help the poor.

What is interesting is that this money was often given willingly, regardless of national boundaries and differences. Indeed, early in the Jerusalem assembly, seven men were chosen to work for the poor and needy in the assemblies there so the twelve apostles (including Matthias) could focus on the work of the Gospel.

The early Christians gave money to compensate teachers and preachers for their efforts in the assembly. For example, in 1 Timothy 5: 17-18 Paul says to Timothy *'The elders who direct the affairs of the church well are worthy of double honor, especially those whose work is preaching and teaching.'* Scripture says, *'Do not muzzle an ox while it is treading out the grain,'* and *'The worker deserves his wages.'* But Paul is not talking about a salary here and there is no indication of the elders being in so-called 'full-time' ministry. Even so, this is exclusively for teachers and preachers, not musicians, organists, secretaries and administrators, drivers, assistants, and so on and so on.

Verses like 1 Timothy 5: 17-18 were the justification for the Church Gravy Train we have today. Many churches have *'happiness'* pastors, *'encouragement'* pastors, *'maturity'* pastors *'outreach'* pastors, and *'welcome'* pastors,' and all are salaried workers, complete with bonuses, cars, homes, and a panoply of benefits. This bizarre categorization of faith makes some more famous cults seem innocuous contrasted with the demise of once-great denominations. Paul set a good model by working for a living when he visited the Thessalonians. He even made more of an impact on the community because of this lifestyle. There are no rules for tithing in the New Testament, or in church collections. These all come from a bizarre reading of selective texts from the Hebrew Bible. How can they claim that Jesus does need our money if there is no text in the Bible to justify it?

Stop encouraging the Church Gravy Train with your money. Most Christians do not realize that there is no economic reason for churches to even ask for money. Given their charity status and tax exemptions, even the worst church could break even with sensible business decisions. Instead, laziness and incompetence reign along with massive corruption. There are a few churches that have worked it out and that is fantastic to see. I have seen a few over the years, thriving in an economic system that punishes efficiency and rewards corruption. How they survive in a system that seeks to cripple initiative, good business practice, and efficiency, is truly a miracle.

What suffering has the church endured except being the cause of it? How many lives have been destroyed by the church and their friends in society? For example, how many people have had to marry behind the altar because they chose to marry a non-Catholic? In other situations, how many lived with the shame of a thousand sins because the church decided to make an example of them, while the priests gorged on abundance and corruption? How many walked along a street only to see people crossing the road to avoid meeting them because they went to the wrong church? Can you imagine how many people had their lives ruined and destroyed because of church slander, gossip, and lies, and how many were victims of the priests and their cult worship?

Christian Fascists, hiding behind their charity status will cause trouble. Christian Fascists are still on their holiness crusades to undermine the law. Even today, in our secular world, they believe themselves to be above the law, and that the law does not apply to them, and they hide like cowering dogs behind old statutes and laws that protect their precious investments. Their hatred is seen in their crusade against homosexuals and transgender people. If some of them had their way, they would prosecute them, ban them, or even kill them, and say that they are doing it all in the name of Jesus. It was not long ago, that churches supported medical treatments that were forced upon gay men which makes the Covid jab seem like a walk in the park.

Does Jesus need our money? No. Christian Fascists want to use the church to advance their political agenda. Whenever churches seek power, they end up becoming violent, oppressive institutions. They assume a life of themselves, and the message of the Gospel is lost.

The early Christian assemblies were simply gatherings of people at a house. That is natural and normal, and this could be easily the case today. You could simply gather over coffee and read the Bible. You don't need a liturgy, or songs, or music, or the Mass, or sermon. In addition, you don't need any of those things to simply gather, talk and pray. If you host it at a local café or restaurant on a quiet day, you are helping the local community and they are meeting nice Christians as opposed to the people they already know who go to church.

Jesus is their ticket to the good life

It is a common belief today as it was in the past that only rich people go to heaven. Many assume this is the case. Jesus is their ticket to the good life. Many Christian Fascists teach it all the time. They say that the way to God is through faith. If you have great faith, then you can have everything you want. Then if you get what you want, it is proof you have faith. If you have this faith, it is proof you will get to heaven. For them, faith is the key to wealth, which is proof of being right with God, and therefore, it guides one to heaven.

How they spin it depends on the tradition. In some older churches, only wealthy people are welcome, though they might tolerate a few poor people. Their members are drawn from the rich families of the town, their children attend the right religious schools, and they expect a particular style of worship, a special kind of homily, and a menu of opportunities to parade their wealth before others. They attend because they are wealthy and their god or their version of their deity is the god who will bless their wealth, their narcissism, and nothing he says in the scriptures will question their power or their wealth.

Others, often in the Pentecostal tradition, are taught, God wants the best for them. If he wants the best for them, then he will give them what they need, and they can get anything by faith. If they do not have it, this means they lack the faith to ask for it and it means they are poor because they have no faith. Though it is generally true in the West these days, the Church of England, or Anglican Church in poor nations, is most certainly the church of the political and economic elite. It is a sign of prosperity and membership in elite society.

This belief that only rich people go to heaven has a downside. If you are a Christian and you are poor, it means that you do not have enough faith. It means that you do not have God's blessings, you are not stepping out in faith. This also means that God is not listening to you, that what you are asking for is not in faith. It means that you will, ultimately, be excluded from heaven.

This is complete and utter rubbish. Yet, many Christian Fascists have made a fortune lying to people with their weird and wacky ways for the fast track to wealth and heavenly blessings. I read about one the other day. It was talking about a secret Bible code that will unlock your wealth. You only need faith and all you want will be yours. It is no surprise because the Bible has been ignored, twisted, or bypassed by the church to preserve and promote its power on earth.

An essential part of this earthly kingdom is that it requires money, lots of it, and the church has gone to great lengths to argue that politics and an earthly kingdom are the way to God. Wealth, however, doesn't matter to God, he doesn't need our money, and all belongs to him anyway, but the church convinces itself that it is not God who moves mountains, but it is money.

Jesus told his disciples in Matthew 19: 24-6, "'*Again I tell you; it is easier for a camel to go through the eye of a needle than for someone who is rich to enter the kingdom of God." When the disciples heard this, they were greatly astonished and asked, "Who then can be saved?" Jesus looked at them and said, "With man this is impossible, but with God all things are possible."*

The disciples of Jesus, like many people today, believed that if someone was wealthy, then it meant that God was blessing you and this meant you were on the right path for the fast track to salvation. If the rich cannot be saved, then who can be?

The church has thought so too, over the years. They have accumulated wealth and sought prosperity, and overall, churches have made many people rich. Google the Vatican treasury. Look at the grand cathedrals of Europe. Ponder the huge mega-churches of North America and Australia. Listen to the sermons of many priests, ministers, and pastors that promise the blessings of God if you give them money, your money, and lots of it. Jesus will never ask you for money, so why does the church?

Nowhere in all the Gospels does Jesus ask his disciples for money. Jesus even said once that he had nowhere to sleep. He often slept outside, relying on the charity of friends and his followers. He often stayed at the homes of friends such as Mary, Martha, and Lazarus. When he died, he only had the shirt on his back. Many ministers I have met over the years have wardrobes full of designer clothes, and only the best. Jesus never asked for money, so why do you pay money week in and week out to the church, and where does your money go? Many Churches love Jesus only because Jesus is their ticket to the good life. Being a Christian is often associated with being wealthy. Many Churches see the door of faith opening to prosperity and success.

In Australia for example, during the failed lockdowns, many thousands of priests, pastors, and ministers were recipients of government money. I was not among them. I did not receive one cent from this 'Job Keeper' slush fund, and slush fund it was. Millions of dollars went from the government to the Australian church in one of the largest direct transfers of financial assistance to the church in Australian history. Much of it is hidden cash, as the amounts are not widely known, and many churches are reluctant to publicize the exact amounts. For the church, Job Keeper was not welfare -as most kept their offertories open – it was a bribe to shut down criticism of the lockdowns, human rights abuses, and martial law.

This Job Keeper payment had a remarkable effect on the ministry of most people in the church in Australia. It silenced them. The church was very quiet. It said very little. Usually, you cannot shut up the church, they are always complaining about something. Yet, during the pandemic, the churches overall said nothing about the lockdowns, the vaccine passports, and the mandates, except to support them completely. Was it because they were bought off? Was it a quid pro quo? Virtually no Christian leader dared to criticize the government policy on Covid. Today, more people are dying from Covid than during the height of the lockdowns and the church remains quiet! Remarkable. At least they are consistent.

The only way many churches define Christ is the advocating wealth accumulation in his name. Paul only asks sometimes for daily expenses but most of his offerings are for the poor back in Jerusalem, so Paul is one of the men tasked with raising money for the poor. Paul often went without food for the sake of the Gospel and often worked in his trade, as a tentmaker. He didn't make those cheap camping tents you use on those family getaways, but those huge tents you see in the Middle East. Paul was a tradesman, and one of the best, and he was happy to work for a living. It was how he often met people because he was living amongst them, not hidden away in the monastery. Like Peter, and Jesus, he knew a trade, and he was probably known more for being a craftsman than being an evangelist.

Churches need a good dose of economics 101. As you know, the churches pay no taxes to the state. They all hide behind the charity rules so they can get as many exemptions as they can. Still, even there, most churches cannot break even. Many churches teeter on bankruptcy and are rarely in the black, many cannot manage money properly and have standards so low it would send shivers down the spines of businesspeople. In addition, many churches make terrible business decisions, often lose money, often squander money, and are always demanding more from you. We all pay the price of this cultural incompetence. If you gave a business $1000, they would make a profit, if you give the church $1000, they will be begging for more because they would have lost the first $1000. There is little or no financial oversight or regulation of the church sector. They are laughing all the way to the bank. They tell you to pay tax, but they do not.

Jesus is their ticket to the good life. If Jesus did not seek a kingdom on earth, what is the church doing? The way the church lives on earth is not building the kingdom that Christ spoke of. Jesus spoke of a spiritual kingdom worked out in the lives of his people, one that was characterized by people laying down their lives for others as Christ did for us. For many in the church, their vision is different. They don't believe Christ will return and expect that their power will remain. How they live is their way, it is not the way of Christ, they are building their kingdom on earth brick by brick, cathedral by cathedral, monument of stone by monument of stone.

Nonetheless, even some Christian Fascists have discovered that the Church is a millstone around their neck. Speak to any priest, minister, or pastor and you will find that they spend most of their time trying to keep the church afloat, rather than doing any real work in the ministry. Many have forgotten what that even looks like. Many are also too scared of their congregation to challenge them in any way since those people pay their salaries. These vile creatures remind them daily that they exist solely because the 'good people of the church' are giving them their hard-earned money.

Those buildings, those church structures, those properties are nothing short of an obstacle to any real Christian work, even the work of religious atheists. I have seen the effect of this on many people over the years. It destroys them emotionally and psychologically. The church doesn't care about the damage and these people (many of whom are Christian Fascists) are thrown on the scrap heap as garbage, while new people are recruited, fresh blood to be squeezed.

The way most Churches treat their ministers, pastors, and priests, is a disgrace. No, I go further. It is a crime. I strongly believe that if governments seriously investigated abuse and overwork directed at clergy, then a great many congregation members would face terms of imprisonment. These include false allegations, gossip, slander, threats, abuse, harassment, and actual violence. There is no protection for clergy in the church, only abuse, a culture of intimidation and toxicity.

A starting point might be for the state to assume ownership and control of every heritage property in the nation. These belong to the nation, not the churches and they cost too much to maintain anyway.

If you are working for the state and you are listening, take note. Please relieve the churches of all the heritage properties. Churches don't need them and usually don't want them. They are more museums and relics than churches anyway; they represent a time in our history that is often full of shame, built during the indigenous genocides, sectarian hatred, or xenophobia, and they have become idols for the rest. In addition, they are also churches that oversaw the appalling abuse of children, and most of those places are still open. The victims can return to the scene of the crime and wonder why those buildings are still there. Please take back the buildings, the churches don't need them. The nation may, so they can pay for them if they want them. If not, they can make nice flower shops, cafes, or homes. At least, get them to pay land tax.

Jesus said that a man cannot serve both God and money. The church doesn't believe that. I heard a sermon by a popular priest who told his congregation that if they gave enough money to the church this would secure their place in heaven. He is still a priest there, he doesn't believe in the resurrection, and he doesn't believe in God, but he likes the money, and he likes his job. He is not alone. Money is the main reason many become priests. It is a step up in salary and reputation, especially in the wealthy churches. Like the Pharisees, they like their position in society.

A few priests love to control people and so they gravitate to the confessional and the path to abuse. Overall, however, it is the love of money that drives most to the pulpit. They are easily manipulated by their churches and few last the distance, few survive the gossip and slander culture. The Church rewards mediocrity and conformity. Chances are your local minister is a mediocre and ordinary person, with few redeemable qualities.

Many priests go into the church young before they have had any life experience. In Protestant churches, where the youngest people are drawn to leadership, the fact that preaching to people is a weekly duty is, at the least, the Millennial's delight. A few enter the ministry as they call it, later, after they have worked for a while. Only a few give up a solid career to enter the ministry. For most, being a minister is a step up, and if you play your cards right, you can hit the jackpot. You can have the good life and employ volunteers while you take regular holidays hankering after your retirement when you will go on the government pension.

It is very different from the life of Christ or Paul. Tradition says that all the apostles bar one were martyred for their faith in Christ. The most severe punishment most priests receive in the West is a paper cut. That is, if they sit down, shut up, and do as they are told. Most do, and so they survive. They live a life of profound mediocrity, underachievement, and disappointment. You see it in their faces. Once in the ministry, many priests, and pastors poke fun at the life of Jesus and his disciples, or the Bible in general. The popular target is Paul the apostle. Many churches love to criticize him. I don't know why. Perhaps he is too honest and church leaders don't like honesty. Paul-bashing is a distraction so you cannot see what they are doing with your money. While you are laughing at your jokes about Jesus, Paul, or Peter, they are lining their pockets and having a little chuckle at your expense.

Jesus is their ticket to the good life. It is, after all, only money. But Jesus came to give us life so we might have it to the full (John 10:10). It is not about money. It is about peace with God, life, hope, a new beginning, a new relationship with God, and freedom, true freedom. The Church cannot give it to us. Only God can. Jesus said, 'If the Son of Man sets you free, then you shall be free indeed.' (John 8: 36).

How to end Christian Fascism and save the Gospel

The greatest threat to the Gospel in the West is the Church. The Greatest strength of the Church is Christian Fascism. The way to save the Gospel is simple: end Christian Fascism, for the last time. There will never be a better time.

During Covid Hysteria, more money was passed from the government to the church directly than at any other time in the last century such as in Australia. Job Keeper was the biggest slush fund for the churches in a century. Thank God for the coronavirus because it brought wealth back to the church. Coincidentally, it was also a time when the church ceased to comment on public policy related to Covid except to praise the government. These statements are all on the public record. Almost no Christian leader in Australia spoke out against public policy or martial law, or the vaccine mandates. Fascinating.

This martial law ended on April 17, 2022. It passed without much statement. The Christian Fascists expect it will be business as usual: money, more money, and more money. While businesses struggle, churches continue to ask governments for more assistance, more protection, and more patronage. Meanwhile, church attendance continues to plummet. As an economist, as well as a Christian, I foresee astounding, catastrophic economic oblivion for most Churches in the West. Reform is essential or churches will be extinct in a generation, if not much sooner.

Today, more people are dying from Covid (April-November 2022) than they were dying during the lockdowns or during the pandemic. Yet, the churches are open now, and church vaccine passports have been largely tossed aside. Yet, Australia is less safe than it has ever been. The churches once again are saying nothing. They seem to take their memos directly from the government these days. Maybe they do. What went on and why was it evil?

There is not a denomination untouched by the crime of institutionalized child abuse. The argument some of the churches made before the *Royal Commission into Institutional Abuse* (2015) was that churches could not be sued because priests or ministers were not legally employed by the church, they were not employees, but were self-employed. The church was adamant that the employment condition of the priest could not be changed for anything. It was absolute. It is a lie of course. Priests are, in practice employed by the Diocese and appointed by the Diocese, and the idea that priests are self-employed is a lie. It is tax fraud.

Covid Hysteria changed everything. The Church accepted a change in employment status for money. The attitude of the church changed dramatically when the Covid Hysteria came along. You guessed the reason – they wanted money. They were self-employed when money was expected, but then they backflipped and became employees of the church so they could receive money. The sordid slush fund of Job Keeper was made available for salaried church workers. In April 2020, the Australian government made an exemption to the rules, and for this one time accept that for the purposes of Job Keeper, church priests and ministers would be seen legally as employees and not as self-employed, so they could benefit.

We don't know how many took Job Keeper because the churches

are very secretive about their finances, but many did. Throughout the pandemic, the churches continued to ask for money even though their ministers were covered by a government wage subsidy. To my knowledge, many secular businesses have repaid Job Keeper, and that was the right thing to do. How many churches have? We don't know because they are very secretive about their money.

If Churches can take Job Keeper, they must change their position on child abuse. The basic message of the Australian church in Covid is this: the victims of child sexual abuse in the church in Australia are not as important as the financial well-being of the priests and ministers. Let that sink in when you think about going to church or paying more money into church coffers. Every church that abused children should be shut down and pulled down, and all the money should go to the victims. Better still, sell the buildings, all the propertied assets of the church, and follow Christ.

Sell all the church buildings and give the money to the victims. After all, what is a building but bricks and mortar? Imagine the message that it would send to the world, that the church is serious about dealing with the crimes of child abuse. The church will fight tooth and nail to protect every property because the least valued property is worth more to them than all the victims of child sexual abuse. This seems to be their thinking. It is difficult to reach a different conclusion. I was astounded that the Churches accepted Job Keeper even though their weekly offertories were still in place. People did not stop giving to their church during the pandemic.

The church is not a charity. The church is a service provider. Without the priest, there is no church, and it would be disgraceful hypocrisy if the churches insisted that their institutions exist independently of the priesthood or public ministry. But you will still see them argue this, as they are the most corrupt institutions in any nation. It would be like a hospital with no patients or a tank without shells. There is no real difference between a priest, a doctor, a psychologist, or a counselor, and yet it is the priest whose livelihood is exempt from taxation. This is occupational discrimination and is a disgrace.

Take your, local doctor. They are often in a practice and pay income tax and their practice may pay business tax. They provide advice to patients, often they prescribe drugs or tablets or a routine of practice, or a specialist referral. To become a doctor, they train for many years and are often those who err on the side of caution. The same could be said for the counselor, the psychologist, and any other similar professional. They provide medical services and pastoral services, and they all help the community. This is, even more, the case for doctors and nurses in a hospital. Yet, they all pay tax.

How is the priest different from a practical point of view? They provide advice to their 'patients' or congregation, they provide resources for people to read, point people in the right direction and provide pastoral care, at least in theory. Why should priests receive special treatment in a secular nation when they clearly perform the function of being service providers? Job Keeper in Australia proved that churches are not charities but service providers. The church is a service provider, not a charity. There are lots of genuine charities and they do good work, but the local church is not a charity and should not be treated as one. Churches say that they *'help the community'* and therefore deserve special treatment. Are they helping the community for money? I thought they were acting out of love, and I don't remember love coming with a price tag in the Bible. All businesses in the community help the community in one way or another. Do you see local churches sponsoring local events in your town? No, they are usually the only ones asking for money.

The church in the second decade of the twenty-first century is at a turning point, unable to decide whether it is committed to the good news of God's grace or the effort to shape the nation in moral reforms. As the latter is critical to the church's function in society, many churches are part of the ruling class and the lucrative jobs in the Church are full-time positions, and they are highly coveted. It means status and one can find a nice comfortable place to live out a career in the same place for several decades. Priests are a relic of the landed aristocracy, the old regime. The idea was that the priest would in effect represent the bishop to the local people and press them with the laws and regulations of the land. Their position was in the parish and the parish was a geographical area for which they bore responsibility. Everyone in that parish was under their control and their authority. They were an extension of the state and had to be mindful of civil disobedience. This role and purpose for priests is complete nonsense today.

Churches sit uncomfortably in nations that pretend to be secular.

Churches are dishonest about their real identity. Churches are not honest with the government about their real identities. Charity status is a coveted status in society. Many financial benefits accrue to organizations that enjoy this position, including many tax benefits. Many, if not most Christian Churches are not charities in any version of the word or meaning of the word 'charity.' Take for example a local 'congregational' church. This denomination is what we would call 'independent.' It has no real association beyond its building or membership. Many Christian churches are like this. They are independent in the real sense of the word. They are self-sustaining and self-governing. Legally, they are a separate charity. It makes sense because they are independent.

Then we have the traditional church denominations such as Anglican, Catholic, or Orthodox. One would think that they would each be treated in the same manner, as one charity, for example, the Anglican Church charity or the Catholic Church charity. But this is not the case. The great deception of these churches is that legally they are all seen as independent financial charities even though they are part of the same organization. This is unethical and wrong. At the very least, each Diocese should be considered one charity with many branches, not hundreds of independent charities. If not, then sever the ties with the Diocese and end this charade. Take for example a typical Diocese in the Anglican Church of Australia. All ministers must be approved by the bishops, and the leaders of various geographical areas, and no minister is appointed without the approval of the bishops. None of these churches are in practice, independent from the bishop's control. In many cases, salaries and stipends are organized on a diocesan basis, not from within the local church. In practice, these dioceses are operating as one organization with many branch offices, not as independent churches with no association with each other. Legally, however, every local parish church is its own independent charity. This is tax fraud.

The way forward of course is to give more authority to real charities and strip churches of fake charity status. Not even proper charities are treated in the same manner. The Salvation Army for example has many branch offices, and so does Anglicare, one of the most powerful and successful social service providers in Australia. No one would think of every single Anglicare office as being a separate charity, acting independently of each other. They all work in concert. These real charities make an astounding contribution to society. They are real charities. The local church, however, is not a charity. It is a building where a group of people gather for one hour a week and have morning tea afterward. They might run an English language class. Legally, this church has all the powers and authority of a charity.

The church charities have virtually no real financial oversight and are therefore susceptible to corruption of many kinds. The average parish church is small, or medium and is run by locals. There is no tax office breathing down their neck. There should be. The ATO is a blessing from God. Taxation is a Christian's delight, and the Australian Tax Office is God's instrument of righteousness. Due to their special charity status, these churches do not have the authority of the tax office to guide their decisions and restrain temptations.

There are no counseling or psychological requirements for priests. Most priests have no training in many of the skills they require to perform even the most basic pastoral functions. There is no protection for Christian ministers, pastors, or teachers. In the old days, the local priest ran his or her parish, but these days some Churches have become like little unions, with so many people on the church gravy train.

The state must insist upon mandatory training not only in theology but psychology and counseling with fieldwork and nursing homes. All priests must have a trade or a qualification aside from their theological degree. There must be regular protection for them under the law. For example, priests should have the right to sue their employers and congregation members in a court of law. They must have the right to collectively bargain and join or establish a union.

The state must step in and reform the church by force if necessary. It is time to make churches service providers. Competition in the marketplace would lead to the growth in productivity in churches willing to make changes for the good of themselves and the community. Many churches would thrive in a competitive marketplace, paying business tax, land tax, and income tax, hiring priests on competitive salaries, and following the laws of the land. It is time to bring the church kicking and screaming into the real world. It has been done before. It should be done again. Courageous are the political leaders who will do it. They have God's blessing. The church as it exists today is a complete disgrace. Priests should lose the right of priests to perform marriages. Priests are automatically given the right to do marriages. This needs to stop immediately as it provides an unfair advantage to those who are properly trained. At the very least, all priests or ministers who wish to do marriages must be trained in the same way to be able to provide the best service for their congregations and the community.

The church court systems are illegal and must be abolished. The only legitimate legal system in a liberal democracy is the one established by the state. These laws are both comprehensive and adequate for the governing of a nation. Christians usually make the best citizens because they tend to live a productive and quiet life. The churches all have their secret, star chambers, secret tribunals, church courts, disciplinary bodies, and heresy boards, all of which are completely corrupt, illegal, and operate independently of the state. These tribunals and church courts are a relic of the day when the church wielded real political power but now these courts are out of place in a liberal secular society. The current legal system with its rules and protections is fully sufficient for any real crimes that might arise such as theft, assault, or harassment.

The state must investigate the abuse of church courts over the decades. The churches cannot be trusted with their tribunals. They have wreaked havoc in the lives of thousands of ministers and priests over the years, with their secret courts and complaint systems, and their abuse of power and position. Most people brought before these courts are completely innocent, but they are victims of church politics. They have their lives and reputations destroyed and the process of prosecution is always political and never applied consistently.

The child sex abuse scandals brought to light appalling abuse that made little dent in church coffers, and the churches are still laughing all the way to the bank. I am confident that if there was a serious investigation of church finances by the state, a great many church leaders would spend the rest of their lives in prison. In response to the Royal Commission, churches added to their secret tribunals and courts more courts for safe churches. But churches are not safe places. For every person who is a religious nut and who goes to church and bows each week to the priest, there are a thousand people who have been kicked out, abused, or thrown out of church due to personality differences or lack of love.

Churches in the West are toxic institutions of abuse and criminality. It is time for the state to step in, reform, and abolish this antiquated sector for the sake of the people who suffered and continue to suffer from unaccountable church power and control. The end of the Church in its current form will not mean the end of Christianity. It will mean the end of Christian Fascism. This is a good thing. It will finally mark the end of the stain fake Christianity has made on the West. It will mark a new beginning where church workers can exist in safety in a legal system of rights and responsibilities like every other profession in society. Maybe then, the good news of God's grace can flourish.

The churches must be taxed

The churches must be taxed. Churches must do their bit for society. During Covid Hysteria, Christian Fascists insisted that they would get vaccinated out of their love for others. They said that vaccine passports were an act of love for society. If so, then they must also pay tax. If they voluntarily pay tax, then they are also acting in love for the society they pretend to support. The reason is that the verse in the Bible they often used to promote vaccines is Romans 13 where Paul insists twice that the Church must pay tax (13: 6-7).

It is time for churches to come clean and cough up the dough, for the nation. Christian Fascists love to tell people what to do. They love to abuse people and harass people, especially minorities. Yet their own Bible tells them to do their bit for the nation out of love. If they do not pay tax, then they are not acting out of love, are they?

Churches must be taxed. For a start, land taxes should be paid on all property to all levels of government, as a contribution to society. Why should churches be exempt? Churches often own a lot of property. Much of it was given by the state long ago. Churches should obey the law and do their bit for the nation. After all, they expect everyone else to pay. The Pope often makes fun of capitalism and the market system and yet his Church around the world bypasses the tax system. It is hardly a justified criticism. He criticizes a system that his church is not part of because capitalism has granted his church tax exemptions. Strangely, the Pope has never argued that his church should follow Paul and pay taxes.

Church taxation proves religious freedom. Churches will oppose taxation because they will say it is an attack on religious freedom. How can something everyone is expected to do, affect their freedom? Taxation affects everyone. Surely, their exemption from the tax system is an attack on religious freedom because it enshrines principles that discriminate against people who choose not to believe in organized religion. It is perfectly consistent with what they call religious freedom. It is not an attack on religious freedom. I pay tax. *Freedom Matters Today pays* tax. I have faith in God and yet I can pay taxes. Why should the churches get special dispensation because they invent traditions that are not in the Bible, and hide behind political power?

God demands taxation and non-payment is a sin. In fact, it is Christian. God wants the taxation of the church. It is in the Bible, the same Bible these hypocrites quote to prop up their unbiblical notion of the separation of church and state. The church and state have never been separated. It is the taxation of the church that will lead to the true separation of Church and State, by enabling churches to be free at last.

Speaking of the separation of church and state, let us consider the religious schools or the private schools that exist to educate. They exist to do that of course, but they also exist to prop up the Christian Churches. Unlike Churches that are run into the ground by incompetence and stupidity, many of these schools are run as successful models of higher education. These schools are often in receipt of large sums of money from the state and yet, many Churches still want to control the curriculum and philosophy of the schools. It is time to bring that to an end. These schools should of course be thankful for their religious origins and possibly employ some chaplains, but they should be independent entirely from sectarian religious power. I say this for the sake of the children, who should be free to learn, not be forced to conform to the whim of the bishops or the personality of the pastors. The same should be for other Christian institutions tied to the Church such as social service providers, hospitals, and nursing homes. They need to be truly separate. After all, church and state must be separate right? If churches genuinely want a separation of church and state, why do they seek and secure government funding for their religious schools?

Christian Fascists pull out the Bible only when it suits them. Like those that say all that matters is love, these church leaders say that all that matters is the Bible, but they don't believe that either. Money is their god. It is a disgrace to hear Church leaders demand tax exemption from the government and then say in the same breath that they stand up for the poor, the oppressed, and the maligned. It is hypocrisy.

Here is where the rubber hits the road if you like. Romans 13 tells us that Christians should obey the government. This has been used to proof text obedience to every public health directive in the West. It has been used to accuse Christians of disobeying God if they even have another opinion on the coronavirus. Let us not forget that the church always ignores this passage anyway when it suits them.

They were silent over Covid. They will not be silent over losing their money. If the government decided to tax churches tomorrow, I would expect, if they are good Christians, the churches will simply obey the government, right? After all, that is what they have said for two years: *'we must obey the government, we cannot protest, we cannot ask questions, we cannot criticize, we must do as we are told.'* If the government decided to tax the church, that would be their response, right?

Of course not, they will oppose it and say that it is the right of the Christian to oppose unjust laws, but they are not unjust, nor are they unbiblical because in the same Chapter of Romans, Paul tells the church twice to pay tax. Twice. It is unambiguous. All the texts on taxation in the New Testament refer to everyone in the church, including the church itself. Paul makes no distinction. It is impossible to ignore this Biblical principle any longer. It is God's will for his people.

Tax was not a big deal for Paul. Oh, the irony. Christian Fascists hate Paul. Yet Paul was a good citizen. He obeyed the law. He didn't mind taxation. He didn't fight his imprisonment through the courts or argue about his 'God-given rights.' All good Christians are the best citizens. They obey the law; they love others as Christ loved his people. Also, they promote the peace and prosperity of the nation, and they live in harmony with others. The problem is Christian Fascists. They are the ones who mix faith and politics. Churches must be taxed to finally break their political power. I truly believe that if churches were forced to become service providers, many of the problems that they face will disappear. It would be an ecclesiastical revolution and will open the door to spiritual renewal.

Paul does not expect the church will be granted charity status. Paul does not insist on the rights of churches while he is in prison. Instead, he rejoices (Philippians 4:4). Churches should voluntarily give to the government whatever tax other businesses pay if only to fulfill the law of God. Surely that is enough reason. Paul is telling the church of Rome to pay tax. He is telling the church everywhere that taxation is a normal, acceptable way to seek the peace and prosperity of the city.

If you are the government, and you want churches to pay tax, then know this, God is on your side, he is on the side of the state because he fully expects the church to contribute to society. Taxation is a God-approved method of governing society. You can quote Romans 13. You can even enshrine the text in your government legislation. Most modern churches, churches that are not state-based, would have no problem paying tax, indeed, they will be better off under a taxed regime. The less government money for churches, the more efficient and prosperous they will be anyway.

In the old days, churches were involved in business. These days the tax rules around charities are a noose, not a source of financial freedom. Like companies hiding behind a tariff wall that destroyed their competitive spirit, churches hiding behind the charity rules has meant they are bloated, inefficient, often corrupt, and usually in debt. Note to the state: charity status is not protected by the Bible. Charity status of the churches is not a gospel issue, nor is so-called religious freedom for that matter. Jesus said his disciples should expect persecution if they were his disciples. The apostles said following Jesus would result in persecution. Churches that use the Bible to avoid the payment of tax are lying to God. The payment of tax is not persecution however, it is obedience to the law of God which is what Paul talks about.

A Christianity without Christian Fascism is a blessing. Christianity is a relationship with a living God that exists every day, not something that is bound to a weekly ritual in a place called 'church.' Christianity is a personal relationship with God, and not membership in a church. Faith leads to God while religion leads to the church. The idea that God lives in the church building is nonsense. Christians are united to God by faith, and this is every day. These truths are all found in the Bible, which the Church usually keeps closed, for obvious reasons. What this means is quite simple: you can have Christianity without the church. The church can be done away with entirely. The abolition of the church, the denominations, the tax-free slush fund paradise, the institution of abuse and misery, the source of most sectarian division and hatred for hundreds of years, is good for faith, good for the gospel, and good for the community.

Most Christians would not dare to speak these views aloud. They fear exclusion and ex-communication. I would rather be faithful to God and his word the Bible. Also, I fear God who can kill both body and soul in hell. In addition, I also wish to follow Jesus Christ. Christ had no problem with the state. It was simply irrelevant to the kingdom of God. Jesus said his kingdom was not of this world. Paul said in 1 Corinthians 15: 50 that flesh and blood cannot inherit the kingdom of God.

This means Christian Fascists are liars, frauds, and hypocrites. They hide behind religion for their own selfish, violent, corrupt purposes. They bring disgrace to God, to faith, to all people who seek to live out their lives as followers of Jesus Christ. The Christian Church, though corrupt, is still one of the most powerful institutions in the West and wields incredible political power. It is also the recipe for social chaos. Christians on the other hand, are instruments of peace. There is a difference between the corrupt institutions of the church and the genuine hearts of faithful Christians.

Churches must pay taxes like Christians do all the time. Christianity without the church is necessary to fix their money problem. The average Christian is a taxpayer, and a good one. The average Christian is a law-abiding citizen. No churches pay tax. All churches expect special treatment. All churches expect the laws of the land do not apply to them. Their surrogates, patrons, and disciples in the state and political parties ensure special treatment and protection. These beliefs suggest that there is a disconnect between the lives of ordinary Christians and the Houses of God they frequent.

Churches must be taxed to avoid the temptation of greed. Christians know that money is the root of all kinds of evil (1 Timothy 6: 10). It is not that money is evil itself. Money is a necessity. But it is the love of money that causes most of the problems in the church. Priests like to tell their flock to beware of idols, or things that distract them from supporting the Church. The church, however, has become an idol. It has become a High Place, a place of idolatry. Money is the god of any established church. Go to Germany and see the beautiful Lutheran churches, I mean the beautiful empty, Lutheran churches. Go to France, or any European nation, even Britain. It is the same. There is a massive decline.

Churches are declining because of inner failings. Churches in the West are in decline because people are not blind. This rapid decline is because people are not stupid. People see with their eyes and things do not add up and they see the church and they see the hypocrisy and they see the money and they listen to the sermons and things do not add up. They see that money is all that matters to the church. It is not Christ, nor his exclusive claims about himself. The church has built its monuments of stone, brick, mortar, and gold, and the priests wear robes or the best Italian suits.

Most of the spectacular collapses of Christian Churches in the West have been over money. Those that are about something else, are often tied to questions of money. Money has done more damage to the Gospel in the last 100 years than anything else. Like the alcoholic who can't hold his liquor, the church is the same with money. They are the worst people to be entrusted with it.

Why do the Churches ignore the teaching of Christ on wealth? It is astounding to me to read what Christ taught about money and then go to Church. These verses and teachings are the first to be deleted from any church. Let me use the words of Christ himself: a rich man can't enter the kingdom of God. Impossible (Matthew 19: 23-4). The love of money is the Achilles Heel of the Western Church.

Imagine a church admitting its failings and wanting to change. It would be marvelous if things were different. Imagine a world where churches recognize their corrupt and violent history, the pain they have caused, and decide to prove their repentance in actions, not words, imagine that. In Australia, they still deny their complicity in the genocide of the Indigenous people across the land, and they still deny their role in the suffering of Indigenous people ever since.

Imagine a church that said, *'churches must be taxed.'* Imagine a church in the West that offered to pay property taxes and paid income tax simply because they wanted to contribute to society, to walk with people, alongside people, and so they may sympathize with the struggles of ordinary people. In addition, imagine a world where churches are not corrupt, where they know how to run businesses properly and judiciously, and become places people want to congregate instead of avoiding.

Imagine a church where ministers and priests had practical skills. Furthermore, imagine a Church where priests had a real job and had respect in their community. The early disciples were fishermen, Matthew was an accountant by trade, Paul was a tentmaker, and Jesus was a carpenter. I could go further. Barnabas was a merchant, and so were Aquila and his wife, they were in the fabric trade, and some of the women who knew Christ during his public ministry used their finances for the disciples. Their faith was expressed or bore fruit through the lives they were living in the world.

Priests are a relic of the landed aristocracy, a stipend class of people who often get everything free, especially the wealthy denominations – free houses, free rent, free transport, often cooked meals, and their kids (if Protestant) can go to the best (church) schools. In poor nations, many believe the church is the ticket to the good life and priests are highly respected positions of wealth.

Imagine a church where priests tried to follow Jesus instead. Jesus gave us his throne to become a man. Churches refuse to pay taxes like everyone else because they live in the past and do not want to give up their power. Did not the Son of God give us his throne in heaven to walk among us, to share our suffering? Make up your own mind. Do you think priests are giving up enough? Are they making the appropriate sacrifices for God, following in the footsteps of our Lord? Did Jesus insist on his rights, his money, his position, his tax exemptions? The one who did not insist on tax exemption or charity status was Christ himself and whom does Paul say that he is?

'The Son is the image of the invisible God, the firstborn over all creation. For in him all things were created: things in heaven and on earth, visible and invisible, whether thrones or powers or rulers or authorities; all things have been created through him and for him. (Colossians 1: 15-16).

This Son gave up all for us, so we might have all. Remember this when you go to church and see your minister wearing the designer clothes, and the nice shoes, or the priest wearing the nice robes, while asking you for more money to fill his belly. Ask him to show you his wounds in his hands and feet, and the side where the spear was thrust, and ask him to show you how his blood was shed for you. Don't forget, as you pass him your weekly offertory, or include him in your will, that he sold you out during Covid Hysteria, and will do so again for money, and the last person he cares about is you.

10 WHAT DOES GOD DO DURING THE WEEK?

After a busy Sunday, what does God get up to?

What does God do during the week? This is a question I have always wondered about. People go to church on Sunday expecting to meet God. They believe that he lives in the building they attend. Their rituals celebrate this expectation. When the service is over, the place is tidied up, and everyone has left, what does God do? How does he spend his time? What are his hobbies? What is he up to?

Christian Fascists don't ask that question because they don't believe he exists anyway. They don't care what he does during the week, and they don't expect to meet him on Monday because they don't believe he turned up on Sunday. Christian Fascists fake the rituals and cover them with words like the 'mystery of faith' because they don't have any.

In addition, they convince themselves that they can conjure up the image of God with magical incantations. Others shout at him during their sermons. Whatever the method, their image of God is their own creation, made in their own image. That's the point of Christian Fascism. God is whomever you want him or her, or it, to be. The only prerequisite is that God doesn't turn up.

When people go to church, they say they are meeting with God. OK, where is he? Where does he sit? Where is he hiding? Perhaps when people turn up on Sunday, God pops across the road for a pint at the local pub. Would you want to meet the people who go to church for all the wrong reasons, every week, for years? I know God has patience, but he has seen it all, he knows all the excuses, he knows all the complaints, he knows all the gripes, he has heard the same stories, the same old gossip, the same old problems.

He has given them the Bible. They leave it closed. They think it is a joke, a collection of make-believe fairy tales written by ancient Jews. He gives them his Spirit, but they don't believe in the supernatural. He gives them the blessings of the heavens, but they don't want them. They want material things, and revenge on their enemies, and payback, and scores settled. He gives them unity in the Gospel and racial harmony, but only the racially pure can attend their church services, and for them, Jesus is a white man with blonde hair and blue eyes, and the service is in English, and minorities are welcome as long as they know their place. Welcome to church! It is no wonder God pops out for a pint on Sunday morning.

Not all people who go to church are Christian Fascists. In every place, there are always a few genuine Christians holding up the light of Christ in the darkness. As for the rest, most cannot tell the difference between the church and Christianity. They quench the Spirit. After all, why listen to God when their priest can tell them all the answers? After all, he went to Bible College. Most are committed to their sect, devoted to their particular and peculiar way of doing things. Most are true believers in their church and are knee-deep in the Culture War especially if they live in America, Britain, Australia, or Canada.

There is a more important question. If God exists outside of the church, why do you need to go to church to 'meet him'? More discerning Christians who attend an assembly run by Christian Fascists will leap to the defense of those who most assuredly despise them and their faith. Christians always leap to defend the Fascists in their midst. It always surprises me. They did last time, and Christians will pull out their unopened copy of Dietrich Bonhoeffer's *Cost of Discipleship*, as proof that only a few diehard Germans were fascists. The truth is, as it was last time, Christian Fascists mock the faith of Christians and would sell them for a dime. They did last time too. Many Christians do not see the malevolence and evil of Christian Fascism, nominal faith, or legalism. It is perhaps a sickness of the Western Church. It is, like Covid Hysteria, a delusion, hypnosis, or blindness. It is a sad inability to discern evil when it appears because people do not want to believe that their church is imperfect, or that they might bear responsibility for its demise. It is perhaps because Western Christians often downplay or deny spiritual realities and the person and work of Satan. He may be of theological significance, but not practically relevant. They might say, of course, God doesn't stay in the church building. Of course, he is at work in the world. They might even dare to speak of the Holy Spirit and his presence in all Christians, and that we have no right to judge nominal believers. What nonsense.

We are not to judge moral failings of others, but we are to call out false teachings, we are to call out corruption, we are to protect the weak and the vulnerable from bullies and liars. Churches will expel the 'immoral brother' but not the heretic. They will kick out the single mum but welcome the man who denies the resurrection. They will cast out the gay person but welcome the wife-beater with open arms. They will humiliate the transgender person but will celebrate when another religious hypocrite turns up on Sunday. This is the church. They love their money and celebrate morality instead of the grace of God.

It is our need for salvation that Christ came for all of us. In Australia, everyone is a migrant, except of course the Indigenous people whose ancestors were massacred, murdered, and persecuted by farmers, settlers, and soldiers who regularly attended the Church of England on Sundays. At some point, every single person came to Australia from abroad, it doesn't matter if that was five generations ago or yesterday. Everyone is in the same boat so to speak or came in a boat, or by plane, as Australia is an island nation. Australians have a shared common identity as a nation of migrants. There are no exceptions.

In the same way, all need the salvation of God found in the Lord Jesus Christ. This includes people whose families have been at church for five generations, and it includes the person who turns up for the first time on Sunday. The salvation is the same, the need is the same, the Savior is the same, and the results are the same, a transformed life, a life touched by the grace and mercy of God. Jesus came to save all, even the self-righteous hypocrites who sit in their well-worn seats in church, molded to the shape of their bums, and who scoff and scorn at all who have not discovered the art of polite church hypocrisy. Churches have their morality codes of who is in and who is out, and they ignore matters of truth and error. This has been the case for centuries, dating back to the days of true church power, national churches, and the origins of Christian Fascism. Nevertheless, even in this cesspool, God's flock must be protected, the truth must be defended, and spirits need to be discerned.

Sadly, most Christians, thanks to the mainstream thinking of Christian Fascism, think that God is external, not inward, or present. During the week, he is *'out there, somewhere, doing his thing,'* like some child looking for his lost toys. They might believe that God is active during the week. But this begs the question then, doesn't it? If God is active during the week, and outside the church building, why attend the services at all? After all, people go to church to meet God and worship him. If God is outside during the week, there is no need to go to church to meet God, is there?

A true Christian believes that while God is everywhere, he is especially present with us and in us. God is not external but internal, God dwells in us by faith. God lives in us by his Holy Spirit. Paul tells us that our bodies are the temple of the Holy Spirit (1 Corinthians 6: 19). When we meet other believers, Christ is present in our midst, when two or three gather (Matthew 18: 20). Each Christian has been blessed by the same power that God used to raise Christ from the dead (Ephesians 1: 19-21). Yet, many Christians believe they must go to a church building on Sunday to meet God, the God who never left them and never will.

The attitude of many Christians to God is the same attitude people have towards monsters. It is one of the reasons I have great difficulty believing in monsters. The real monsters are people, not monsters. There are those movies where there is a dark, scary house, and in the house is a monster. He lurks and waits, and the camera pans towards the door which is opened by the teenagers. They walk slowly through the creaking building. We know that just around the corner is a foul fiend, a creature of deformed horribleness. Then, suddenly, at the right moment, the beast leaps out and the children scream, and the lights go off.

Fine, scary stuff, but my question is this: what does the monster do the rest of the week? Surely, he is not waiting for the kids to turn up. He must get sore legs just waiting behind that door. What does he eat, and how does he spend his time? Does he play board games? What about friends? Does he drink coffee or tea? This is how most people view God. He is waiting at church on Sunday for people to turn up.

This way of thinking is the idea that God exists for them. God is only as big as our need for him to be. The purpose of God's existence is to serve them, wait upon them, fulfill them, satisfy them, and work for them. God's purpose is to be there on Sunday when people turn up. He is waiting for them to turn on the music, adjust their skirt and ties, and clear their throat; he is waiting for the electricity to work and the sound system to turn on, waiting for the sermon and the minister or pastor to speak and waiting for the elevation of the polished silverware of the Mass. He is there to bless their kids' program, approve their budget, and rubber-stamp their five-year plan. God is molded into the church service, he is the purpose-made God, a God adaptable for every variation, every style, every tradition, and every sect. God fits all shapes and sizes made for him, and he does what he is told when he is told to do it.

Many priests think they control God. They announce their power every time they perform the blasphemy of the Mass. The astounding arrogance of the priests who incant the prayers to invoke the Holy Spirit and bring him out of heaven to transform the presence of Christ into the wafer and wine. It is G.O.D., God on Demand, a cluttering of words thrown together by the ancient liturgists to force the Spirit down out of the clouds away from his inaction to do as he is told, to bring meaning to something no Biblical text authorizes. It elevates the priests who stand over their altars drinking the blood and eating the bodily sacrifice of a man who said he would not eat the Passover again until his second coming and nowhere said that his suffering would be prolonged beyond one day.

Many ministers and pastors think they control God. The astounding arrogance of the preachers who think their words and their long sermons are words direct from the mouth of God. Just listen to them along with the crowds waiting on their every word with bated breath, jotting down every nuance, and copying every personality trait, claiming to follow Jesus, but gaining disciples for themselves. Churches are known not for the faithfulness of their people but the sermons of their ministers or pastor. I also stand corrected; they are also known for the position they take during the

Culture War. In both cases, the Christian Fascism of traditional liturgical national Christianity or the Christian Fascism of the evangelicals, these Christians have a faith where God is made in their image.

All Christian Fascists are the same. They not only create God in their image: they make him one of them. He becomes a white Jesus or a rich Jesus, or a Jesus who likes children or a Jesus who likes old people, or a Jesus who likes hymns or a Jesus who likes choruses. In some churches, you must kiss the icons, and perform elaborate baptism rituals for your kids, in another church, you must sit on hard pews and never smile, in another, you cannot have the Mass unless you are a church member, in another, you must listen to a 40-minute sermon and never question the pastor, in another, you must speak in English and believe in the monarchy of England, in another, you must sing in a particular way and wear the right sort of clothes.

We are all made in the image of God. This is how the author of Genesis speaks of it (Genesis 1: 27). Christians believe that through Christ, we bear his image in every-increasing clarity (1 Corinthians 15: 49). This suggests that the way the Bible speaks of God and our relationship with God should shape the way we see God each day.

Our petty, pathetic, sectarian squabbles are immature. Even mature Christians, however, will fight all the wrong battles, for all the wrong things. They fight amongst themselves like little kids in the sandpit. Also, they hate each other and despise each other like estranged siblings. They all work against each other like jealous co-workers. Throw nationalism and religion into the mix and they have all gone to war against each other.

Churches are now full of bitter angry people who hate each other. It is no wonder numbers have fallen. These days, evangelical fascists are obsessed with everything about sex. Sex is to the postmodern church what alcohol was to the pre-war church. Sex before marriage, sex in marriage, divorce, gay-sex, transgender sex, and all kinds of sex. Get this right, then you are a true believer, fall foul of the new morals' crusades in the church, then you are worse than Judas. Their obsession with sex is a deflection from the real sins tearing the church apart: factionalism and greed. Factionalism is rife in most churches. Let me explain what I mean by practical church factionalism.

Every church attracts the same types of people. If you go from church to church, you can easily find these types. They are so predictable. There is always the 'in crowd,' the chosen, the ones with the ear of the priest or the minister. There are also always the hard workers who have slaved away for free in the kitchen and other places for years. They usually go without much thanks but without whom the church would grind to a halt. There are weirdos or crazy people whom nobody likes. They are on the margins of the church. People tolerate them. Every church has intellectuals and rich people who attend over whom the ministers and priests fawn and prostrate. There are the families who have been there for several generations, who block every new initiative, and who are the powerbrokers of the church. Some famous families keep appearing in the church every generation. They say, *'do you know the Smiths, or do you know the Watsons, or do you know the Simpsons?'* In every church you must take a side, you must join a clique, and you must support a faction.

God doesn't work for the church. He is in his world, with his people, accomplishing his purposes. Christianity's biggest problem has always been the church, the greatest threat to faith in the world. It is impossible to defend the disgrace that is the church, and it is impossible to cover up its mistakes. The church has been the greatest source of division, war, and conflict, especially since nations created national churches. In WW1, Germans and English Christians prayed to the same God on either side of the trenches on the Western Front. In the English Civil War, the Puritans of Cromwell, and the Church of England supporters of Charles I prayed to the same God before Naseby. Both sides would happily kill each other and then go to church on Sunday and take the Mass or hear a Sermon. The Western Christian Church has made no decisive difference in any major political, economic, or social event in centuries. Don't listen to church propaganda, do your research on this, if you want. Overall, the church has been irrelevant.

God is at work in us during the week, transforming our lives, shaping our actions and words, and encouraging us in our discipleship. God is the God of peace and action. His action brought peace and his peace enables us to act. This action was the death of his Son, Jesus, whom the author of the Hebrews calls the 'Great shepherd of the sheep,' who died a horrible, sacrificial death for sin. The death of this Jesus brought about a new promise between God and people that cannot be revoked by any person on earth, not even a priest or a pope, and peace with God is possible for all who seek it. Not only is there peace, but the God of peace gives us everything we need in life, and he continues to work in our lives effectively and meaningfully. None of this has anything to do with Sunday church. This is life with God, with God, during the week, every day for all who seek it (Hebrews 13: 20-22).

During the Week, what does God think of us?

People often say that we need to bring someone to church so they can hear about God. The church is where the magic happens. It is great PR. During the week, the church is closed. Christian Fascists melt into the community during the week. They emerge on Sunday dressed up, or wearing their religious smiles, and doing their religious things. The creation of the church buildings, the institution of religion, complete with its rituals, tax havens, and traditions has dramatically transformed our understanding of who God is, how he exists, and how we relate to him. God doesn't need the church to work in the world.

God never leaves his people, and he doesn't live in a church. The most underutilized and neglected resource in Christianity is the people of God, the ones who turn up on Sunday and go home again. They think, wrongly, that the building is a church when they are the people of God. Also, they think they are meeting God, whereas God never left them. They think that God wants them to give him money, whereas God wants them to serve him with their lives.

Cultivated by tax-free structures, and the nature of middle-class life in the West, Church has become the new 'High Place.' People know churches not by the people who attend, but by where the building is located. Whatever rhetoric some employ, the substance of the gathered people of God is lost in translation. As far as I can tell, the tax status of churches is usually interpreted as a 'Christian right' rather than what it is, tax fraud.

In ancient Israel, before the Exile to Babylon, for whatever reason, many refused to worship at the temple of Jerusalem, preferring to worship God in shrines they built locally under trees, or on hills, hence the name, the 'high place.' For some reason, the people could not obey God and built their church buildings where they decided how one was to meet God, on their terms, in their way. These high places reflected local customs and tribal loyalties, and for centuries were difficult to remove, even during periods of revival in the temple cult. These tribal loyalties, these local churches, with this inherited tradition and steadfast refusal to accept God's way of worshipping together, have many parallels today in the way nationalistic or tribalistic churches have formed.

What was Christianity's biggest mistake? It was making an idol of the church by trying to capture God and force him into a building. In the 'high church' sect of the Church of England and Roman Catholic Churches, there is the bizarre tradition of placing little red lamps above the altar that remain lit during the week. These lamps indicate the continual presence of God the Holy Spirit. The ones I have seen have red cellophane wrapped around a light bulb connected to an electric switch than is usually turned off. In reality, the Spirit is among his people, and he never leaves them, and he is constantly pointing them to the Lord Jesus Christ.

As I said, the High Places were the ancient locations where Israelites worshipped Yahweh outside the temple of Jerusalem during the time of the first monarchy. We know that the Law of Moses did not approve of them, and they were places of cultural, ethnic, and folk significance for the local people. In addition, we know that the High Places included many pagan and cultural practices from the land around them, traditions that arose in various places. We know the High Places were extremely popular and they became the excuse for profligate lifestyles and alternative approaches to the worship of God. None of the prophets approved of the high places and they called the Jews to a communal and personal understanding of God, reviving the idea of the Spirit of God who moved among his people.

Today, in God's world, the church and the Spirit wrestle against each other. In many ways, Churches today are to the Spirit what the High Places were to the Temple. God lives in us through his Spirit, and he does not dwell in houses made by human hands. We are the Temple of the Holy Spirit, not the church building.

This is not however the view of most Christians. They downplay the role of the Holy Spirit, the fellowship of the Spirit, the actual union of a believer with Christ, and the communion with God found through faith. They have replaced it with the Church, an external, dead, lifeless thing that has no capacity for accepting God. It has no heart. It is not a person. It is a thing, bricks and mortar, dust, and memories. We know Christ does not dwell in the Church because of the hatred most churches have for each other. Their attitude is that God only dwells with them, only accepts them, and rejects everyone else. Speak to a liberal Christian and pretend to be an evangelical or vice-versa. It is only a matter of time before an argument breaks out, fellowship is broken, and who knows, even a scuffle.

God at Church is distant. If God is 'in the building' then it must mean that he is distant from people most of the week. It must mean he places space between himself and them. Most traditional church buildings have what they call an 'altar.' Contemporary churches usually have a stage or a pulpit or stand for the speaker. Both traditional and contemporary churches assume that the priest, minister, or pastor has a special connection with this elusive, impersonal God who seems to be always angry with us and wondering where we have been during the week.

God at Church is elusive. The God of the Bible seems, in most churches to be distant, and far away. The institutional church, the church of buildings, denominations, parties, factions, and bigotry, has a history of enmities longer than anyone can imagine. For centuries, these different churches have competed over their versions of membership in the kingdom of God. It has been a violent, awful, brutal struggle between men and women whom all claim to worship the same God.

But all these kingdoms look remarkably like the kingdoms of earth. These earthly kingdoms, made of brick, stone, marble, glass, brass, and gold, are indeed strangely beautiful. This is not, however, what Jesus had in mind when he said that he was the Way, the Truth, and the Life. Christian Fascists hijacked the Gospel and the message of Christ. They had no intention of bringing people to the Father since they were too busy building their temples on earth and how beautiful and empty many of them are now.

The God of the Church is often Christ-less. Jesus has a habit of saying things to us that get in the way of our plans and expectations of God. Jesus and his words often get in the way of the church. Our view of Christ is obscured by what the church often says about Jesus because we are aware of their failings, and their faults. Jesus is kept at bay through rituals and regulations. Seminaries were invented not to train leaders, as none of the disciples or early Christian leaders (aside from Paul) were trained in anything beyond life experience. Seminaries were invented to recruit sectarian leaders to enforce conformity, ensure compliance, and fight turf wars over property, money, wealth, and ecclesiastical power. It is loyalty to the church and its power that draws most people to the Christian ministry, a long and torturous path full of loyalty tests.

Only Jesus Christ can overcome the Mass Formation Psychosis of Christian Fascism. The last thing they want for you is your freedom, and they will do anything to preserve their power over you, your soul, and your money. It is a formidable system; it is almost impregnable. Most people cannot tell the difference between the Church and Christianity because they keep their Bibles closed.

The reality is different. We are blessed in Christ in the heavenly realms with every spiritual blessing (Ephesians 1). Also, we are adopted into God's family and have God as our Father and Jesus as our brother (Romans 8: 15, Galatians 3: 26). We are united with Christ (Philippians 2: 1). Also, we have the Spirit of God, and the love of God poured into our hearts by the Spirit (Romans 5: 5). We have so many good things by our new life in Christ. These are all recorded in the Bible. You do not need the permission of your priest or pastor to read about them. God always keeps his Word, and his promises are sure and certain.

What does Jesus mean when he says he is the Way?

Jesus is the Way, not to wealth and prosperity, but God. We need not only to depart from politics and from our love of money or whatever other idols we have so that we can see things clearly. Some Christians have got it right in the West based on a clear reading of the Bible. Jesus is the Way to God because he died on the cross for our sins. He took our place, died in our stead, on behalf of us. The old word was vicarious, meaning, in our place. Jesus is and was defined as the way to God because he died for our sins. There is a linear progression from that event to the possibility of us knowing God through that event. The emphasis was on a personal decision to follow Jesus.

All this is a faithful reading of the New Testament and there is nothing wrong with that. Faith is personal. Faith is not private. At some point, it must become public. I think of the two men who have my deepest admiration in the New Testament. They were two secret disciples of Jesus. They kept quiet throughout his public ministry because of their fear of others. Fear makes people do many things and stops people from doing many things as well.

These two men knew Jesus, and followed him, albeit secretly. Nobody knew, possibly only a few of the disciples. Then came the betrayal of Judas. Out of the blue, a clever stratagem by a small group of Christ's enemies. There was the kangaroo court and the swift execution. This would have been the time to stay quiet, the time for these secret disciples to say, *'Ah well, Jesus is gone now, I should get back to my old life, so no one knows I followed him.'*

But these two men did the complete opposite. They made their faith public on the day Christ died on the cross. One even went to Pilate and asked for the body of Jesus. He buried Jesus, someone with whom he bore no earthly relation, in his own family tomb hewed out of the rock. The other man helped him bury Jesus. The disciples of Jesus, including Peter, had either fled, denied him, or were in hiding. Joseph of Arimathea and Nicodemus decided to follow Jesus after his death. This was the worst possible time, at a time when the hatred for Jesus was at fever pitch. Both men did not believe Jesus would rise from the dead, but they wanted to identify with him in his death which they did so. How can I say they did not expect him to rise again? Why did they bury him and spend 34 kg of perfume on a man they thought might rise again?

The West can tolerate Jesus as Savior but not as Lord. They can tolerate the idea of someone saving them to enable their lives to go back to normal. They can accept the idea that Jesus came to help them achieve what they want to do in life when they want to do it. But Western Christianity has tried to avoid the other sense in which Jesus is the Way to God. This has to do with his claims of divinity, not simply his claims to be the Savior of the world. Jesus is the way because of his death. He is also the way because of his birth and his entrance into the world.

Christ is not simply the way to God, but he came from God. He was the way from God to the world. Jesus was born of Mary. He was conceived by the Holy Spirit and is from heaven. In heaven, he was the Word of God and was God. The reason many Christians downplay the incarnation of Jesus and focus only on the cross is simple. They prefer to see him as Savior but not Lord, or King. If Christ is king, then other kingdoms fade into the background, and you can focus on what is important. If Christ is king, then serving him is our duty, and the focus of our lives, and his word, the Bible, not the American Constitution, is our guide through life, with many commands difficult to hear, and even more difficult to apply, such as to love your enemies and do good to them.

It is perhaps why many American and Australian Christians seem content with recruiting Christ in their Culture War since they have generally forgotten that the early Christians believed Jesus to be God, or God with us. They believed in the kingdom of God, a real kingdom where Christ is king, not a political kingdom with parliaments or presidents, but a spiritual one of the heart, the mind, and the soul. I would say quite plainly that Jesus doesn't vote because he is the king. Jesus doesn't believe in democracy. It is not worth saving, but you are, all of you. The Culture War is repulsive to God.

Jesus repeatedly in John's Gospel makes himself equal with God, there is no denying that, there is no skirting around that fact, that John asserts quite openly and regularly that Jesus claimed to be God. He said to one of his disciples: *'if you have seen me, you have seen the Father,'* (John 14: 9); to the Pharisees he said *'I and the Father are one,'* (John 10: 30); and to them he also claimed the name of God, the holy name of God, inscribed in capital letters, LORD when he said that he lived before the advent of Abraham himself, saying *'before Abraham was, I am,'* (John 8: 58).

The existence of Christ before his advent nullifies an earthly church kingdom. John is convinced that Jesus is God, and he summarizes his view succinctly in the first verse of the entire work. In a sense, it is the most important verse of the Gospel. It is why the Gospel is so disliked by the church because it raises so many problems regarding their kingdom on earth, the opposite of the kingdom of God. If Jesus is God, then what does he care for bricks and mortar. John says: *'In the beginning was the Word, and the Word was with God, and the Word was God.'*

John views Jesus as the Word, who was *'with God in the beginning.'* The greatest word of Jesus was himself. Before he was born, he lived as the Word, and that Word pre-existed before his birth to Mary as God the Word, or Logos in Greek. John is clearly referring to the relationship between Jesus and the Word, that Jesus through his creative power, testifies to his divinity. He ascribes to Jesus creative power, the power that created the world, and yet it is not a recounting of Genesis 1 to 2, he simply says that *'through him all things were made; without him nothing was made that has been made,'* (John 1: 3). For John, Jesus was the creator of all things. If you see in Jesus the face of the Father, then you see in Jesus the creator of the world.

I don't know if you have ever heard these words. Jesus claims to be far more than a good man, he firmly claims to be God. This is the God who came from heaven and became one of us, so he could live our life and die and rise against and return to heaven. John says that in Jesus there is life and there is hope for all people, stating from the very beginning of the Gospel that faith or salvation is not based on what you do, or a set of rules, or baptism or the Mass, or ritual, but simply your attitude of heart, your conviction and worship of the one who came from heaven, the Word made flesh.

What is the obstacle between you and God?

What is the obstacle between you and God? Most Christians say they believe that Jesus came into the world to restore a lost relationship with God. In other words, the gospel, the good news about God is that God has provided his way to bridge a gap between people and God, which is sin. Jesus died for us on the cross, and became sin for us, taking on himself all the sin of the world. As a result, all who trust, or believe in Christ as the Savior sent by the Father, have eternal life. That is certainly what the New Testament teaches. The righteousness of God is appropriated by faith, and in God's eyes, through the death of Christ, we are seen as righteous.

If you have not heard this message at church, then you ought not be surprised. Indeed, for reasons of money and power, the church often avoids the central reasons for Christianity to focus not on the problem between God and his people but on the obstacles between people themselves. A religion about others that is not anchored in our relationship with God is the door to personal disappointment and social misery. God sent Jesus not only to restore a relationship with himself, but also through this reconciliation to bring about peace between people. Christian Fascism flourishes when Christians give up on the goodness of God's grace and focus on the strenuous and exhausting pursuit of personal holiness outside of the cross of Christ.

The Church has betrayed the deposit it should have guarded. What is the obstacle between you and God? The good news that there is hope found in Jesus Christ should be good news. But like in most things, money and power get in the way. The Church has done its best over the years to obscure, undermine, remove, condemn, mock, destroy, and mistranslate the gospel of God. Instead of the purity and wonder and simplicity of the gospel, we have a putrid quagmire of filth in the Church, run by a cadre of corrupt men in love with power and money, a culture of factions, and divisions, a language of bigotry and hatred, and doctrines of shame and guilt which people are forced to drink in rituals and ceremonies designed to keep God distant, and the Bible closed.

Christ removes the obstacles and brings freedom. Jesus places no obstacle between you and God, the Church does that. In addition, Jesus came to remove the barrier of sin so that we could know God and he did that by his death on the cross. Therefore, there is no freedom for us to know God. Jesus does not and the Gospel writers do not place any obstacle between you, your life, and the possibility of knowing God. The church does that, the barriers they put in front of you, the rules they expect you to obey, the navel-gazing and introspection they expect you to engage in, the restrictions they place upon you, and the lists of the unredeemable they read out to you.

Becoming a Christian in today's church is like an obstacle course with lots of hidden traps and holes one can fall into. Few make it through. The Pharisees, Jesus said, keep the door to the kingdom of God closed, and while they do not enter, they also prevent others from entering (Matthew 23: 13-15). For, this is the most powerful image of his confrontation with these men, of this ancient sect. They had, to use a modern phrase, lost the plot, lost their way, and Jesus calls them on it.

Christian Fascists use all kinds of excuses to shut down the Gospel. Christian Fascists have all kinds of excuses to shut down the Gospel for the sake of social and cultural change. They are not interested in the good news of new life in Christ. They want to force the behavior of people to conform to a church that has lost sight of the grace and mercy of God found in Christ. What is the obstacle between you and God? Christian Fascism and their desire to turn the good news into daily news. This daily news is what excites people because it is primarily about other people, whereas the good news of Jesus is about what God has done for me. The kingdom of God does not turn on what Joe Biden said today, or Donald Trump, or the latest death statistic in Covid, but it turns on the person and work of Jesus Christ.

When I returned to Australia after many years abroad, I thought that the Gospel would be alive and well. When I left, certainly in evangelical circles, there was optimism for the future. But I was wrong. In less than a generation, the church found power and ambition not to build the kingdom of God but reshape the nation. I was involved in the Constitutional reform movement in the 1990s and helped start the debate on the future of the Christian blessing in the Preamble to the Australian Constitution, *'humbly relying on the blessing of Almighty God.'* Even at that time, most people in power were agnostics and atheists, as the ruling class usually is. The Preamble is not in the actual Constitution and reflected the significance of the Church of England and the Roman Catholic Church in the lives of most of the rich white men who wrote it. In the 1990s, the issue was a minor skirmish, but many in the ruling class wanted the phrase removed to reflect the shifting demographics. At the time, most churches had not even the slightest interest in public Christianity. That was the old world.

When I returned, it was like I was returning to a different nation entirely. Australia had been reshaped by American imperialism and the War on Terror. The Church had given up on the gospel and was obsessed with sex, marriage, and a war against feminism. The new view was that Australia's past was Christian and pure, while the present was pagan and putrid, contaminated by a mixture of social sins caused by the usual suspects: women and minorities, especially Muslims. On 11-12 December 2005, at a local beach in Sydney, thousands of young white men rioted against anyone who *'looked like a Muslim'* whatever that meant. Many were hunted down and beaten. Churches outwardly condemned the riots, but privately applauded them. When I spoke to Christians about it, all I heard were the tired old cliches, the language of bigotry and prejudice.

For many Christians even today, Sunday is when you get dressed in your best clothes and 'go to church' which is the great act of identifying with Christianity. One is required to 'do' nothing, except sit, and sing, and converse, and smile, and then go home again. People have so identified church attendance as being synonymous with Christian identity that they forget that attending a church service tells us nothing about a person's relationship with God. If I enter a garage, that does not make me a car, so why would simply entering a building on Sunday every week make me a Christian? I discovered that the fascist Billy Sunday said that back in the 1920s. These days, the Culture War that began in America, is in full swing. We live in an era of pretend morality, public morality, selective morality. Oh, how self-righteous we have all become, how perfect we are, and how sinful others are, who do not live up to the standards of perfection we demand of them.

What is the obstacle between you and God? The Culture War, which takes attention away from Jesus Christ. Christians get led astray by every whim and wisdom of the sages of our age, who are the media and their political operatives. These days, it is all about gender, sex, and identity. The identity of a Christian is in Christ. There is a lifetime of pondering and thought wrapped up in those words. But no, let's protest everything under the sun. We walk under a dozen banners, but few walk one day behind Jesus. We support endless petitions, but rarely write our name under the scriptures and say: 'here we stand.' A gutless and cowardly generation, rent asunder by partisan politics and sectarian hatreds. And you still say the West will prevail. Beyond slaughtering tens of millions in war, and sowing a century of vendetta, I do not see a clear foundation for the future of the Gospel in the West.

Like a Jack-in-a-Box, Jesus is useful. In other words, all that Jesus has to say is boiled down to our debates on gender identity. We are only interested in Jesus if he is useful to our Culture Wars and our desire to control politics. Fascist Christians and the world agree that the answer is public morality. It is all about what we do.

What is the obstacle between you and God? The obstacles to knowing God is always something that can be intrinsically measured and something we do. It has nothing to do with God, or the Gospel.

For God, the most important thing to do is to accept that he sent the Son into the world to be the Savior of the world. John says instead that 'In him was life, and that life was the light of all humankind,' (John 1: 4). The most important thing about the advent of Christ, the arrival of Jesus into the world is that he came at all, because in his arrival we see the reason for his arrival and that is he is here to deal with the darkness of the world and destroy it. For God, it is all about what he did, and what we do changes nothing. Building a kingdom on earth is an illusion. It will end in dust.

The Culture War is an Echo of the Religious State that controlled the West for a thousand years. It is simply a pale reflection of the religious wars of the past when the church held the sword. Take divorce, for example, the stigma associated with it for generations, the laws against it, the condemnation of the church concerning it, and the social exclusion that divorce brought, especially for women. Every generation has its holiness crusade, its loyalty tests, and its pogroms to persecute the undesirables. There has never been a time in history when people simply sat back, loved each other, and got on with life. There is no point trying to engage with the idiocy of the church holiness crusades.

These Culture Wars are a distraction from the good news of Jesus Christ, an obstacle to personal freedom from fear, sin and death, guilt, and shame. They also take our minds away from what is essential. Jesus said that where your treasure is where your heart is. In these holiness crusades, the mind is refocused on something that is not central to our life or our relationship with God.

As I have said before, beware of mixing your nation with the Bible. It will not end well. America is not the light on the hill, the gospel is. America is not God's nation, the people of God are, and they come from all nations. The Bible doesn't even mention America. Maybe it does in Revelation. Who knows what will happen? We should put our trust in God and not in a nation that falsely claims to follow God. History has shown that empires fall and then come to nothing. Constantinople, Rome, Greece, Assyria, Babylon, the Ottoman Empire, the British Empire, and the list goes on. The world quaked in their presence, and the desert sands consumed their memories.

The cultural system we have now is unsustainable, and the Culture War is cannibalistic in nature and will consume itself. Since

9/11, the political landscape is a succession of crises to sow fear, distrust, and instability. Many young people have lived only with the war in the Middle East their whole lives, and a political culture that is designed to unsettle them. Your heart, mind, and soul are not the property of the state, nor the playground for politicians and bureaucrats. A mind is a precious place, and so are the heart and the soul. What these fraudsters have not told you is that their instability will never end. Covid was just the latest episode. It is now the war in the Ukraine, climate change, cancel culture, and then war with China. You will go insane if you have not already. Now, the ruling class is openly talking about nuclear war. The goal is to keep you afraid, to make you fearful, and to force you into a life of constant anxiety. What is the obstacle between you and God? It is Churches that prevent you from knowing God in Christ and turning you away from the cross.

Fascism leads to weariness, Christ to hope

Fascism leads to weariness, Christ to hope. The Word made flesh is the good news, God's kingdom will outlast the nations destined for dust. The church's constant loyalty to the state, its devotion to loyalty tests, nationalism, xenophobia, and the new public morality will not make a nation strong.

The point of Covid Hysteria was to provoke distrust among you, fear among you, and the idea that your enemy could be your friend or your lover. When a woman marries a paranoid obsessive man, he will go out of his way to destroy every positive relationship she has. He will work on her family first, destroy those bonds, then work on her friends, and then relationship by relationship, destroy everything until he is her god, until she worships only him, and believes that he is without any flaws, that he and he alone can be trusted, that he never lies, and loves her like no one else.

That is the government. It is always what people in power do when they have lost their way. The old systems of liberal democracy, authoritarian society, or even socialism offered stability and degrees of opportunity for people to live out their lives without inordinate fear. Fascism, both secular and sacred is inherently unstable and will not last.

What governments have done during covid is wicked. Lockdowns are over, the martial law is over in Australia and yet more people die each day from Covid than ever before. Calling Covid 'the flu' means that the last three years were unnecessary as there has been no major rediscovery or reevaluation of the nature of the disease in the last twelve months. Covid is not the flu, people continue to die from it, are hospitalized by it, and continue to languish in suffering from it, but now the government simply doesn't care because the economic costs of lockdowns coupled with the failure of vaccines have already driven the West towards a revival of 1970s-style stagflation. 'Living with Covid' is simply another deceitful cover-up of state failure. The lies of the state are manifold. There was no success with vaccination programs if people continue to die even if they are vaccinated. The vaccines cannot provide safety if people continue to contract the disease the vaccine, be hospitalized, and die.

The level of mass formation psychosis in Covid Hysteria is astounding, but we can just add it to another series of lies from the state. They lie all the time. In this unsustainable system, Covid Hysteria will be replaced by another fear machine, and then another and then another, the goal being to control your mind, your thoughts, your every waking moment, so they can break you, and then they do not have to force you to do anything, you will simply volunteer.

It is time for God's truth to smash these delusions and for you to see that you are being deceived. This is God's world, not theirs. The light shines in the darkness and the darkness has not overcome it, it never will, it never can. This is because Jesus is the Way, the Truth, and the Life. This is essential.

Whichever monkey oversees the bananas is not that important. Listen to the politicians in their election campaigns. Here is fifty dollars here, a hundred there, another hundred here. This is what democracy has become. Santa Claus is here early friends with his bag of goodies, and this is as good as it gets. All the parties believe in the same fundamentals now. There is virtually no difference. The so-called two-party system is one party with two sides, and they take it in turns. The minor parties are all fronts for the two major parties. They are protest votes or controlled opposition. Nothing will change each election cycle.

This is not democracy at work. This is a one-party state

pretending to be a democracy. At least in Asia, they do not pretend. Singapore and Japan both have fake versions of democracy, and they work quite well. At least they are honest about it. China will probably evolve in the same direction. The anti-China rhetoric of the West is becoming more facile with every passing day as new details emerge of the Australian 'secret government' under the former Prime Minister Scott Morrison or Trudeau's secret decisions, or Biden's allegation that all Trump voters are enemies of the state. People in power in the West are not even pretending to support robust democracy, free speech, freedom of association, or the press. All Western nations are dismantling the old democratic institutions in favor of a system, not unlike an authoritarian, fascist regime. America condemns Russian 'autocracy' and yet supports Saudi Arabia, and Australia condemns Chinese 'autocracy' while helping Papua New Guinea undermine the 2019 referendum that saw a majority of people on the island of Bougainville seek independence.

Politics is a fact of life, but it is not the heart of life. The Culture Wars have made politics essential. They are not. They are irrelevant. Fascism leads to weariness. Nations come and go. It is time to get out of the political insane asylum for that is what it is and focus on what is essential in life. Time to take back your life. Politics is irrelevant. You are empowering these people in power with your time, your thoughts, your mind, and your soul. They lie to you, and yet you still trust them, and like the abusive husband, they want total control. People in power are like spiritual vampires, they feed on your soul and only take it, and they are draining you of your life, one day at a time.

If God does not lie to lie, why do you trust the government? The government said the vaccines would protect you. They don't. Our leaders said that the vaccines would stop the spread. They don't. And they said that you cannot die if you have the vaccine. This is also a complete lie. They cannot say they didn't know. Science has been available for two years. They just chose to ignore it for ideological purposes. They lied all through the last two years.

Yet, many of you worship them as living gods, completely infallible and without flaws or blemishes. If you refuse to see the truth about the state, then you only have yourselves to blame. Take their trinkets at the election, watch them every night on TV, listen to them on the radio, send your children off to fight their wars, live with their policies, never criticize, or protest, and worship them as your new gods.

Jesus however came to dispel the darkness. He did. So why do you still close your eyes and stumble around? Jesus is the light of the world. When John refers to Jesus as the light, he is not simply saying that Jesus died for our sin, but that the arrival of Jesus brought light into the world. The light he refers to is the presence of Jesus in the world from his birth in the back room of Joseph's Bethlehem home, to his baptism by John, to his excruciating and painful death on the cross, and those final days with his disciples as the Risen Lord.

We are not the light, Jesus is the light, but he is light for all people, and the light of Christ shines in all the darkness of the world. Jesus also shines in the church where they try so hard to extinguish his message or trick his followers, but there is light in all places and every good thing in the world comes from the light. No verse summarizes the coming of Jesus as the Way from God as this one: *'The Word became flesh and made his dwelling among us. We have seen his glory, the glory of the one and only Son, who came from the Father, full of grace and truth.'* (John 1: 14).

For John, the Word became flesh, the God of the Hebrews walked as a man on earth, amongst his creation, wearing the clothes of creation, so he could be one of us. This is the Way of God, from the eternal Word to that of a man. Christians believe that Jesus was born human but is also God, that he existed before he was born and that he became a man. The old word for that was the incarnation, the incarnation of Christ, Jesus entering the human world, our world, to become one of us. The point is this: Jesus is God made flesh, God made human, and he dwells with us today. He is here, he is amongst us, he is present whenever two or three are gathered, he indwells all believers, he is the one who hears our prayers and takes them to the Father.

Where is God during the week? With his people, with anyone who trusts and believes in him, and he is always with us. He is with us spiritually, but always in person, always real, and always risen. The Christian Fascists go to church because if God is there, they hope he stays there and doesn't follow them home.

When Jesus was tempted by the Devil, the temptations were really about Jesus not using his divine power, for he never used it to promote himself or to meet his own needs, and only exhibited his divine power for the good of others (Matthew 4: 1-11). The Devil was telling him that there was no reason he could not be visibly divine and human at the same time, but this would have invalidated his mission. He came to live a human life, experience our life, and identify with us in his death.

The full identity of Jesus was veiled on earth but he saw himself as the Son of Man. He says so often enough in the Gospels and thus identifies with an ancient character mentioned several times in the Hebrew Bible or Old Testament. Much of his conversations in John's Gospel have to do with the Patriarchs, who were the great leaders of ancient Israel. Jesus believed them to be real people who lived long ago. Jesus was a great fan of the patriarchs. His ministry was in Israel where the Patriarchs lived and died.

One of them was a man called Jacob, whose name meant 'to deceive,' a rather unpleasant man who tricked his brother out of his birthright and then ran off to hide with his relatives. He was not, one would say, a good person. The Bible is very honest about his deceitfulness, and it is doubtful you would want Jacob as a recruit for your Culture War or holiness crusade.

On his way to his relatives, Jacob has a spiritual encounter, much like Paul in the New Testament, a remarkable experience that he spends the rest of his life pondering. It is the story of the origin of the town of Bethel in Israel. After his encounter, Jacob says that he was afraid, and *'Surely the LORD is in this place, and I did not know it...How awesome is this place! This is none other than the house of God and this is the gate of heaven.'* (Genesis 28: 16-17).

What was his encounter? Genesis records: *'And he dreamed that there was a ladder set up on the earth, the top of it reaching to heaven, and the angels of God were ascending and descending on it. And the LORD God stood beside him and said, 'I am the LORD, the God of Abraham, your father, and the God of Isaac, the land on which you lie I will give to you and your offspring.'* (Genesis 28: 12-13).

This was a most remarkable encounter as Yahweh, the God of Abraham and Isaac spoke to Jacob as one would a man, that God would speak to him directly without the need of an intermediary, and the clear distinction in the text between the LORD and the angels. The Patriarchs had a personal relationship with God. God is a person, he appeared to them, he walked with them, and he talked with them as one would a man.

Jacob's response to all of this is also remarkable. God does not tell him how to respond or what to do, but he decides to anoint the rock on which he slept with oil and to rename the place from Luz to Bethel which means the house of God, simply because that is where he met God face to face in his dream. For Jacob, this House of God was the discovery of his relationship with God.

One of the first things Jesus says in the Gospel of John is this enigmatic statement to Nathaniel, a new disciple. In verse 51 of Chapter 1, he says: *'Very truly I tell you, you will see 'heaven open, and the angels of God ascending and descending on' the Son of Man.'*

He is making a link between the LORD God who appeared to Jacob and himself as the Son of Man, God among his people. He identifies with Bethel, the house of God, where God appeared to Jacob in the flesh, where God meets us on earth. The point is that the Son of Man came from heaven and that the angels descend and ascend upon him in the same way as they did for Jacob. It is a bold affirmation and deeply controversial for Jesus to identify with the LORD in this way, but he does. Jesus is the way to the Father, but he also came from the Father. He is more important than many could imagine.

Yet, we believe he is only here to help us in our Culture War. The God of the universe is revealed and all we care about is electing our President or Prime Minister. The God of heaven walks among us and all we care about is the bricks and the mortar of our churches, the dust on the pews, and preserving the memories of those who have died. We need to lift our gaze and rediscover the real Jesus.

Is Jesus a footnote to faith?

Dear Fascists,

How are you?
I hope you are well.
I have a few things to say so you are clear about where I stand.
Jesus is not a footnote to faith.

Jesus is not a footnote of my faith, he is the end of faith, that is, he is the purpose of faith, the object of faith, and the one who makes faith possible. He is the Way, not just to God, but from God. When he says to his disciples that he is the Way, he is talking about himself, and I hope that is clear.

The most important thing in my life is not your political party, your politics, or your Culture War. I don't care about left or right or up or down. They mean nothing these days anyway, and political affiliations make no sense in the world you have created.

Not everything in the world is about your political agenda. People will be weary of your fascism. It will not sustain itself. It will eventually wither and die or be consumed by fire. Fascism always is. A society based on politics is without meaning. The result will be exhaustion as people squabble and fight over the crumbs under the table. The future for many people is a world of censorship, indoctrination, brainwashing, factionalism, jealousies, dislocation, and introspection, as they question their motives, their thoughts, their values, and their souls against the latest truth proclamation from people in power, where the goalposts change every day and the rest of the world watches on.

Be prepared for a world of anxiety, fear, distress, and abuse. It will not be an easy ride. A world where propaganda controls everything will lead to a dark world, not light. Jesus is not a footnote to faith. He is central to life.

Remember, that political democracy in the West, has only been around for a century or so. Remember also, that Christianity was born when the world was ruled by a dictator and local governors and kings were appointed. It was into this world that Jesus came.

He did not promote democracy or political freedom, but he did speak of freedom, and he did bring it, but it is not the realignment of political virtues, but a freedom of the heart, the mind, and the soul, available to all as he is the Way the Truth and the Life.

Freedom is not new. It is not owned by democracy. It predates the rise of America and Britain, it is ancient. Paul's teaching on freedom is itself a commentary on the debates over freedom dating back to more ancient times. The people of the past were not stupid, or inferior, or uneducated, they were just before us. Some of their societies were incredible, culturally rich, sophisticated, beautiful, and edifying. In some ways, they were freer than we are. Try losing your smartphone for a day, or don't look at it for one hour. They would laugh at us today and our silly arguments over freedom in the West and say, *'we were talking about all of these thousands of years ago, and you talk as if you own freedom or something.'* The Western link between democracy and freedom is classic misinformation. It is classic fake news.

Dear Fascists, I know you mean well. But deceit is not the way to run the state. It is far better to be honest about why you are doing things, and the reality of life. Eventually, we discover the political truths. We know that we were lied to about Vietnam, we were lied to about Agent Orange, we were lied to about the War on Terror and so-called weapons of mass destruction, we were lied to about indigenous people, we were lied to about many things, but for most of us, we were duped at the time, we were victims of mass formation exercises or propaganda exercises promoted by people in power.

I know in fascism, people need to be controlled and manipulated through ideas, words, phrases, fears, and anxieties. Covid is just the latest example of that. I am aware of your goals and plans. Let me tell you about mine.

The first goal is to encourage people to open the Bible, read it for themselves, and make up their own minds. Since the 1950s, many churches have begun 'bible studies' and most of them are modern versions of the older catechisms. In other words, they function to activate and inculcate sectarian values. I want to do to the Bible Study what King James did to the Bible. He wanted people to read the Bible without the copious Calvinist notes on the side that was present in the then popular Geneva Bible. In the Geneva Bible, whenever people were open to the Spirit, there was Calvin to force them to toe the line, hate Catholics, and love the Reformers. Calvin had it all explained, and they didn't need to think for themselves.

Bible studies these days are like the Geneva Bible. These studies employ the techniques of embarrassment and threats of exclusion to make sure there is conformity. Most are closed, and most are comprehension-based, with a series of prearranged questions that have a particular goal. There are right and wrong answers. This is fascism in practice. This is not Christianity in action. When Jesus read from the scroll of Isaiah that fateful day he returned to Nazareth, the eyes of all people were upon him because he was also required to provide the commentary. He was a nobody and yet he was asked to give the sermon. The synagogues of the first century were freer than most churches today.

We should let God speak through his word. We should simply work our way through a book of the Bible, read a passage and reflect upon it and let God speak to us. We should respect what others say when they read the same passage. God speaks through his word in different ways. There are often many things that one can get out of a passage. The Bible often contains more than one 'point' and there are often many treasures to discover. To prevent others from hearing what God is saying to them is trying to stop God from speaking.

My second goal is to revive the ancient pattern of simply following Jesus Christ. Jesus calls all to follow him, and no one who has begun to follow him ceases on that path. Christians can gather anywhere to pray or read the Bible. They need not go to church, step into a building, or join a denomination. A restaurant, a bar, a café, or a home is a suitable place to meet. Why meet in the Church building and give Christian Fascists more people to abuse? I hope for an everywhere Christianity, a gathering of Christians in every cafe, every restaurant, every space, everywhere, all the time. As I have said, the Church on Sunday is not the 'church.' It is not in the Bible. The church is not a place, but an assembly of people. Any group can be an assembly of Christians, a gathering. Whenever two or three are gathered, that is a 'church' that is assembling in the name of Christ, and Jesus is present. You do not need the authority of your priest to do this, or the authority of the government. You have the Spirit of God if you believe, so go out into the world, into your community and take the Gospel to all the people there.

My third goal is to plead with the government to end the support for Christian Fascism. I hope that through these reflections you have been able to see the difference between a Christian and a Christian Fascist. Anyone who talks about the Culture War, public morality, church traditions and beliefs, the importance of sectarian values, or points away from faith and a personal relationship with God the Father and Jesus Christ whom he sent, is a Christian Fascist. There are many fake Christians in the church today. Most churches are crawling with people who do not believe in God, and who are there for every reason except the one Christ ordained, to be places of prayer and encouragement.

Dear Fascists, please reform the Church, for the sake of the nation and the good news of God's grace. I will encourage Christians to stop supporting these institutions of abuse and create their own ways of gathering and praying and encouraging. Christians make the best citizens. Christian Fascists make the worst citizens as they mix religion and faith. Most churches could easily become self-sufficient financially, but they are run by people who are inept, incompetent, and bad with money. Many churches could be self-sustaining but instead are money pits. Indeed, many church workers could find real employment and still be effective in their Sunday worship services. Sadly, the only way forward for real reform is if the state came in and took over these reforms, especially in taxation. Churches are service providers, not charities. The law should reflect that. They need to pay land tax, income tax, and business tax and lose their tax exemptions. The only practical way forward to save the church from its addiction to money is for you, the government, to step in and fix it. Christian Fascists are not Christians. They are trouble. you should know that. You needed to buy them off during Covid Hysteria. Their cost will just go higher and higher. Already, they are lining up for their so-called 'religious' freedoms. How much money do you have? They want it all. Money is their God.

So now you know my three goals: studying the Bible, following Jesus, and overcoming Christian Fascism. Freedom Matters Today looks at freedom from a Christian perspective. While we will live in peace and obey the law, do not expect us to prop up your society, cover up your mistakes, fight your wars, or play games in your Culture War and your re-imagined history. We believe in the Bible, we believe in prayer, and we have a faith where Jesus Christ is the Way, the Truth, and the Life. Sin is the disease, and Christ is the Cure. We seek the peace and prosperity of the nation, nothing more, and as far as it is possible, we will seek to live at peace with all people.

The only thing of any importance to us is the good news of Jesus Christ and the freedom that comes from knowing him and knowing God the Father who sent him. Because Jesus is the Way, the Truth, and the Life, we have freedom from fear, freedom from guilt, freedom from shame, freedom from sin and death, and freedom from prejudice.

We stand for the truth, and this truth is not a set of doctrines on what to do or rules to follow, but this truth is a person, the person of

Jesus Christ. Stop telling us what our faith is and telling us what we ought to believe as Christians. Stop telling us what rules as Christians we ought to believe and follow. Stop using the Bible to promote your political ideology. It is unwise. It is foolish. Stop telling us what God wants us to do. We do not see your name written in the Bible, we do not see your ideology or your democracy or your fascism, or your nationalism in the Bible.

Truth is a person, and for me, it makes sense that this is the case because then it takes the emphasis away from me and what I might believe or say or do, and places the emphasis on Jesus, what he did, who he is, and why he came. What we think of Jesus is the heart of the Christian faith, it is the heart of the good news, and it is the heart of the mission of God's gathered community around the world.

Everyone needs to make up their minds about Jesus, who he is, what he did, and why he came. This is essential. People need to decide about Jesus, not about anything else, and those who insist that the Christian Gospel is not about Jesus but something else, are promoting a different Gospel entirely. Our faith is about another, it is not about us. Our faith is simply a trust in another, Jesus, who was sent by God, came from God, is God, so that all who believe in him might have eternal life.

This is the Gospel. This is plain and simple. It is not complicated, and it puzzles me why Christians make it complicated and confusing and that is perhaps they fear that the Gospel may be true, that God accepts everyone if they believe in the Son, and though we love to tell others about Christ, we are often selective in the people we would like to enter the kingdom of God. Saying that truth is a person is not a new thing to say and I am not the first person to say it. The first person to say it was Jesus himself when he said in John chapter 14 verse 6 that *'I am the way, and the truth, and the life, no one comes to the Father except through me.'* I am glad Jesus is the Way and I am not.

We will continue to pray for the nation, fascist or not, and pay taxes as we should. But answer me, dear Fascists, if their Bible tells them to pay tax out of love for their nation, why do you let the churches off the hook? Surely, everyone needs to make their contribution to the nation, out of love for others. Churches are addicted to their money. Only you can help them. You will be following God's will as well as serving their best interests. Maybe with less money, they might think more of the God they pretend to believe in. The starting point is to put the fear of God back into the church and only you can do that.

American Christians often pointed to Trump as the *'New Cyrus,'* a man anointed by God to restore power to his people, but a more important question is: how has the wealthy, opulent, bloated American church suffered? If God, in his wisdom needed Cyrus to set his people free, he also needed a role for Babylon to raze Jerusalem to the ground. This was also the will of God, as recorded in the prophecies of Jeremiah who failed in his mission to call Israel back to God. God even called Jonah to speak to Nineveh, for all people need to hear the love, mercy, and forgiveness of God, as he has no favorites. Remember this, dear fascists when the churches come begging for special exemptions and tax breaks.

Yours sincerely,

Michael J. Sutton,

Founder, and CEO of *Freedom Matters Today.*

The Last Supper the Church ignores

The New Testament contains the last supper the church ignores, a meal of significance the church tries to forget (John 21). The account of the Last Supper in the Gospel of Luke already provokes serious questions about the way the Western Church invented the Mass and ignored the text. In Luke's gospel, there are two cups, not one, passed around and Jesus explicitly tells his disciples that he will not eat or drink this meal until the arrival of the kingdom. (See Luke 22: 18). Why would Jesus participate in a meal that he said he would not participate in? Furthermore, Luke is describing the Passover and the imminent execution of Christ. What Jesus is saying is to his disciples, he is not instituting the Mass, and his point is that he is the fulfillment of the Passover, assuming the role of the lamb of God, the scapegoat. Death is on his mind, as he knows that it is only a matter of hours before he dies. The church stripped the event of its beauty and pathos, and its human vulnerability and clothed it in idiocy, and bizarre traditions, making sure that everything Jewish and Hebrew was purged and removed. As I have said before, the Mass is the beating heart of Christian antisemitism.

Beyond Luke's Gospel, there is a meal the church usually ignores because it provides practical advice on how to follow Jesus and does not support the ritual of the Mass. After the resurrection, Peter decided to go fishing and went back to the Sea of Galilee with some of the other disciples.

They didn't have much luck in the night, but in the morning, there was a man on the shore who could see the shoals of fish swimming around and probably had a better vantage point. He told them to throw the nets over the other side. Being good fishermen, they followed the advice, and John records that they caught 153 fish. Interestingly, he notes the number, perhaps because it was the largest haul they ever caught. John saw it was Jesus on the shore, who had himself been fishing the night before, caught some fish, and had a barbeque ready for his mates when they came ashore.

It is easy to see why this is the last supper the church ignores. It is so ordinary and full of life. Peter was so excited he swam ashore to see Jesus. Jesus didn't rebuke the men for fishing. He didn't make fun of them and tell them they were fishing in the wrong place. Jesus didn't even rebuke them for not believing in him. He went ahead of them and made them breakfast. Our Lord had it all prepared.

This is the true Mass, a breakfast with Jesus, sitting near him, enjoying a meal with him, and listening to him. It is not sitting in fear in a darkened hall, with a huge stone altar out of the front, with priests in funny clothes chanting and incanting like a wizard, with hocus pocus and spells. It is not listening to a man drone on for an hour, then quietly standing up and grabbing a cup of coffee, having a polite chat, and then going home.

It is easy to see why this is the last supper the church ignores. Jesus blesses ordinary life, not the ritual of the church and the silliness of the Mass. This is real life, and the church is not able to stand there with the collection plates. The point of the breakfast with Jesus was that they were with Jesus. He was with them. He is with us. We are with him if we trust in him as our Savior and Lord. He is Life. Jesus is with us every day, in spirit. One day he will return in person because he has never left in spirit. It will just be different. The last supper the church ignores is significant because it is about

Jesus and his disciples, not about the church and its power.

Throughout the Gospel of John, John makes the connection between Jesus and life itself. Jesus is life. Life testifies to him because he is life. He wrote in the first chapter of his first letter the same thing: *'That which was from the beginning, which we have heard, which we have seen with our eyes, which we have looked at and our hands have touched—this we proclaim concerning the Word of life. The life appeared; we have seen it and testify to it, and we proclaim to you the eternal life, which was with the Father and has appeared to us.' (1 John 1:1-2).*

In other words, Jesus is eternal life, and to know him is to enjoy eternal life because we know him. The link between life and knowing Jesus is firmly established in John's Gospel. Jesus says in John's Gospel, that *'everyone who believes may have eternal life in him'* (John 3: 15); and *'for God so loved the world that he gave his one and only Son, that whoever believes in him shall not perish but have eternal life.'* (John 3: 16).

Jesus says later: *'Very truly I tell you, whoever hears my word and believes him who sent me has eternal life and will not be judged but has crossed over from death to life.'* (John 5: 24).

Imagine that you never have to go to Mass again, you never have to seek God's approval because you already know God and have already passed from death to life because you know Jesus. You never have to enter a church building again and sit cowering in the chair, fearful of a wrathful God who disapproves of your every mistake and who is unforgiving, because God has said that you have already passed from death to life. The church makes it about power and money. Christ makes it about life and death, and he is the bridge between them.

Jesus brings true hope and the end of fear. Jesus says, *'For my Father's will is that everyone who looks to the Son and believes in him shall have eternal life, and I will raise them up at the last day.'* (John 6: 40). Our Lord says, *'Very truly I tell you, the one who believes has eternal life,'* (John 6: 47). He sums it up no more clearly than later in the Gospel. *'Now this is eternal life: that they know you, the only true God, and Jesus Christ, whom you have sent.'* (John 17: 3).

Just like church, eternal life is not a place. It is a relationship. Eternal life doesn't happen when you die. It is a relationship with

God, and it begins now, and you can have a permanent relationship with God that occurs every day. You do not need to go to church to meet God because you already know him, you talk to him in prayer, you read his word in the Bible, and you encourage one another to grow in the faith as you share about what God is doing in your life and what you are learning, and how God is encouraging you in your daily life. Now, in the same way, that we cannot reduce God down to the Culture War, we cannot reduce our relationship with God down to our Sunday church experience. That is not life, that is one hour of our week. What Jesus is saying is that he is life.

Knowing him is having eternal life and trusting him is experiencing eternal life. What Jesus is saying, and John is saying is that knowing God is enough and this is the blessing of God. Nowhere does God promise material blessings or money or anything. If you have them, praise God, if you receive them, praise God, but do not think for a moment that Jesus came into the world to give you money. He came into the world so you might know God and that God might know you. That is life, knowing Christ, and following him.

The Christian Fascists don't like the gospel because they fear that if you meet God and believe in him and find eternal life, then they won't be needed anymore, and you might grow in your faith without them, and you will not pay them money out of a sense of guilt, that you are paying God off for your many weaknesses. These soul catchers would prefer that you don't find out about God. They tell you that it is all about the ritual or the Mass, or the sermon, joining a particular faction, singing a particular song, wearing the right clothes, or supporting the right political candidate.

Freedom from fascism is found in following Jesus. Christian Fascists are right about one thing. If you know God, then you don't need them at all. You can find freedom from fascism by finding Christ and following him. Find other people who know God, who want to grow, who ask questions, and who are genuine people. Look for God's people, they are everywhere. It might be hard to find these people but, in every city, there are God's people. Look for them. You do not need a priest, a minister, or a pastor if you know God.

Don't go to church, follow Jesus instead.

Remember, Freedom Matters Today because you matter to God.

ABOUT THE AUTHOR

Michael J. Sutton is the founder and CEO of Freedom Matters Today, which looks at freedom from a Christian perspective. He holds a Ph.D. from the University of Sydney (2002), a Master of Divinity from the Australian College of Theology (2017), a Diploma of Bible and Ministry from Moore Theological College (2017), and a First-Class Honours Degree in Economics (Social Sciences), from the University of Sydney, 1995. He spent ten years of his working life in Japan as a lecturer and researcher in international relations and economics in Sendai, Tokyo, and Kyoto. He lives in Sydney.

WHAT IS FREEDOM MATTERS TODAY?

Freedom, Matters Today is a tax-paying, educational service provider that looks at freedom from a Christian perspective. We are apolitical and non-sectarian. To date, we have identified six themes: freedom from fascism and tyranny, freedom from fear and despair, freedom from past and prejudice, freedom from guilt and shame, freedom from sin and death, and freedom from war and conflict.

Our slogan is simply don't go to church, follow Jesus instead. Being a Christian is not about going to a building on Sunday but about having a relationship with God. Religion leads to the church, but faith leads to God. God gives us true freedom.

Our books are works of originality and rely upon the arguments and perspectives of the author. They avoid name-dropping or name-calling. There are few, if any, footnotes. If you require verification, Google it. This book is based on our blog and podcast written and broadcast between February 28 and May 8, 2022.

For further information about Freedom Matters Today, listen to our podcast, broadcast weekly, or visit our website at freedommatterstoday.com. We explore faith, life, and what it means to follow Jesus

Remember, Freedom Matters Today, because you matter to God.